THE AMERICAN SOLDIER IN WORLD WAR II

THE AMERICAN SOLDIER IN WORLD WAR II

CHESTER G. HEARN

MBI Publishing Company

This edition first published in 2000 by MBI Publishing Company,
729 Prospect Avenue, PO Box 1, Osceola, WI 54020-0001 USA

MBI Publishing Company books are also available at discounts in
bulk quantity for industrial or sales-promotional use. For details
write to Special Sales Manager at Motorbooks International
Wholesalers & Distributors, 729 Prospect Avenue, PO Box 1,
Osceola, WI 54020-0001 USA.

Library of Congress Cataloging-in-Publication Data Available

ISBN 0-7603-0969-8

Printed in Italy

Credits
Project Manager: Ray Bonds
Designed by Interprep Ltd
Picture researcher: Anne Lang
Archival photographer: Rolf Lang
Color reproduction by Studio Technology

The Author
Chester ("Chet") G. Hearn is a former soldier in the U.S. Army, who
has written more than a dozen books on U.S. military history, three
of which have been "alternate selections" for the History Book Club
of America. He graduated from Allegheny College with a B.A. in
Economics and a minor in History, and spent much of a civilian
career as an executive in industry. He now spends all of his time
writing and researching – when he is not afloat on Lake Erie,
Pennsylvania, or at a local pool keeping in shape for competitive
swimming.

Contents

PREPARING FOR WAR

During the summer of 1940, nothing eclipsed the attention of the young men and women of America – not even the war in Europe – more than the battle waged in Congress over the Burke-Wadsworth bill, the precursor of the Selective Service Act. Never had the nation been called to arms during peacetime, but France collapsed in June and the bill went to the floor for debate. The torrid heat of July only made opponents of the legislation madder, while in Europe Germany's *Luftwaffe* turned its attention from France and battled for control of the skies over Great Britain. As one supporter of the bill said, "Every time they bombed London we gained a vote or two in the House or Senate."

President Franklin D. Roosevelt, consciously aware of America's preference for isolationism, trod lightly on the issue and took a poll. Much to his surprise, 71 percent of the public favored the bill, including strong support from the very men – especially those without jobs – who would be drafted by the bill.

Despite fierce opposition from American mothers, who threatened to hang advocates of the legislation in effigy on the Capitol lawn, Roosevelt signed the bill on September 16, 1940, and the contentious Selective Training and Service Act became law. For an undetermined period of time, the odious

Men and Women in Uniform		
	1939	1945
U. S. Army/ Army Air Corps	190,000	8,300,000
U. S. Navy	125,000	3,380,000
U. S. Marines	19,000	475,000
Total	334,000	12,155,000

"draft" and its frightful notices would consume the daily apprehensions of more than 20,000,000 American males as they daily dipped their hands into boxes containing the mail. Before the war came to an end in Europe and the Far East, 18,000,000 men would pass through armed forces medical processing centers. Of that number, the draft would hustle more than 11,000,000 men into all branches of the service and reject 6,500,000 for being either physically or mentally unfit.

But, for the peacetime force of 1940, conscripts would serve only one year – just long enough for the Army to whip them into shape for combat. During the summer of 1941, the program almost suffered political death, saved by a single vote in the House.

Like canteens, boots, and helmets, the fighting man of World War II became GIs, or "general issue." They came from all walks of life, but the first million men inducted in 1940 were those between the ages of twenty-one and thirty-six. Pollsters asked whether they objected to a year of military training, and 76 percent of them approved of the idea. Some replied, "If I'm likely to fight, I'd rather know how." When the Japanese attacked Pearl Harbor on December 7, 1941, men drafted in 1940 were still in training camps.

Ripple effects from the Great Depression had left many men

Below: Some recruits receiving their first induction physicals found the experience of wandering about nude among strangers a difficult adjustment to make, but they soon got accustomed to it.

unemployed, and serving their country gave them a self-esteem lacking in civilian life. Those with good jobs or in college considered the draft an imposition on their careers, but, during October, 16,000,000 men began registering with the local draft board. They came in from farms, gas stations, milk routes, factories, and fishing boats to fill out a complicated eight-page questionnaire. Farmers got a break, but men making their living as actors, musicians, bartenders, or delivery boys were among the first to go. When Frank Sinatra received a deferment "because of a punctured ear drum," Army Chief of Staff George C. Marshall ordered an investigation and demanded to know what doctor had conspired to make the crooner IV-F.

Joseph Crousen of Texas thought he would beat the system and joined the Marines. Some years later, when asked why he enlisted, Crousen, now a retired warrant officer, replied, "Ah'll tell you why ah signed up. By Gawd, ah was hungry, that's why! Someone had told me Marine food was pretty damn good. Ah must have liked it, ah ate it for twenty-five years."

In November, 1940, 6,500 local Draft Boards each inducted about ten men into the Army. The Navy, Marines, and Coast

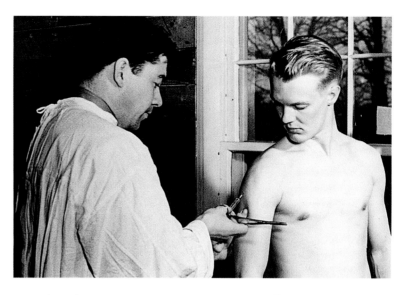

Guard preferred filling their rolls through voluntary enlistments and succeeded in doing so until mid-1942, after which they became more reliant on the draft. Young men entering the peacetime Army had no inkling of what to expect. They frolicked through the physical, laughed as the company barber shaved off their hair, picked up a foot locker that would contain all their earthly belongings, and settled into a clapboard barracks from World War I where winter winds whistled between the slats and sometimes froze the water in the latrines. Letters home describing the rigors of basic training sent a stream of draft candidates into other

Above: Most inductees looked away when receiving shots. Anticipation of being stabbed with a dull needle tipped with a hook caused many recipients to faint at first bite.

Left: The first army haircut was always a close shave with clippers that bared the scalp. After that, the inductee could keep his hair.

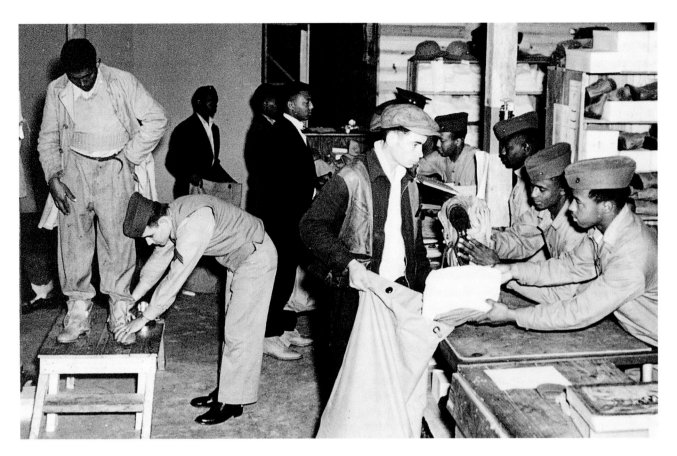

Above: After fitting the recruit for shoes, the soldiers dispensing uniforms looked the inductee over, estimated his size, and began dumping clothes into his duffel bag, leaving the recipient to hope they fit.

branches of the service.

Some sought ways to avoid the draft. With war approaching, a comrade of cartoonist Bill Mauldin urged him to join the National Guard. "You'll be among friends," he said, "you'll stay out of the infantry, and you'll solve your civilian unemployment problem." But Mauldin soon learned that life was not that simple. Men in the National Guard were first among those called to active duty.

During the first year of the draft, the Army inducted only the fittest specimens, culling out those overweight or under-weight, those with bad teeth or imperfect eyesight. A month before Pearl Harbor, Army doctor's believed that "A registrant who qualifies today and is inducted into the Army can feel distinctly honored." In 1941 physical standards began to drop, and by 1942, all the former rejects found themselves buck privates in Uncle Sam's training camps. Those overweight got thinner, and those underweight got tougher. There is no record to show the number of men classified IV-F by virtue of having venereal disease, but the Selective Service soon discovered a large number of draft dodgers had purposely infected themselves with gonorrhea.

Left: Selection of U.S. Army uniforms and equipment. On the left are herring bone twill olive green fatigues that replaced khaki drill "chino" service dress in 1942, when the GI was issued with a one-piece overall that was found to be impractical for jungle use. The gun is the M1918 A2 BAR. Elements of the final combat uniform are on the right, a two-piece olive drab poplin uniform introduced in spring 1945. The gun is the M1 Garand.

After that, the Surgeon General lowered his standards. By war's end the Army, using sulfa compounds, had treated and cured 200,000 draftees of simple gonorrhea.

Competition for the fittest draftees evolved into a battle between different branches of the service. After the Japanese attacked Pearl Harbor, Navy recruiting officers hovered around induction centers and over a period of a single month enticed 35,000 men away from the Army. They skimmed off the cream and sent the remainder back to the draft board. In late 1942, when the Navy became more reliant on the draft for manpower, they obtained a concession to enlist seventeen-year-old volunteers as reservists. Once trained and eighteen, they were transferred to active duty.

Because the Army could not draft men under the age of eighteen, General Lewis B. Hershey complained to Congress that "he would be lucky if he could get two out of three in that prime age group." The Army grumbled about the quality of the men sent to training camps, draftees grumbled about the Army's training methods, and both groups berated the Selective Service.

The poor relationship had a downside. Men working and needed in defense plants feared they would be drafted into the Army and abandoned critical factory jobs to enlist in the Navy or the Marines. Those enlisting in the Army Air Force rendered themselves draftproof, knowing they might not be called into service for training for as long as a year.

By 1943, the Selective Service began inducting fathers in their mid-thirties, taking them from jobs in banks, hospitals, stores, and other non-defense occupations. So repugnant did the thought of drafting fathers become that a poll conducted in 1944 revealed that by a three-to-one majority, Americans preferred drafting single women to married men. Despite the furor raised against the policies of the Selective Service, German Army leaders rated the American infantryman as superior physically to any other soldier on the battlefield, and for the most part, better educated.

By mid-1942, "Greetings" from the draft board meant a quick trip to an

induction center for a stripped-down, assembly line physical. Most of the men had never been far from home. Nakedness and strange surroundings caused nervousness, elevating heart rates and blood pressure. Others could not produce a urine sample. At day's end, an officer swore the draftees into the Army

Above: One of the GIs' biggest gripes was inspection – rolling up their bunks, tidying up their foot lockers, and making everything look neat, just so some officer could wander through the barracks and find some small transgression.

SELECTIVE CHRONOLOGY OF WAR: 1940

Feb 26: Air Defense Command is created by War Department to integrate U.S. defenses against air attack.

Apr 21: Capt. Robert M. Losey, an Air Corps Weather Service Commander, is killed by Germans in Norway during a raid. An official military observer, he nevertherless could be classified as the first American military officer killed in hostile action during World War II.

July 10: the Armored Force is established by the U.S. Army, combining elements of cavalry, infantry, and artillery, originally with 242 officers and 7,015 men, and 393 light tanks.

July 19: Naval Expansion Act is signed; it is a measure to strengthen U.S. defenses, and calls for construction of warships, naval aircraft and auxiliary shipping.

Aug 1: Training of the U.S. Army's first parachute troops begins at Hightstown, New Jersey.

Aug 17: The first regular-serving U.S. pilot to die in action in World War II is Pilot Officer William M. L. Fiske III, who is serving with RAF in England. He dies of wounds received in aerial combat during the Battle of Britain.

Aug 27: Congress authorizes calling into active service individual members and units of Reserve components for a period of 12 months.

Sept 16: America's first peacetime program for compulsory military service comes into being with the Selective Training and Service Act, providing for the enlargement of the armed forces as well as for draft quotas and the training of draftees; the legislation provides that 900,000 selectees are to be taken annually; men between the ages of 20 and 36 are required to register for tours of duty one year in length, a requirement that is extended to 18 months in August 1941.

Above: The Air Force turned out early in the morning for calisthenics. They needed the fitness training because so much of their time was occupied sitting and flying.

When a draftee received orders to report to a training camp such as Fort Dix, New Jersey, or Fort Bragg, North Carolina, it was without reference to any physical incapacity. All men were physically equal, whether they were strapping two hundred pound athletes or one hundred and ten pound weaklings who had never lifted anything heavier than mother's Monday wash. The British and Germans graded their men by a dozen fitness categories, but not the U.S. Army. When the first American divisions landed in North Africa, the typical infantryman struggled ashore with more than one hundred and thirty pounds of equipment.

Orientation began a few days after a recruit stepped off the bus at one of the reception centers, but first came the forty minute Army General Classification Test (AGCT), where examiners attempted to classify inductees by their "useable intelligence." The test placed men into five classes, those with a score of 130 or more being Class I, the highest, and those with a score of 69 or below being Class V, the lowest. To be eligible for Officers Candidate School required a grade of 110 (Class II) or higher, and those with the highest grades were often transferred to the Army Air Force.

to prevent them from enlisting in the Navy during their last two weeks at home. Draftees brought lurid stories home about the medical examination, advising their friends on how to fail the physical by ingesting a handful of aspirin to elevate their heartbeat. Others upped their blood pressure by swallowing Octagon soap. After army doctors discovered the schemes, they passed thousands of men into the service with legitimate health problems regardless of symptoms.

Right: Part of the training involved obstacle courses, and for some of the men the exercises represented more physical exertion than anything they ever did in civilian life.

Whenever possible, the Army attempted to fit a soldier to a job similar to one performed in civilian life. After basic training, a heavy equipment operator might find himself in the 4th Armored Division; a mechanic in a company motor pool; a cook in the regimental mess; or a hospital orderly in the Medical Corps. General Hershey, always looking for fighting men, observed that he never saw "a draft questionnaire...in which the guy said he shot people for a living." By war's end, most "guys" did, because only 15 percent of the Army's classifications could be matched with civilian occupations.

After the test the dreaded inoculations began, using, as draftees believed, a "square needle so dull that its point formed a hook." Fear of the "hook" caused occasional faintings and a jolt of smelling salts. Then came the "shortarms inspection," where an Army doctor examined the draftee's genitals. After confirming the absence of venereal disease, doctors offered sage advice, counseling that "Flies spread disease, so keep yours buttoned."

The first draftees received a mixed collection of clothing left over from World War I, where the average man was one inch shorter and fifteen pounds lighter. It made no difference whether the uniform fit. As long as it could be stretched and buttoned or not fall off, it fit. Footwear was a different matter. Some reception centers made inductees hold two pails of sand – the weight of an average pack – while standing under an X-ray scanner before issuing boots. As one man discovered, "The Army of 1941 showed almost as much interest in a soldier's feet as in the condition of his genitals." By mid-1942, 14,000 men poured through reception centers every week.

After the inductee finished his indoctrination at the center, he went to a training camp. By 1945, the War Department operated 242 camps, but in 1940 they were mainly old structures left behind from previous wars. By 1941, forty-thousand-acre camps, cities in themselves, were being built across the country. Barracks grew at the rate of one every forty minutes – usually a two-story affair with fully appointed latrines to house sixty-three draftees. Once the new crop of neophytes settled into the barracks, a platoon sergeant took control of the men and plunged them into their exercises.

Some ill-chosen campsites gave the soldier a taste of combat conditions. A GI

Left: The Coast Guard had their own methods for drawing recruits. Here, they unloaded a specially built ship on the streets of Detroit to lure young men into the service, though not the boy walking with his mother.

Below: Naval personnel get a quick course in how to shoulder a weapon, allow for distance and windage, and orient the two sights on the barrel to the target.

wrote home from Fort Benning, Georgia, describing it as filled "with mud and dust at the same time." Another soldier stationed at Camp Barkeley, Texas, grumbled that "mosquitoes were so large and so discriminating that before they bit a man they sat on his chest and checked his dog tags for blood type." A letter from a private on bivouac wrote from "Somewhere in the Goddamn Alabama woods." Another GI moved into a new camp that a week later washed away in a flood. The spontaneous humor of the typical GI would sustain him well in the jungles of Guadacanal and the deserts of North Africa, because after the Japanese bombed Pearl Harbor, training took on a new importance.

During the early months of the war, men had little opportunity to become proficient at their trade. They spent more time correcting campsite deficiencies than preparing for battle. Some men built their own grenade course, and because of a shortage of live grenades, practiced by throwing stones into the pits. Others never learned to field strip, clean, load, and fire an M1 rifle until they reached North Africa. Because of the scarcity of 105mm fieldpieces, five crews had to share a single gun, but with war, all that began to change. What the new soldier did learn was the elements of drill and military courtesy, most of which lapsed into unimportance on the battlefield. By the time the first draftees finished basic training, they knew a little about fighting, but barely enough to keep from getting lost in the woods. If nothing else, they were now physically fit and part of a squad, a platoon, and a company, and they understood the chain of command. They had pulled guard duty in the middle of the night, peeled potatoes, slopped the mess hall floor, and scrubbed latrines. They had marched twenty miles with a rifle and pack, bumbled through bayonet practice, stumbled through night fighting, learned to compensate for windage on the firing range, and could almost fix a position with a map and compass.

From the barracks of the Army emerged a quasi-military society unlike anything the country had ever experienced. It included men born with "silver spoons in their mouths" and hillbillies who had never worn a pair of shoes or seen a bar of Ivory Soap. The

---

SELECTIVE CHRONOLOGY OF WAR: 1941

Feb 4: United Services Organization (USO) is founded.

Mar 11: Lend-Lease Act is signed, allowing sale, transfer, and exchange of defense materiel to nations "whose defense the President deems vital to the defense of the United States." Lend-Lease aid to Allies during World War II exceeds $50 billion.

May 27: State of unlimited national emergency is proclaimed.

June 16: President Roosevelt orders closing of German and Italian consulates in U.S.

July 7: U.S. troops land in Iceland to prevent Germany from occupying the island and using its as a naval and air base against the Allies.

Aug 18: Bill passed by Congress permitting Army to keep draftees in service 18 months or longer; previously, active service was for 12 months or less; following Japanese attack on Pearl Harbor, military duty was extended for duration of the war.

Nov 20: Japan presents final demands for keeping peace in Pacific. Demands include: U.S. to abandon China, freezing of Japanese assets to stop, resumption of trade between U.S. and Japan, U.S. naval expansion in Western Pacific to stop.

Nov 27: "War Warning" goes out to commanders of the U.S. Navy Atlantic, Pacific, and Asiatic Fleets.

Dec 7: Japanese forces attack Pearl Harbor in "a day that will live in infamy."

Dec 8: U.S. Congress declares war on Japan.

Dec 11: Germany and Italy declare war on U.S.

Dec 22: The first American troops arrive in Australia aboard an Allied convoy from Hawaii.

new society contained goldbricks, brownnosers, mama's boys, loudmouths, and "sad sacks," the latter being a creature who "did his best, but he was not very bright, always had bad luck, and was often victimized." Those who had never experienced the joys of bathing were hustled into the washroom for a "GI shower," a harsh scrubbing with a stiff brush that turned the skin beet red. College grads who attempted to remain aloof received a Ph.D., meaning "post hole digger." Most men tried to fit in, but some Yanks and Rebs engaged in private skirmishes that drill sergeants brought to an abrupt end by invoking the "buddy system," thereby making the antagonists dependent upon each other.

Heterogeneity brought men of different backgrounds closer together, but what the Army never quite understood was the mind of the GI. Draftees found themselves physically in the Army but mentally unreconstructable civilians. The reluctant buck private thought more about his civilian past and his hopes of the future than he did the Army. He was also better educated than the infantryman of World War I. When the War Department sensed deep unrest among draftees, it authorized Hilton H. Railey of the *New York Times* to carry out an investigation at various camps. After traveling 8,000 miles, Railey concluded that the typical draftee of 1940 was "a different breed of cat." They questioned "everything from God Almighty to themselves," mainly

because they were so well informed on the issues and discriminate enough to differentiate between the importance of certain types of training and traditional Army harassment.

One draftee recalled watching a bull-of-the-woods drill sergeant stand nose to nose with a malcontent and bellow, "You never had it so good! You get three square meals a day and boots on your feet." Instead of replying, "Yes, sir!" the poor fellow politely said, "Thank you," and the sergeant had to walk away to keep from throwing a fit.

To better gage the morale of the GI in training camps, General Marshall organized a detail to open and read soldiers' letters before sending them forward. When discovered, the practice only made the GI madder. An independent observer summed up the

Above: A selection of U.S. firearms issued during the war. Rifles (top to bottom): Model 1917 .30-cal, Model 1903 A1 Springfield .30-cal, Model 1903 A3 with grenade launcher, M1 carbine .30-cal, Model 1903 A4 in sniper configuration, and M1 Garand with bayonet and scabbard above. Handguns (top to bottom): M1911 A1, M1911, S&W Model 10 .38-cal ("Victory"), Colt Model 1917 .45-cal, and S&W Model 1917 .45-cal.

Below: Firing from the kneeling position was more accurate than from the standing position, enabling a soldier to anchor his elbows on his knees to steady his weapon.

attitude of the draftee, writing, "The American soldier is a much more complicated character than he is ever given credit for. He cannot be written into the script as though he were a civilian wearing a brown suit with metal buttons, nor can he be regarded as a 'soldier' – a being whose reactions are totally divorced from civilian emotions."

A buck private would pass up an opportunity to see a movie on the base and pay twice as much to see it in town just to "get away from the Goddamn Army." His reasons were often justified. One Indiana soldier wrote home, "The other evening we lined up for retreat and the corporal verbally burned us in hell with language because one of the fellows had not buttoned... his shirt pocket. Yet, there stood the corporal in front of us with his own shirt button open. Its a job to keep your mouth shut on occasions like this." No wonder GIs disparaged rank. But with all his personal differences with Regular Army personnel, the GI also expressed pride in defending his country.

After about eight weeks of what the Army called "branch immaterial training" (later simplified to "basic training"), the draftee stood inspection before the company commander and was now ready for the second phase of his training. After

Below: Judo instruction for Marines included defensive measures against the bayonet. Cpl. Arvin Lou Ghazlo, USMC, teaches Pvt. Ernest Jones a quick parry at Mountford Point Camp, N.C., April, 1943.

the war, combat veterans listed the least helpful types of training, citing close order drill, bayonet exercise, marches and hikes, military courtesy lectures, inspections, and chemical warfare training.

In 1942 the War Department divided its Army into three branches, those being the Army Ground Forces, Army Service Forces, and Army Air Forces. Each branch set up its own phase two training programs, the Ground and Service forces being quite similar. For obvious reasons, the Air Force required an entirely different program of training, though all of its members first went through the same basic training.

Soldiers assigned to Army Special Forces became the teachers and technical experts – engineers, maintenance men, diesel mechanics, troop and landing ship instructors, supply personnel, and ordnance experts. Others became cooks, bakers, clerks, and special communications technicians. They all received a crash course in the basic

Below: At Fort Benning, crew of a medium M-3 tank clamber on board in April, 1942 – part of the training course that "made them smart and proficient soldiers."

infantry weapons, the M1, carbine, and Browning Automatic Rifle (BAR), but most of them served behind the lines and not on them. The only troops unimpressed by the men in Special Forces were combat soldiers, who viewed those in the Quartermaster Corps as a bunch of inept "goldbrickers" whose first priority was to look after themselves.

The role of the Army Ground Forces was to meld men into divisions that could be formed into field armies. When General Marshall became chief of staff in 1939, he brought a new vision to the organization of the Army. Instead of the old "square" division consisting of four regiments and 20,000 men, he pared it down to a "triangular" division of three regiments and 15,000 men. Leaner and more flexible than the square division, the triangular concept contained greater firepower because of the inclusion of an artillery and a tank battalion.

An infantry division contained three regiments, each having three battalions of about 850 men subdivided into three rifle companies, one heavy weapons (mortars and machine guns) company, a headquarters company with six 105mm howitzers, a service company, and an antitank company. Marshall's concept of

Above: Parachute training at Fort Benning, Georgia, enabled the GI to land in lovely open fields – not in the trees so many of them encountered when landing in France on D-Day.

opportunities. Marshall capped the army's size at 90 divisions and 11 field armies. Sixty-two divisions went to Europe and 22 to the Pacific. Capping the number of divisions placed a heavy burden on the American soldier, especially in Europe, because it forced him to spend more time in battle than his British or German counterpart.

In advanced training camps men learned to perform roles that supported the needs of the division. Those having transferable civilian skills began to fill the unit's vacancies. Eventually training was continued overseas, acclimatizing men to fighting in jungles, in deserts, or along mountain ranges such as those in Sicily, Italy, and southern France. But not until 1942 did the Army have the right trainers – battle-hardened veterans from combat in North Africa and the Solomons, men who understood tank warfare, booby traps, land mines, sniper tactics, and the importance of personal hygiene on the battlefield. Not until 1943 did training centers have all the equipment needed to provide the soldier with the tools of war or training films that depicted live action. As one historian noted, "It is doubtful that the draftees appreciated the moving parts of the M1 rifle as much as the moving parts of Betty Grable...." This was certainly true of the GIs still in stateside camps, where some remained as long as two years. After D-Day, divisions moving to France

a division containing three regiments of three battalions did not come by accident. He believed in the holding attack, with one regiment to fix the enemy in place, a second to seek a vulnerable flank, and a third in reserve to support the other two or take advantage of created

Right: At Camp Lejeune, N.C., Afro-American troops receive their first lessons in drill, a basic training exercise that soldiers seldom ever used after leaving training camps.

continued to train a few miles behind front lines before going into battle. In 1944, when some soldiers got their first taste of combat, they were able to say, "It was no worse than maneuvers."

By 1943, draftees no longer hurled rocks into grenade ditches. Infantrymen crawled through infiltration courses where live ammunition zipped thirty inches over their heads and simulated grenades and mortar shells exploded a few yards away. They scaled 1,500 foot obstacle courses in three and a half minutes while carrying a thirty-pound pack, yelling as they went. They crawled over eight-foot walls, slid down ten-foot poles, leapt flaming trenches, scampered through water mains, hurdled five-foot fences, tottered over twenty-foot cat-walks, cut their way through barbed wire, and charged over jagged four-foot obstructions. In squads and platoons, they circulated through simulated killing grounds, kicking down doors in house to house combat and firing M1s at pop-up targets.

One observer noticed that as a platoon of privates moved through a mock Nazi village, "The wonderful, horrible, strange thing is that they want to try themselves at the real thing....They were all terribly excited by the village fighting. It was the kind of training they like. It has purpose. It is always obvious that when the lieutenant says not to do it that way it means life or death for them to learn it, and in the Nazi village they hang on his words."

There were casualties. Artillery shells

Above: U. S. Marines of the 51st Composite Battalion gather in an anti-aircraft installation to walk through the procedure of operating the gun and setting the timing on the shell.

Left: At Greenville, S.C., men of the Air Service Command Signal Corps work together studying, sending, and receiving Morse code messages using "dits" and "dahs."

SELECTIVE CHRONOLOGY OF WAR: 1942

Jan 9: U.S. Joint Chiefs of Staff is established, as is Combined Chiefs of Staff (U.S. and British) to undertake high-level control of war effort.

Jan 15: The American-British-Dutch-Australian Supreme Command (ABDA) is established.

Jan 26: First U.S. troops arrive in European theater, in a convoy to Northern Ireland.

Feb 19: President Roosevelt signs an executive order making wartime detention of Japanese-Americans possible; within weeks, 112,000 Japanese are removed to secure internment camps, where they remain until Dec 17, 1944.

June 1: Machinery which had been put in motion 10 days earlier results in the start of an effort to recruit blacks for combat service with the U.S. Navy and Marine Corps; the Navy's effort is directed at absorbing 1,000 men a month; the Marines are to recruit a whole battalion of 900 men.

June 17: The first issue of *Yank*, a weekly magazine for American servicemen in World War II, is distributed.

July 31: U.S. Army Transportation Corps is established under emergency wartime authority, with responsibility for moving men and materiel for the Army, Navy, Army Air Force, and other agencies.

Aug 16: One of the nation's most famous military units is formed when the 82nd Airborne ("All American") Division is activated in Louisiana; less than a year later it becomes the first unit of its type to go overseas and the first airborne division in combat.

Aug 19: Four American Rangers, attached to British Commandos, become the first U.S. troops to fight on French soil during the war; their mission was to knock out a six-gun battery in the gunpits around Dieppe during the amphibious assault on the northern France coastal town.

Nov 8: U.S. troops are involved in Allied landings in North Africa as part of Operation Torch; the assault involves 100,000 troops, 258 ships, and hundreds of warplanes.

Nov 12: The draft age is lowered from 20 to 18 under terms of legislation enacted by Congress.

become a cohesive force in an infantry company composed of men who had trained together and had come to trust each other. Soon they would become part of the fighting traditions of a regiment, a brigade, or a division, whether they landed in New Guinea, North Africa, or Europe.

An infantryman might not always like his officers – the handiest object for venting his vexation – but he had come to respect the men who fought beside him. They had been through the hell of training together. They shared each other's attributes and weaknesses, and for the rest of their lives they would be buddies.

After a furlough home, GIs traveled by train to one of eight camps that served as staging areas for ports of embarkation. Three of the largest, Camp Patrick at Hampton Roads, Camp Planche at New Orleans, and Camp Stoneman at San Francisco, geared up to pass units through in one week. When ships were scheduled to leave port, the number of AWOLs (men absent without leave) escalated. After Military Police discovered that regimental officers had granted passes for the soldiers to "see the

exploded prematurely, mortar shells roved off range, hand grenades went awry, and, on rare occasions, parachutes failed to open. "When training casualties occurred," one historian wrote, "the mails were flooded with protests." But all the losses were not training casualties. There were those of another type – misfits who could not adapt, psychoneurotics on perpetual sick call, drug addicts, compulsory thieves, and homosexuals who could not control their impulses, most of whom became "Section 8" discharges.

Those who made it through training went off to war with one of the Army's 90 divisions or as replacements for regiments already in the field. They had

town" on the day of embarkation, the practice stopped.

Private Robert H. Welker, assigned to a ship going to Europe, recalled being rooted out of bed early one morning, "lined up and given boat numbers. Then about ten o'clock a platoon of military police drove up and surrounded the company area, standing armed and ready about every fifteen yards. We were 'under restriction' for movement to a port of embarkation; we were on our way."

To ensure that timorous GIs found no opportunity to go AWOL, MPs herded them onto buses or trains, conveyed them directly to the pier, and formed them in columns near the gangway. Irving Berlin had not gotten around to writing lyrics for World War II, so the port band played familiar tunes from World War I, like "Over There."

Each soldier had a number chalked on his helmet, and as the company sergeant tolled off the man's last name, he answered with his first name and initial. Checked off the list, he then labored up the gangplank wearing all his gear – rifle, cartridge belt, bayonet, canteen, pack, gas mask – and dragging a mightily stuffed

duffel bag. Once on board, every soldier received a form letter from President Roosevelt, which read, "You are a soldier of the United States Army. You have embarked for distant places where the war is being fought." One private crumpled up the leaflet and tossed it in the trash can, remarking, "Tell us something we don't know, Mr. President. You must think we're all a bunch of idiots."

Accommodations on board a troopship made life back at the barracks seem plush. A set of six bunks, stacked one on top of the other, swung on chains or standees. Between each was a two-foot crawl space, making it virtually impossible for a man to change position once he crawled into his bunk. A soldier found no place to sit and spent as much time as possible topside. Some troopships practiced "double bunking," providing one bunk for every two men and forcing them to sleep in shifts. Liners like the *Queen Elizabeth* and *Queen Mary* practiced "triple bunking," but they ran without escort and crossed from one side of the Atlantic to the other in six days.

Joseph Florian, attached to the S-2 Intelligence Section, 95th Bomb Group, had the good fortune to make the crossing on the *Queen Elizabeth*. He recalled bidding "farewell to the magnificent skyline of New York City to the blasting

Above: At Washington, D.C., a group of servicemen are directed onto buses at the Greyhound Station by Military Police, who perform the dual role as guides and making certain that nobody changes his mind about taking the bus.

Left: The 108th Medical detrains at a siding and begins the trek to the point of embarkation. Soldiers traveling long distances, such as those coming from Wisconsin, arrived by train.

Above: Stacked in four-tiered double hammocks, soldiers traveling on a crowded troopship could barely roll over without colliding with someone else or finding a foot in their faces.

horns of every ship in the harbor. Little did the 16,000 troops, who were packed like sardines in a ship designed for 3,000 passengers and crew, realize that it would be exactly two years, almost to the day, when they would see the same sight and from the same ship, on their return journey."

The worst carriers, the crowded Liberty Ships, wallowed through the ocean for three weeks before passing through the Strait of Gibraltar. They were used extensively in the Pacific to shuttle troops from one island to another, leading one division commander to drolly observe that a Liberty Ship provided good training for the hardships of campaigning.

Most servicemen, having never been to sea, felt their stomachs begin to roll, followed by an overwhelming surge of nausea. Queasy soldiers took to their bunks but only got sicker. They ignored

abandon ship drills, almost welcoming an enemy torpedo to end their misery. If those on the top bunk vomited, contents from their stomach dribbled down upon the lower bunks. Those who rushed for the head found it blocked by ailing comrades. Men not afflicted became sickened by the stench. Soon there was no escape from the odor but on deck.

GIs lost track of the days because each miserable hour seemed like eternity. Life on board a troopship provided a rare occasion where men volunteered for KP duty just to get away from the berthdeck. One Yank wrote, "We'll win this damn war but I can't face the trip back."

Most servicemen crossing the ocean did not go directly into battle. They landed in Northern Ireland, Great Britain, Australia, or on one of the Pacific Islands. They filed into new training camps, there to be consolidated into an invasion force. But, in the early stages of the war, some

Left: Disembarked in Northern Ireland, this group of resolute American soldiers in early-issue uniforms demonstrate their determination as they head to new quarters to prepare for fighting the Germans.

of the troops were "combat loaded" so they could come off the ships fighting, such as the division under General George S. Patton that sailed from Hampton Roads and landed on the shores of Morocco.

A soldier's life in a foreign country – be it friendly or hostile – became an education in itself. Some would die, but most would live, and the experiences of their generation would transcend their own expectations of life, death, and war. There would be a multitude of heroes and a few "yellow bellies," but mostly there would be millions of courageous young men in uniform who deserved the right to be proudly called American soldiers.

Bill Mauldin epitomized the combat soldier, writing that "you don't become a killer. No normal man who has smelled and associated with death ever wants to see any more of it. In fact, the only men who are even going to want to bloody noses in a fist fight after this war will be those who want people to think they were tough combat men, when they weren't. The surest way to become a pacifist is to join the infantry."

Below: Life in Great Britain goes on behind the walls of a town while thousands of Americans with equipment and artillery move down the thoroughfare on their way to a new encampment and further training.

DAYS OF BOREDOM AND BATTLE

Right: The U.S.S. *Pennant* was one of the many ships converted by the Navy to haul soldiers from San Francisco to the South Pacific, a long, tiresome journey in cramped quarters.

Below: Fliers and crew of the VCS-7 Navy Unit sit around the coffee pot with English personnel, all waiting for orders that would direct them to their next mission.

In war, there was probably no man more anonymous than the typical GI or more visible than Sergeant George Baker's cartoon persona of "Sad Sack." Picturing a soldier as he stumbled through the sands of North Africa, slogged through the mud and snow of the Ardennes, or hunkered down in a jungle foxhole on Guadacanal, the cartoons captured an image and nothing more. Thoughts roaming through the mind of the typical soldier remained, for the most part, unexpressed.

Probably no correspondent covering the war understood the GI better than Ernie Pyle, a middle-aged newsman who followed the soldier into the front lines and wrote thoughtfully and with distinction of the "mud-rain-frost-and-wind boys" until being killed himself by a sniper's bullet on a grim, lonely island off the west coast of Okinawa.

Dozens of reporters studied the psyche of the fighting man and tried to get inside his mind, but Americans had a way of suppressing their thoughts and laughing off their troubles. When

Corporal Henry Singer told Ernie Pyle, "I just want to get this goddam war over with so I can go home," he probably spoke for millions of others. Nothing more needed to be said. But Singer reached into his pocket, handed Pyle a letter from home, and said, "Read it." His girl had married some guy who worked in a munitions plant. Pyle said he was sorry and handed back the letter. "You keep it," said Singer. "I don't need it anymore. Besides, she was getting a little too fat for me."

Unlike the Allies, Americans developed a different style of fighting. As one reporter from the *New York Times* observed, when the British went into battle, they sang; when the French went into battle, they shouted; but when the GI went into a fight, he did so quietly and suddenly. German prisoners testified to the fear they experienced toward "these silent soldiers moving remorselessly

Above: Not every squad received training before landing on a battlefield, but veteran cadre of the 92nd Division make certain that this squad gets a dose of simulated action at Fort McClellan, Alabama.

Left: Two American prizefighters, Jackie Wilson (left) and Sugar Ray Robinson found themselves in the same Aviation Squadron at Mitchell Field, New York, where they decided to fight a common enemy instead of each other.

forward." Japanese infantryman fighting in the jungles of the South Pacific or on the rocky ridges of Iwo Jima never lived to express their fears because the typical Marine learned to beat the enemy at his own game, and on some islands killed them all. "Killing ain't never easy," said a Marine named Getz, "but I still have relatives in Germany and I'd rather be killing Japs than them."

When bored, GIs wrote letters, especially to sweethearts they left behind. V-mail worked astonishing miracles, reaching the farthermost outposts on earth in about ten days. Getting the mail from the command post to the man on the front line was not so easy, but every "Mail Call" produced a reaction more spontaneous than hot food from the mess tent. Sometimes with the mail came terrible heart-wrenching news that began with "Dear John" and ended with "I know we got married more than a year ago but I'm pregnant with another man's child, and I guess I'd better get a divorce because the guy really wants to marry me." After reading words to that effect, one soldier said, "We were out on some island in the Pacific that no one heard of,

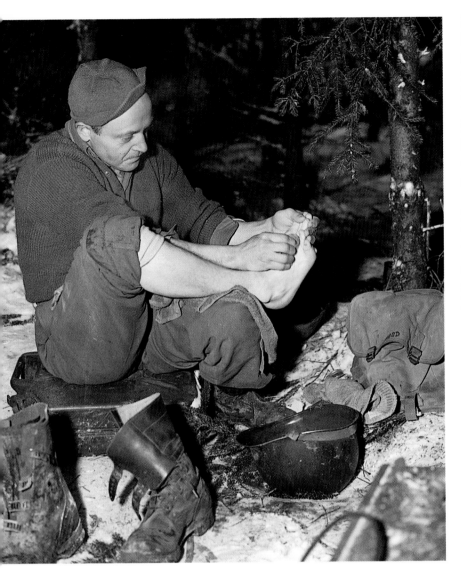

killing civilians in massive numbers. Strategic bombing runs, though aimed at enemy factories, also targeted enemy morale. The American airman soon shed his concerns, especially after the August 17, 1943, attacks on the German ball-bearing factories at Schweinfurt and the Messerschitt factory at Regensburg where casualties among B-17 crews reached enormous proportions.

One co-pilot, flying into a hailstorm of bullets and flak over Regensburg said, "The fear was unpleasant, but it was bearable. I knew that I was going to die, and so were a lot of others...." He had never seen so many German Bf 109s and Fw 190s at one time. They were everywhere, "queued up like a bread line and let us have it." He made it back to the airfield, but others were not so lucky.

Nothing could be more stressful than the life of a flier over enemy territory. A combat soldier on the ground might go through the war in two or three campaigns and fight in a dozen battles. A bomber crew flew 35 missions to complete a tour. The boys in the air knew their chances of survival were far less than 100 percent. They dealt with the prospect of a short life in different ways, mostly in some form of denial. Young fliers relied on eternal optimism, reassuring themselves each day that no harm could come to them. Others kept mentally or physically busy, deflecting concerns over personal mortality through various forms of social activity. As one flier recalled, booze at a local pub filled

Above: Cpl. Lloyd C. Hood of the 101st Airborne Division takes time out to wash his feet, an important hygienic measure to ward off such maladies as trench foot.

and I couldn't get to a telephone if I had to. I never felt so damned abandoned."

For the flight crew who flew bombers over Germany, one of the most difficult psychological hurdles for them to bridge was the knowledge that they would be

Right: The best place to avoid artillery fire is in a bomb crater. Here three riflemen from the First Army take time out from battle to smoke a cigarette while keeping out of sight.

with young women provided the principal catharsis.

Not all GIs were men. Some were women. After the Army entered North Africa, the Nurse Corps followed right behind it, landing at Tunis. They lived in tents erected in bivouac areas just like the men. Most nurses were lieutenants, and they tended to congregate together.

Nurse Eugenia Rutkowski of Detroit, Michigan, had never been under fire until one night "all hell broke loose." Alarms went off, anti-aircraft guns opened, and bombs started falling around the compound. "Talk about being scared," she said, "I sure was," so she started to run for a foxhole in the tent area. A Britisher sprinted by her, shouting "keep pumping," so she followed him, not into a foxhole but into a German bunker built by Rommel's men. Just above the bunker a battery of French anti-aircraft guns opened like a bank of drop hammers, making her ears ring. She noticed that nobody paid any attention to the racket, yet she shook all over. When a lieutenant offered her a chair and a glass of wine, she took them. Reflecting later, she wrote, "I could not believe this introduction to war," but, like all rookies experiencing hostile fire, Lieutenant Rutkowski got over it.

When another untested lieutenant, Edward Jones of the 29th Reconnaissance, went ashore at Normandy, he could not remember being the least bit scared though everyone around him

seemed to be "in a desperate state of nerves." A few days after landing, it occurred to him that soldiers all around him were being shot and killed and he could be next. Then fear set in and "you get a sort of hollow feeling in the stomach and a type of funny ache between the shoulders." Jones could not explain the sudden rush of fear, except to say that "It is just that each of us had a different method of expressing it."

A soldier's reaction to seeing dead comrades brought off the battlefield never changes. It is grim and of few words. Ernie Pyle watched one night as mules brought five corpses down a mountain trail to a road near the front lines in Italy. A soldier came along with the mules, informing those on the road

Above: After the U.S. Army captured Naples, Italy, landing craft rode up to the beaches to unload men and equipment, along with a special treat of nurses running ashore with their trousers rolled up above their knees.

Left: A selection of uniforms of female U.S. service personnel including (left to right) field jacket bearing insignia of 8th and 9th Army Air Forces; M1943 field jacket with American Red Cross insignia and (below it) wool olive drab blouse; nurse's seersucker jacket, trousers, and cap, with utility bag; service jacket with plain civilian buttons, non-combatant's shoulder insignia (left sleeve) and Air Transport Command insignia (right sleeve), plus garrison cap, service skirt, rayon government issue slip, and low quarter Oxford shoes.

Right: America's women needed no encouragement to care for her country's sick and wounded servicemen; they joined up in droves and were sent to all fronts. But, as the war intensified, the Army Nurse Corps felt the need to enlist ever more help.

that one of the dead was their company commander, Captain Henry T. Waskow, of the 36th Division. Two men unlashed the captain and laid him beside a stone wall. Then they laid the other four bodies beside him. In war, nobody buried bodies, so the men began to leave. As one infantryman passed by the captain, he paused, looked down, and said, "God damn it!" The next man came along, looked briefly at the fallen captain, and lamented, "God damn it to hell anyway!" Then a third man came by, who Pyle thought might be an officer. He stooped and spoke to the captain softly, as if he was still alive, and said, "I'm sorry, old man." And then they were gone.

Nobody recognized the other four bodies though eventually someone would. If they were men who had fought with the unit since landing at Anzio or Salerno, chances are their names would be known to members of their company. If they were replacements, their only identification might be dog tags. Of replacements, one infantryman said, "I have seen men killed or captured when even their squad leaders didn't know their names."

Sergeant J. Gaizetti had been fighting around Cassino since early February, 1944, where he distinguished himself during several days of bitter street fighting. Wounded during the campaign, he rejoined his unit, and on June 4 found himself in St. John's Square the day

More nurses are needed!
ALL WOMEN CAN HELP—LEARN HOW **YOU** CAN AID IN ARMY HO[...]
U. S. ARMY NURSE CO[...]
CALL AT YOUR LOCAL RED CROSS CHAPTER OR WRITE THE SURGEON GENERAL, U.S. ARMY, WASHINGT[...]

Rome was liberated. In a letter home he described the square as being "so fully crammed with thousands of shouting people that there was no room for one more sardine." Being of Italian descent, he still spoke a little of the language and soon melded into the crowd. For three

Right: Somewhere in England, Maj. Charity E. Adams and Capt. Abbie N. Campbell inspect the first contingent of Afro-American members of the Women's Army Corps assigned to overseas service.

Left: Paratroopers of the 82nd Airborne Division in Sicily prepare for the invasion of Salerno, which took place on September 13-14, 1943.

days he disappeared. When he caught up with his unit, nobody asked any questions, and if they had, Gaizetti would not have given them truthful answers.

One rainy night near Delle Tombe in Italy, Captain August G. MacDonald cautiously led the advance when a flash of lightning illuminated a German officer leaning forward from a slit trench a few feet away. Startled, MacDonald made a flying tackle, drove the German back into the hole, and beat him repeatedly with his fists. When the man no longer moved, the captain looked him over. The German had been dead for four days.

When the tanks moved ashore on Omaha Beach, the crews inside had been trained to fight, but nobody told them about the hedgerows. Normandy's countryside puzzled them. When tankers crawled up to a hedgerow, they often paused to consider their next move. One American tanker with the 3rd Armored remembered being stalled with a column behind a hedgerow where Germans had pre-sighted their mortars. When shells started dropping, mass confusion ensued mingled with "horrifying screams of stricken men....We immediately saw death and destruction in its most violent form." Dozens of men jumped from their tanks, "running like hell for the rear."

Survivors learned a lesson. If you are on the attack and in the enemy's front, never become a stationary target.

Americans found a marvelous way of amusing themselves by inventing a bald-headed guy by the name of Kilroy whose fingertips clutched the rim of a wall while his long nose drooped over it as he peered vacuously at you. Every GI must have

Below: En route to a drop near Salerno, an officer of the 82nd Airborne gives last minute instructions to paratroopers as they approach the objective.

Above: In camps established in England, messes operated out of huts and served hot meals, but men brought their own mess kits, filling them as they passed down the chow lines.

carried a piece of chalk because the words "Kilroy was here" appeared on rocks, walls, tanks, and enemy helmets everywhere from Sicily to Okinawa. Generalmajor Franz Sensfuss of the 212th Volksgrenadier Division led his command into the Battle of the Bulge and told his men that if they captured a soldier named Kilroy, he wanted to personally interview the prisoner himself.

The combat soldier celebrated his delivery from the jaws of death in many different ways. When granted a respite from duty, some headed for the nearest drinking hole or the nearest bordello, and not necessarily in any order because there were always girls on the prowl in the

pubs and bistros. Others looked for the biggest poker game in town and gambled away six months pay in a few hours. Some sharpies pocketed three or four thousand dollars a night, more money than they could earn in a year back home, but to them the amount meant less than the fun of winning because tomorrow they could all be dead.

American soldiers were generally considered better paid than their counterparts, Allied or enemy. Service pay varied, being based on years of service, years in grade, duty in the United States, duty abroad, combat duty, and so on. After Pearl Harbor, Congress jumped a private's pay from $21.00 a month to $50.00. Every other grade received a commensurate increase, along with increases based upon his length of service. An Army corporal, captured in Italy, found himself being interrogated by a German general and two captains. One of the officers questioned him on his pay. After hearing the answer, the general turned to his captains and chuckled, "He's paid more than you!"

Considering the circumstances, the American serviceman was looked after pretty well. Every Army Overseas Unit operated a PX, which followed the soldier as well as possible. This was not feasible near the front, so in 1942 theater commanders authorized the issue of toilet paper, chewing gum, toothpaste, and cigarettes free of charge from the quartermaster supplies. The GI was offered cigarettes everywhere he went – the local draft board gave him a carton,

Right: A selection of GI's rations, including (in the large boxes) K-rations, not much-liked but considered by Dr Ancel Keys of the University of Minnesota to comprise a balanced meal for breakfast dinner, and supper. The GI liked better the gum and Chesterfield cigarettes, and appreciated the pack of "Waldorf" toilet paper.

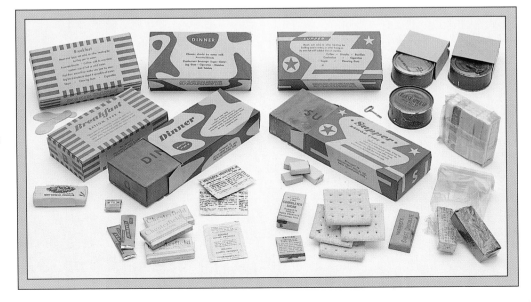

the Red Cross distributed cartons shipside, assault troops received a carton just before the D-Day landing in France. Once ashore, the quartermaster passed out one pack a day, and there was a four-cigarette pack in K-rations.

Like everything in the Army, if it did not have a number, it had an alpha, and rations were no different. The standard Army rations, or A-rations, were for soldiers eating in a mess hall. They were hot and freshly cooked, served cafeteria-style three times a day, and consisted of all the foods that a GI might eat in civilian life, starting with a breakfast of eggs and pancakes, bacon, juice, and coffee, and ending the day with perhaps a pork chops, mashed potatoes, mixed vegetables, bread, coffee, and a dessert.

All other rations declined in palatability compared with A-rations, but not in nutrition. Unit messes operating out of a tent in the rear prepared B-rations, consisting mainly of canned meats – such as the ubiquitous spam – and tinned vegetables, such as peas, carrots, and, though not a vegetable, corn.

Standard combat, or C-rations, contained six 12-ounce, self-heating cans of meat (more spam), stews, and vegetables. D-rations, which the GI called D-bars, were 4-ounce chocolate bars, often hard and stale, which served as an emergency supplement.

K-rations, considered the worst of the lot, contained ingenious compounds which, if nothing else, were nutritious. They were developed by Dr. Ancel Keys of the University of Minnesota, consisted

of three boxes labeled breakfast, lunch, and dinner and contained a balanced and edible meal, all self-contained and ready to eat, with a pack of Chesterfields thrown in for good measure. The food was usually dry and contained bars, looking much like a chocolate brownie, that took up to a half hour to chew through and contained dried meat and dried fruit mixed with a few spices or sugars to give them a little taste.

K-rations did vary: one officer's K-ration contained "a dinner ration (canned meat or stew), soybean meal crackers, a stick of gum, three Chelsea cigarettes, a package of lemon powder, paper-wrapped lumps of sugar advertising Joe's

Above: 2nd Lt. W. Murray, platoon leader, Khaki Combat Team 5707th Composite Unit, picks up a sack of C rations during Merrill's march near Naubaum, Burma, in April, 1944.

Left: A selection of the accoutrements a GI might have had about him, most of them issue items, but some available to the troops through private purchase or institutional donation. Some were designed primarily to keep up the troop's morale, maintain their spiritual well-being, and keep them occupied during periods of inactivity. Most useful of the lot was probably the two-piece mess kit on the right.

Steak House, a few pieces of candy, and finally a can of cheese laced with bacon bits. He thought it was great!"

U-rations, or unit rations, were supplied in a thirty-pound box and were sufficient to feed five men for one day. They were distributed mainly among men involved in vehicular transportation.

Every ration kit came with a tiny can opener, one of the most ingenious devices of the war. Barely one-inch long, the point could pierce a tin and be worked around the can in amazingly short time, putting to shame the more sophisticated devices in mother's kitchen back home.

What a soldier drank depended upon where he went. Arab traders sold a horrible home brew which, if consumed in any quantity, rendered the drinker as senseless as a person clubbed on the head with a baseball bat. In Italy, they drank grappa, a milder form of self-induced misery. In the jungles of the South Pacific there were no watering holes, but there were Seabees. Those coming from Appalachia or the South were well-schooled in the fine art of making "moonshine." Seabees built stills almost as fast as they built airstrips, and they could make "white lightning" out of anything that would ferment.

Seabee Jim Rothermal admitted brewing "raisin-jack" on Guadacanal by blending a gallon of raisins with four gallons of water, adding five pounds of

sugar and a little yeast, and then hiding it in a foxhole to "let it work." In twenty days the concoction was ready to drink. "One batch was outstanding," said Jim. "I filled a soup bowl full, drank it down, and in twenty minutes I could barely walk." Achieving a state of semi-consciousness in less than a half hour became the benchmark for a successful brew.

Some of the soldiers learned to make their own "hootch" by taking a coconut, punching three holes in it, pouring in sugar, and plugging it up until it

Left: Men of the First Battalion, 163rd Infantry, embark from LCIs at Aitape, New Guinea. With them came the Seabees, always ready to build airstrips and roads with their heavy machinery.

fermented. Real drunks filtered Aqua Velva through bread, a trick they learned from the natives. But the moonshiners on Guadacanal made good money selling their distilled spirits at $20 a bottle while real whiskey, bootlegged by Seabees, sold for $40 a fifth. William Schumacher of the 25th Army Division admitted that on Guadacanal some men drank because "there wasn't anything [else] you could do except fight."

Nobody ever counted the number of Marines who went on patrols drunk or with a canteen full of stuff that could get them drunk. Bloated Japanese corpses lay all over the jungle, and the stench was enough to drive anyone to drink. To keep from gagging, Marines broke cigarettes in half and shoved them up their nostrils. If they came across an enemy too sick to evacuate, they shot him, justifying the act as a mercy killing. Afterwards, a drink sometimes helped.

On the body of a dead Japanese soldier, a Marine corporal on Guadacanal found a letter written home by Private

Below: With the Fifth Army in North Africa, four tankmen hitch a ride with their tank on a flatcar – using shelter halves and blankets for a canopy.

Right: Moving up through Prata, Italy, men of the 2nd Battalion, 370th Infantry Regiment, face the rugged mountains they yet have to climb.

First Class Ray Herndon of Waterboro, S.C. On Tuesday, September 15, 1942, Herndon lost his life on the south side of Edson Hill on Guadacanal. Having been mortally wounded in the stomach, he fought off an enemy attack so his buddies could escape from being caught in an exposed area. A day later, the squad returned and killed several Japanese. Searching the bodies of the dead, the corporal turned up a blood-stained letter that Herndon had written to a sweetheart but never mailed.

"I know I am sick with the fever, and if they don't take me off this island soon, I can't predict the future. This is a hellish place to be, but to stay alive, you have to fight every day whether you can stand or not. The sneaky devils are all around us, but we're getting to understand them better than they understand us.

I wish we had gotten married before I went off to war. I think of you every day, and I am fighting this war for us and our future. If you still love me after all these long months, then I ask the Lord that you wait for me. Never before have I needed you so much. If I should die tomorrow, I do so knowing that I love you and always shall. Pray for me."

The letter was dated September 14, 1942, the day before Herndon died in battle.

Mention of the Lord became a new experience for a lot of fighting men. They had learned something about Him when growing up, and they began to learn more from chaplains who came with the division. When one night a battalion of Marines got caught in a wicked crossfire, every man in the unit suddenly became "the most religious and holy guys you would even want to find. At night we were all praying and shaking in our holes. We had a chaplain whom the men grew to like a lot. He was killed in a mortar attack. It was a little hard to take." The chaplain had soothed them, promising that "God was with us," but no one in the battalion could quite understand why God had deserted their chaplain.

In the early stages of fighting on Guadacanal, one of the preferred sources of entertainment came from Tokyo Rose, who personalized many of her messages to specific units, and on occasion to specific individuals. At times, the messages could be disturbing to the undoctrinated. Rose played a lot of popular and sentimental music, hoping to increase homesickness and undermine morale. She seldom succeeded and became instead a soldier's source of entertainment.

Once places like Guadacanal became safe for civilians, though fighting in the jungles continued, movie starlets, singers, and band leaders began making appearances. Not too many entertainers traveled to places like Guadacanal and New Guinea, but Artie Shaw brought his band, and popular Joe E. Brown brought his jokes. Bob Hope, Jack Benny, and Ray Bolger turned up at the Munda airstrip in New Guinea, and gals like Martha Tilton and Carole Landis visited the boys at the military hospital at Cape Gloucester, New Britain.

One of the girls with a troupe on New Guinea remembered sharing with eighty women, "one barracks, one latrine, one shower, and one ironing board." While there, the girls made a startling discovery. If the GIs wanted a little hanky-panky, they saved it for their next furlough. What they did not want was sex and smut from the USO shows.

A more off-beat site visited by two traveling units of the USO was Dutch Harbor, a small base in the Aleutians. Dutch Harbor lacked any form of recreation, and it had become a staging area for men on their way to Attu to oust the Japanese. When the chaplain, Jacob Rudin, learned that Jo Bernier and her all girl dancers were coming, he hurriedly built a platform on the dock. Since the soldiers could not come ashore, they all piled into the stern of the transport, which backed to the dock, and watched Jo and the girls tap rhythm into their hearts.

As the show went on, orders came for

the transport to shove off. The emcee turned to the soldiers and promised to keep the show rolling as long as the vessel stayed in sight. A woman with an accordion came to the mike and softly sang "Aloha," and tears flowed like raindrops as the transport pulled away. "I don't believe," Rudin wrote, "that any troupers ever played to a more appreciative audience than did those USO entertainers to the amusement-starved soldiers." The visit made such a hit with the men that Bernier brought her troupe back, joined by another ensemble of two men and three girls.

Battlefields became macabre killing grounds, but not in ways expected by civilized man. The fight for Buna in New

Above: On August 14, 1943, Sgt. Norwood Dorman of Benson, N.C., holding an M1 carbine, emulates the pose of a World War I Italian soldier, part of a memorial in Brolo, Sicily.

Left: American and British paratroopers from the First Airborne Task Force, Seventh Army, swap war stories and enjoy a respite from fighting as they lean against a farmhouse in southern France.

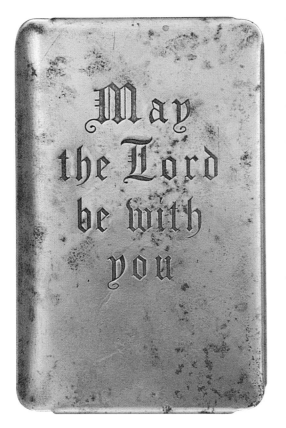

malady that baffled the medics. Men in good health threw down their guns, said they were sick, and refused to fight. They manifested no symptoms but furiously complained of everything from dysentery to acute hepatitis. Examining doctors could find nothing wrong, but the men refused to go back to the front. In his medical report, doctors diagnosed the "goldbricks" as "scared shitless" and shoveled them back to their unit.

Henry Berry chronicled many stories of Marines serving in the jungles of the South Pacific. One of them concerned the 3rd Amphibious Corps, 3rd Marines. On November 1, 1943, a captain took his company ashore on the island of Bougainville. Instead of being confronted with a fire fight on a beachhead, the company settled into a base camp and listened as the action moved deeper into the jungle. Finally it faded away altogether. That's when "That old bugaboo, boredom, set in [and] that old adage about idle time causing problems appeared."

Whether for hygienic reasons or amusement, four of the captain's lieutenants decided to pass the time by getting circumcised. "That's for babies," the captain warned. "Any adult who lets a doctor cut his penis is crazy."

The lieutenants thought they knew better than their company commander and proceeded with the operation. A few days later orders arrived making the four of them captains. They were too vexed by pain and complications to enjoy the promotion. "So I found myself with four

Guinea introduced images soldiers never forgot. Toward the end of the fight, the enemy began falling apart. Dead lay everywhere, but then the wounded and the living began crawling from foxholes and bunkers. They armed grenades, held them to their stomachs, looked you straight in the eye, and blew out their guts. Dick Randall of the 32nd Army Division witnessed the scene, writing, "Those Japs had put up a helluva fight, and now they were killing themselves instead of us. Nothing made any sense. I guess we saved a little ammunition."

The affair on Buna created a new

Right: Services are performed for deceased soldiers at the 3rd Branch Camp, American POWs, at Airyokei, Takao Province, Formosa, circa 1943-44.

newly made captains with very sore peckers. To make it worse, we're on an island with nothing to do. What a mess!"

Enemy snipers had the habit of shooting anybody who behaved like an officer. They would hide for hours with Marines all around them just for a chance to pick-off a captain or someone of higher rank. Too often they succeeded, and new captains without much field experience were always being flown in to take command of veteran units. Some spent too much time dispensing petty discipline just to establish their authority. Squad leader Paul Sponaugle, serving with the 37th Army Division on Bougainville, had a spat with a captain who threatened to court martial him. "I told him [the captain] if he brought up the subject again, I'd shoot him. He didn't bother me any more." Rookie officers forgot that men fighting in jungles had been hardened to killing. Veterans had little patience with dandies wearing brass and on occasion were known to shoot one if the right opportunity presented itself.

When Marines waded ashore for the first time, they did so with men they knew. Either on New Zealand or Australia, they had gone through training together and become friends. As the war waged on, they began to lose their friends and found themselves among replacements, mostly kids who really knew nothing about fighting. Veterans found it easier to become loners than to nurture new friends because they knew the greenhorns would be killed or maimed. "Guess you don't want them to die and hurt you," one grieving Army veteran said. "Its easier to just do your job and not get too close."

Combat soldiers lost all sense of time. Each day was either boredom or battle, otherwise every day was the same. As Frank Chadwick recalled, "you ask someone what day it was, or maybe what month it was, they'd say, 'How the hell do I know?' No one kept track. What for? There was no end in sight." Not until Nimitz bypassed Rabaul and attacked the Gilberts and the Marshalls did the combat soldier begin to see an end to the war. Otherwise, said Chadwick, "we'd be a hundred years old before we got to Tokyo."

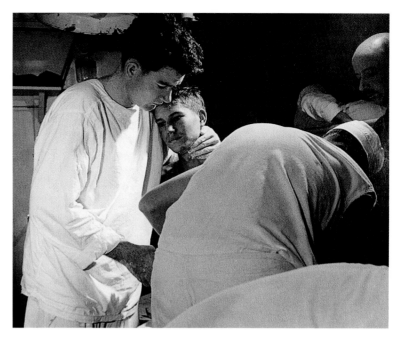

Above: In April, 1945, young Pvt. J. B. Slagle receives his daily dressing of wounds aboard the U.S.S. *Solace* (AH-5) en route from Okinawa to Guam.

During peacetime, sailors developed a habit of not giving much attention to the defense of their ship. On the cruiser USS *Marblehead*, all of that changed after December 7, 1941. One week later Warrant Officer W. E. Jarvis recalled that "Men who had never given much thought to observation [were] now busy scanning the sea and air for Japs. Engineers off duty [could] be found acting as lookouts or asking...the ship's crack gun captains how to operate this or that gun, where the ammunition comes from, and other things they needed to know to fight the ship." Like many of the vessels in the Pacific Fleet, *Marblehead* was an old antiquated cruiser having no sonic equipment for spotting submarines or a short-range voice radio for fast communication with other ships in the convoy. So nervous had

Below: A small selection of shoulder insignia representative of most of the major American commands active in the Pacific theater. The shoulder patch was not only a means of identification, but also a source of unit pride.

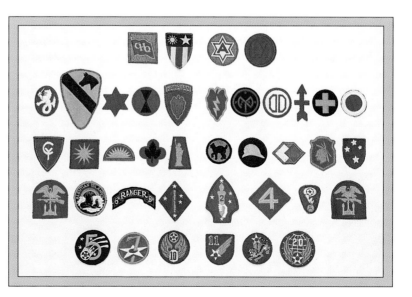

the crew become over their deficiencies that they mistook a school of whales for a pack of enemy submarines.

Sailors lived through weeks of inactivity and boredom interrupted by moments of sudden panic. Iwo Jima, like many of the islands in the Pacific, was surrounded by coral reefs and deep water, and Navy transports tended to anchor in the lagoon. If a vessel moored too close to shore, nobody got sleepy on watch that night. After dark, the enemy would come down to the beach, strip off their clothes, tie three or four hand grenades to their bodies, and with barely a ripple, swim out to the ship. Sentries sat with rifles fore and aft, peering into the water. If shooting started, nobody slept, but nothing upset the nerves more than hearing a metallic object strike the deck and roll out of sight, sometimes exploding, sometimes not.

Seven-man underwater demolition teams (UDTs) operating from ships off Okinawa drew perilous assignments during the days before the landing. The enemy had driven hardwood posts 10-12 inches in diameter into the sand and coral along the beach and interlaced them with barbed wire. Edward T. Higgins had been in the bitter cold water the previous day and remembered suffering severe leg cramps. Before he shoved off for the mission, he pulled on the top half of his winter underwear, hoping it would help keep him warm.

Once in the water, each UDT man pulled five packs of Tetrytol charges weighing fifty pounds each, but Higgins did not think the drag from his woolen underwear would slow him much. As the team neared the beach, bullets began spattering in the water nearby, and a soft voice said, "Higgins, old boy, someone is shooting at you!"

Higgins moved away, swimming toward another man from the team. "He reacted as though I was shoving a floating mine in his direction," Higgins recalled. Then the man turned and hollered, "You son of a bitch, get away from me with that Goddam white sweat shirt! Do you want to get us all killed?" Then it dawned on Higgins that his underwear made a marvelous target, but with five packs of explosives riding behind his torso, he could not take it off. That day, the UDTs cleared 1,300 yards of beach fitted with 1,400 obstacles. Higgins got back to the boat safely but vowed never to wear his underwear on the outside again.

Nothing jarred a sailor's nerves more

than kamikaze attacks, not even submarines. On April 3, 1945, a swarm of enemy aircraft came off Okinawa and attacked the American task force. From the control director on the destroyer *Aaron Ward*, signals went topside and six 5-inch guns swung as one and pointed toward the target picked by the director. At 7,000 yards the 5-inchers opened with the usual dull ba-ROOM, ba-ROOM. At 6,000 yards a small stream of smoke curled from an enemy Val D3A, but the plane kept coming. At 4,000 yards, the kamikaze dipped over for its suicide dive. At 2,000 yards every sailor on the destroyer was saying to himself, "Now or never!"

All along starboard, the little 20mm guns swung into action, and somebody shouted, "Get him! Get him!" One of the gun crews pumped out a 5-inch shell that struck the Val and blew it up almost in their faces. A hundred yards from the ship, the plane dipped into its death dive. At the last minute the pilot catapulted from his cockpit. With an unopened parachute, he hurtled high across the ship and landed in the water on the other side. Bill Radar looked up and saw the face of the man as he passed overhead, and said, "He looked like a mess of raw hamburger."

A short distance away, five kamikazes roared down from 10,000 feet in a vicious, well-coordinated attack on the destroyer *Little*. Gun crews brought down the first plane, but the second struck the destroyer's port side, doing minor damage. But the next three planes survived the fire and slammed into the ship. A bomb landed in *Little*'s after engine room and blew up her boilers. High pressure steam ripped the ship open "like a sardine can." In less than ten minutes, she folded up and sank, taking with her ten members of the crew. Like many fights at sea, the furious action lasted about fifteen minutes.

Every soldier, sailor, and airman experienced a multitude of emotions when pitched into battle. One former squad leader, Louis Maravelas, who fought his war on land, probably spoke for thousands everywhere when he said, "By the time we left [the Pacific], I think my mind had gone over to the clouds somewhere. You lose touch with reality, fortunately not for long."

FROM PEARL HARBOR TO ISLAND-HOPPING SUCCESS

Right: On December 7, 1941, the Japanese attacked Pearl Harbor. Many of the vessels presumed irreparable were eventually returned to service, but not the destroyer U.S.S. *Shaw*, which blew up in the harbor.

As dawn streaked the sky over the Hawaiian Islands on Sunday, December 7, 1941, and soft ocean breezes swept across the island of Oahu, the first wave of 184 dive-bombers, torpedo-bombers, high-altitude bombers, and fighters took off from six Japanese carriers and set a course for Pearl Harbor. An hour later, a second wave of 171 planes, most of them torpedo-bombers, followed.

At the Marine base that morning, soldiers idled about the compound, smoking cigarettes after leaving the mess hall. Sailors on watch on warships moored in the harbor strolled the decks, enjoying the warm, sultry air. Boxes of anti-aircraft ammunition remained locked; officers on watch had the keys. At the Army, Navy, and Marine airfields, a few members of the ground crew hung about the hangars, some waiting for the arrival of a group of unarmed planes coming from the mainland.

At 7:02 a.m., Private Joseph L. Lockard of Williamsport, Pennsylvania,

Below: Naval losses at Pearl Harbor included eight battleships hit and five sunk. Three cruisers and three destroyers were lost along with 2,403 men killed and another 1,178 injured.

manned one of the mobile aircraft detection units on Oahu. After his watch ended, he stayed because he "was interested" in what appeared to be a large flight of aircraft 130 miles slightly east of north and heading for the island. After checking his readings for twenty minutes, he reported his observations to a lieutenant on duty at the Army's General Information Center. The officer had been told some planes were expected from the mainland, so he assumed that Lockard's readings were of friendly aircraft.

A half hour later the distant droning of the first wave of Japanese aircraft became audible, and when a few enemy planes swept over Diamond Head, nobody paid much attention to the big red dot painted on the wings and fuselage. Minutes later, all kinds of hell broke loose. High-flying bombers plastered Hickam Field, leaving the Air Corps with only sixteen serviceable aircraft. Low-flying planes, armed with shallow-running torpedoes, swung over the water and converged on the anchored battleships.

By 10:00 a.m. six of eight great battleships – *Arizona*, *California*,

Nevada, *Oklahoma*, *Tennessee*, and *West Virginia* – either lay on the bottom of Pearl Harbor or struggled to remain afloat. Pillars of thick, black smoke blanketed the harbor. Three destroyers in drydock lay ripped apart, three cruisers sustained heavy damage, 2,403 men died, and 1,178 more lay wounded. On what President Roosevelt declared the "date which will live in infamy," America's ability to protect her interests in the Pacific were obliterated. From a disaster that devastated the Pacific Fleet, one small ray of hope remained. Three aircraft carriers were not in port that day.

On December 8 Congress passed a joint resolution declaring war on Japan, and three days later a second resolution declaring war on Germany and Italy. By then, Imperial Japanese forces had raided or bombed Guam, Midway, Wake Island, and the Philippines and put a force ashore at Bataan to capture the small American-Filipino garrison. The air attack destroyed 18 of 35 B-17s, 56 fighters, and 25 other aircraft at Clark Field on the Philippines. The British also got a dose of General Hideki Tojo's workmanship when Imperial forces attacked Malaya, Hong Kong, Singapore, and Burma and sank the only two capital ships on His Majesty's station in the Far East.

Two days later, 6,000 Japanese landed on the unfortified island of Guam and rolled over 700 Marines and Guamanians

armed with nothing heavier than .30-caliber machine guns. On December 11 a Japanese amphibious force tried to land on Wake Island, lost two destroyers, and was driven off by 450 Marines. Nine days later the enemy returned with a larger force. The Marines fought heroically, killing 700 of the invaders before being

Above: Had the Japanese made an amphibious attack on Hawaii, the American servicemen, armed with .30 caliber Model 1903 rifles and Model 1910 bayonets, were ill-equipped to meet it.

Left: After Pearl Harbor, the loss of the Philippines and the subsequent death march of American and Filipino soldiers from Bataan to the Cabanatuan prison camp became the next worst disaster of the war.

Above: After weeks of defending the tiny island of Corregidor, American forces finally surrendered to overwhelming odds, giving the Japanese the false impression that the GI was not a formidable foe.

statement, "The President of the United States ordered me to break through the Japanese lines and proceed from Corregidor to Australia for the purpose, as I understand, of organizing the American offensive against Japan, a primary purpose of which is the relief of the Philippines. I came through and I shall return."

With the outset of war in the Pacific, the United States suffered an internal malady – command confusion. The Army and Navy finally resolved who would be in charge of what. MacArthur drew command of the Southwest Pacific Area, comprising Australia, New Guinea, the Philippines, the Solomon Islands, the Bismarck Archipelago, and most of the Netherlands East Indies. The Navy controlled all the rest of the Pacific. The arrangement created a defect. Having no supreme commander guaranteed no unified effort, and the Army and Navy would, for the most part, fight two separate wars against Japan. Admiral Ernest J. King, Chief of Naval Operations, had the foresight, however, to pick subordinates much like himself – good strategists, marvelous tacticians, brilliant fighters, and excellent motivators.

overwhelmed. It was a fight to the death and, for the first time since the attack on Pearl Harbor, a Japanese invasion force received a dose of American courage. It would not be the last.

On December 24 a strong amphibious force under Lieutenant General Masaharu Homma landed on the shores of Luzon and nine days later captured Manila, pushing Filipino and American forces to the Bataan Peninsula. On February 2, 1942, Roosevelt ordered General Douglas MacArthur to quit the Philippines and fly to Darwin, Australia. At Darwin the general issued his famous

By the beginning of August, 1942, Imperial forces occupied the Pacific area from the western Aleutians in the north, the Solomon Islands and New Guinea in the south, and the Netherlands East Indies, Thailand, and Burma in the west. The Japanese plan to overrun southeast Asia, exploit it, and build an impregnable defensive perimeter around its conquests

Right: Though U.S. forces did not assault the Gilbert Islands until November, 1943, commandos on the deck of the submarine U.S.S. *Argonaut* return in August, 1942, from a raid on Makin Island.

began to stumble on June 4, 1942, first at Midway and again on August 7, when Admiral King took the first step on the long road back to the Philippines and gained a foothold in the Solomon Islands on Guadacanal, Tulagi, and Gavutu. The summer of 1942 marked the end of Japan's fast and frenzied expansion.

At Midway on June 4, 1942, Japan lost four carriers, and with those carriers went the Imperial Navy's hopes of finishing off the American Pacific Fleet. Instead of driving into India, Japan stopped at Burma to conserve its resources. If the Imperial Army could cross from the north over the Owen Stanley Mountains on Papua and capture Port Moresby, and at the same time build air bases on the Solomon Islands, they could cut the flow of American supplies into northern Australia. During the first six months of the war, though the official strategy of the United States was to whip the Germans first, four times as many men went to the Pacific than to Europe. Had this not been done, Japan's domination of the Coral Sea and northern Australia would have been complete, making it doubly difficult for Allied troops to secure a foothold in the Solomons or New Guinea.

The Joint Chiefs of Staff, after muddling the command in the South Pacific, formed three operations called "tasks." For Task One, they shifted responsibility for recovering the Solomon Islands to the Navy and began to plan an amphibious assault. Task Two, under MacArthur, would advance up the northern coast of New Guinea at the same time as amphibious attacks began in the Solomons. After these operations got underway, the Joint Chiefs would then decide when MacArthur should launch Task Three, capturing the enemy's main supply center at Rabaul, New Britain.

It came as quite a surprise to MacArthur when he learned that on July 22, 1942, 16,000 Japanese troops had landed at Buna on the northeast coast of Papua. He found it even more amazing when the landing force began crossing the impregnable Owen Stanley Mountains and driving toward Port Moresby, the key to controlling the western Coral Sea and a natural staging

Above: During the Japanese air attack on the U.S.S. *Enterprise*, a bomb struck the flight deck of the carrier, killing Robert F. Read, who lost his life taking this picture.

area for invading Australia. The landing occurred at the same time that Vice Admiral Robert Ghormley was planning an amphibious assault on Guadacanal.

What attracted Ghormley's interest in Guadacanal, one of the southernmost islands among the Solomons, was the airstrip being constructed by the enemy. So at dawn on August 7, eight months after Pearl Harbor, he sent the 1st Division of the 1st Marines ashore to seize it.

One Marine with the first wave said, "Oh, my God, when dawn did break, what a sight! All these ships had moved up during the night, battlewagons, cruisers, carriers, tin cans, you name it, it was there....Then, wham! the wind blew and you knew what flew. Those swabbies opened up on the island with a vengeance."

For three hours the Navy pounded the

SELECTIVE CHRONOLOGY OF WAR: 1941

Dec 7: Japanese carriers launch attack on Pearl Harbor, forcing United States into war. Nineteen U.S. ships are sunk or disabled, 188 warplanes destroyed, over 2,400 Americans killed and 1,178 wounded. Japanese lose 5 midget submarines, 28 aircraft, and fewer than 100 men. Two Japanese destroyers also bombard Midway Island.

Dec 8: Japanese forces attack Hong Kong, Guam, Midway, Wake Island, and Philippines.

Dec 10: Japanese land on Luzon, Philippine Islands.

Dec 23: Japanese land on Gulf of Lingayen, Philippines.

Dec 23: U.S. Marines on Wake Island surrender following second Japanese landing.

Above: During the Battle of the Coral Sea on May 7, 1942, the U.S.S. *Lexington* received serious damage. The Japanese thought she was out of commission, only to find her back in business a few weeks later.

minute they saw us." On the nearby islets of Tulagi, Gavutu, and Florida Island, sharp fighting occurred, but on Guadacanal, the Marines landed unopposed. They quickly captured the unfinished airstrip and renamed it Henderson Field. The quiet soon erupted into a fierce campaign involving six naval battles and a jungle fight that lasted eight months.

It took time for American soldiers to acclimatize to the jungles of Guadacanal. Robert Kennington, a 25th Division infantryman, came from Florida and North Carolina and thought he knew something about heat. "Guadacanal," he said, "put both of them to shame. In the jungles the trees block any breeze. You don't get any air at all. You can cut the humidity with a knife. It felt like...127 degrees in the shade." When staking out a new perimeter, Kennington remembered GIs being "felled by the heat before they got to our positions. They just passed out along the trail....We were hit by the heat, mosquitoes, leeches, and a little bit of everything else." Trees in the jungle grew to a height of 100 feet, spilling out vines that sprawled on the ground with "big hooks on them like a rooster spur. When you...ran into one of those vines, you either stopped or were cut up. When tangled you backed out. You learned not to try to bull through them because those hooks were like a razor. I still have scars from them."

War in the jungle became a nerve-racking duel with Japanese snipers. Contrary to war movie renditions of snipers camouflaging themselves in trees, most trees in the jungle could not be climbed; should one be scaled, the dense foliage made it impossible to see anything below. What worried patrols were the snipers on the ground. Under roots of big trees, a sniper would dig a hole straight down like a well, camouflage it on top, and crawl inside with a rifle or a machine gun. If a patrol wandered by, he would rise from the hole and open fire.

shore before the 1st Marines, commanded by Major General Alexander A. Vandergrift, waded ashore. "We didn't realize it at the time," said one observer, "but [the bombardment] was almost a complete waste. The few Japs in the area had hauled ass back into the boonies the

SELECTIVE CHRONOLOGY OF WAR: 1942

Jan 7: Japan begins siege of Bataan.

Feb 1: U.S. Navy launches surprise attack on Japanese bases and shipping on Marshall and Gilbert Islands in effort to protect trans-Pacific supply routes to Australia.

Feb 22: General MacArthur is ordered to leave Philippines, and is appointed C-in-C Allied Forces, Australia.

Feb 23: Japanese submarine shells oil refinery near Santa Barbara, California, the first enemy attack on U.S. mainland.

Apr 6: Japanese land on Bougainville and Admiralty Islands.

Apr 9: U.S. and Philippine forces on Bataan surrender to Japanese. Infamous "Death March" begins, during which many U.S. and Filipino perish on 65-mile trek from Marireles to San Fernando.

Apr 29: Japanese capture Lashio and cut Burma Road, the only passable road between India and China.

May 6: After withstanding a month-long siege, U.S. garrison of 11,500 men on Corregidor surrenders to Japanese.

Aug 7: U.S. Marines land on Guadalcanal, taking strategic Japanese airfield, and naming it Henderson Field; Japanese are not ultimately driven from the island until Feb 1943; more than 5,000 U.S. Marines and Navy personnel are killed in action on Guadalcanal.

Aug 24: Japanese attack on Henderson Field thwarted in Battle of Eastern Solomon Islands; Japanese lose 1 light carrier, 1 destroyer, 90 carrier aircraft, against 17 U.S. warplanes lost and carrier *Enterprise* damaged.

During August and September, the beachhead on Guadacanal continued to expand until 17,000 Marines occupied a seven-by-four-mile strip around Henderson Field. The Japanese wanted

Left: At the Battle of Midway, the Douglas Dauntless dive-bombers with folding wings surprised the Japanese and destroyed four of the Imperial Navy's big carriers.

Guadacanal back in the worst way and poured in reinforcements from their base at Rabaul. Whenever Imperial troopships with reinforcements moved down the Solomons through "the Slot," Japanese battleships and cruisers would hammer Henderson Field to destroy its aircraft.

Marine Clifford Fox remembered the night of October 13 when two enemy battleships, supported by cruisers and destroyers, bombarded the airfield from midnight until dawn. "We had all dug little foxholes," Fox recalled, but "the battlewagons were throwing huge fourteen-inch shells....God, the noise was incredible. Boom. Boom. The earth shook like it was going to swallow us all. I thought it was the end of the world."

A fresh Army division had just landed on the island, but few of the men had bothered to dig foxholes. As soon as the shelling began, a GI dropped into a nearby hole and, after landing on Fox, began "reciting all those Catholic prayers. By that time some people were going crazy.... A sergeant in our unit cracked up. When I got up at sunrise, it looked like some god had swept his giant hand and knocked the palm trees down, leaving jagged stumps in their place."

In the Solomons, Admiral Ghormley moved too slowly to satisfy Admiral Chester Nimitz, Commander in Chief of the Pacific Fleet. Nimitz was a mild-mannered Texan promoted over 28 officers after the Pearl Harbor debacle. He found Ghormley exhausted and defeated, so Nimitz sacked him and put

Vice Admiral William Halsey, the Navy's most aggressive and colorful commander, in the job.

Halsey wasted little time. On October 26, the same Japanese squadron that had bombarded Henderson Field stood off Santa Cruz Islands, east of San Cristobal. Halsey sent Admiral Thomas Kincaid with two carriers, *Hornet* and *Enterprise*, to meet them. Kincaid lost *Hornet* after suffering heavy damage from dive bombers, but American planes from *Hornet* and *Enterprise* disabled two Japanese carriers, two battleships, several other vessels, and

Below: The Navy's PBY-5A Catalina flying boat and patrol bomber served all over the Pacific Ocean, this one landing on a field at Amchitka, Aleutians, during January, 1943.

Right: A PT boat marksman draws a bead with his .50 caliber machine guns off New Guinea on July 8, 1943. The fast but lightly armed PT boats also carried a pair of torpedo tubes.

Below: A selection of uniforms and equipment issued to the U.S. Army GI, indicating the adaptability necessary to clothe and equip a soldier in opposite extremes of climatic conditions. The left-hand group shows early war items for tropical theaters, as issued in 1941-42, while the right-hand group shows pieces of winter service kit, which was standard in the northern campaigns to recapture the Aleutian Islands of Attu and Kiska.

sank two enemy destroyers.

On the nights of November 13-15, two more naval engagements occurred, this time off the north coast of Guadacanal in "Ironbottom Bay," so named for the wrecks piling up on the bottom. The Americans could ill afford to lose another ship, but in the three-day battle the Imperial Navy sank two American cruisers. The Japanese lost two battleships, seven transports loaded with infantry, and limped back to Rabaul with two cruisers heavily damaged. Only four damaged transports bearing reinforcements made it to Cape Esperance on Guadacanal. In Halsey, the Imperial Navy would find a much tougher customer than Ghormley.

For the GI fighting on the ground, war contained a variety of horrors. Jap fighters swooped over the treetops, strafing patrols caught on ridges having little protective cover. "If you looked," said one Marine, "you could see the pilot's face."

On occasion a P-39 Airacobra would fly in low and "get the jump" on the enemy. Airacobras worked well for low level attacks at ground level but could not compete with the Zero at high altitudes. A few rounds of cannon-fire from a P-39, however, could rip apart a Zero. When one fell into a ravine below a ridge, a squad on patrol gave a cheer, but one observer recalled, "it didn't always go our way. A few times we watched our planes coming back from a dogfight. Sometimes they couldn't make it and crashed into the jungle."

While fighting raged indecisively in the jungles of Guadacanal, Japanese forced their way across the tip of Papua until stopped by Australian troops thirty miles from Port Moresby. In mid-September, MacArthur rushed in planes and two poorly prepared National Guard divisions of infantry. He did not understand the Army's new triangular division formation of infantry, artillery, and tanks, so he broke up the 32nd Infantry Division and sent it into Papua without heavy artillery or tank support. This compelled Major General Edwin F. Harding, the luckless commander, to break the undergunned division into task forces and throw them against virtually impregnable defenses.

MacArthur never admitted his mistake, but he learned from it, and to his credit, he learned fast. In casualties, the Papua campaign exceeded losses at Guadacanal by a factor of three and required more than ten months and 40,000 troops to battle the Japanese back over the mountains, capture the Buna-Gona area, and begin the long two-year drive up the northern coast of New Guinea. The enemy retreat across the mountains turned into a rout. Thousands of Japanese died of starvation and disease, and their commander, General

Tomitaro Horii, drowned crossing a river.

For MacArthur, retaking New Guinea became essential. It would open the way for a pincers movement that could isolate Rabaul, Japan's most important base in the Solomon Sea. When Allied forces assaulting Buna reached a state of collapse from jungle fever and hunger, General George C. Kenney taught MacArthur what planes could do by airlifting in 15,000 fresh troops. With reinforcements came a new general, Robert L. Eichelberger, whom MacArthur told to take Buna or to not come back alive. Eichelberger did both. Though naturally thin, the effort cost him thirty pounds.

During the months that followed MacArthur's long campaign along the northern coast of New Guinea, the Army and the Marines started up the Solomon Islands. The key to America's success became the judicious use of tactical air. Unlike Europe, the enemy's air defenses were weak and worsening. For MacArthur and Halsey, every island became a potential air strip, bringing more and more Japanese targets within bombing range. In February, 1943, Marines led the way, landing on the Russell Islands; in June, on New Georgia; in August, on Vella Lavella; in October, on Choisel and the Treasury Islands.

The second part of the pincers plan involved Halsey, who on November 1, 1943, landed troops on Bougainville, the largest island in the Solomon chain. The Japanese attempted to drive away the invasion fleet with four cruisers and six destroyers. Halsey repulsed them with four light cruisers and eight destroyers. The Imperial Navy countered by dispatching to Rabaul one light and seven heavy cruisers and four more destroyers from their main fleet at Truk.

Halsey had no battleships or heavy cruisers to protect his invasion force because they were all with the Central Pacific Fleet. What he did have on loan were two fast carriers, *Saratoga* and *Princeton*. Carrier planes had never attacked a base as heavily defended as Rabaul, which contained some 150 aircraft, but the situation had become so desperate that Halsey ordered Rear Admiral Frederick C. Sherman to throw every dive-bomber he had against Rabaul.

Above: On November 20, 1943, men of the 2nd Battalion, 165th Infantry, find the going rough as they wade ashore at Butaritari on Makin Atoll. The Japanese are firing machine guns from two wrecked ships (right) 800 yards away.

Below: On Kwajalein Island, flamethowers of the U.S. Army 7th Division smoke out Japanese troops hunkered down in a blockhouse where bullets could not reach them.

Right: On October 22, 1944, LSTs unload troops and supplies on Leyte Island in the Philippines, adding an exclamation mark to General MacArthur's promise to return.

Halsey expected Sherman's fliers to be cut to pieces, but the Bougainville beachhead had to be protected at all costs. Sherman launched two air attacks on Rabaul that destroyed half of the enemy's aircraft and forced the Japanese commander to send the rest of his planes back to Truk with the cruisers. Halsey did not want all of Bougainville. He wanted just enough of it to build an airstrip for

more strikes against Rabaul. As one Marine recalled, "Our job was to establish a large perimeter so the Seabees could build an airstrip. This they did. Thousands of Japanese soldiers were left to wither on the vine in the deep jungle."

The land campaign on Guadacanal ended in February, 1943, but fighting in the miserable jungles on New Guinea and Bougainville continued for many months to come. At home, *Life* magazine complained that after a year of fighting, U.S. forces had only advanced from Guadacanal to New Georgia, a distance of two hundred miles, and grumbled that at the present rate, the war would end in 1957. But neither the editors of *Life* nor the Japanese could see the American strategy unfolding before their eyes.

In heavy weather on March 1, 1943, American reconnaissance planes spotted a large Imperial convoy crawling moving with 17,000 troops through the Bismarck Sea toward the northeastern coast of New Guinea. Two days later B-17s and B-25s from Major General George C. Kenney's Fifth Air Force look off from Papua and shattered Japan's plans for holding New Guinea. The bombers struck with a fury, sinking or damaging ten warships, twelve transports, and 102 Japanese aircraft.

The enormously successful attack sent Tokyo an undeniable message. Japanese forces had reached the end of their penetration. Now they would have to constrict their ebbing power to safeguard

SELECTIVE CHRONOLOGY OF WAR: 1943

Jan 29: Battle of Rennell Island opens U.S. Guadalcanal Campaign offensive which ends organized Japanese resistance on the island by Feb 8.

June 30: Operation Cartwheel, amphibious operations against Japanese positions in the Solomons, begins with two U.S. Army divisions and one Marine detachment landing on New Georgia, the objective being to take Japan's most important base in the Solomons; because of mistakes, it takes six weeks to bombard the base into submission.

Oct 6: U.S. Marines land on Kolombangara, near New Georgia.

Oct 9: A U.S. amphibious force of 4,600 ends the New Georgia campaign during the Battle of Vella Navella, paving the way for the U.S. assault on Bougainville.

Nov 1: U.S. Marines land on Bougainville; within 18 days American troops there number 34,000.

Nov 20: Amid a deadly barrage of Japanese fire, U.S. Marines land on Tarawa; they have to wade ashore from 500 to 1,000 yards out, many drowning under the weight of their equipment.

Dec 26: U.S. Marines land on Cape Gloucester and capture Japanese airfield there three days later.

Left: A selection of U.S. small arms and accoutrements. Rifles (top to botom): Model 1903 A1 .30-cal with Model 1905 bayonet and early scabbard; Johnson Model 1941 semi-automatic rifle .30-cal, with Model 1941 spike bayonet; M1 Garand .30-cal with Model 1942 bayonet and plastic scabbard; M1 carbine .30-cal, with two extra ammo clips and obverse/reverse ammo pouches; Model 1903 A1 with M8 8x telescopic sight, for Marines; Winchester Model 1917 trench gun, 12-gauge; Winchester Model 12 trench gun, 12-gauge. The pistol is the ubiquitous M1911 semi-auto, .45-cal.

their conquests. The costly war in China had sapped energy from the Imperial war machine, and along the island fringes, American soldiers were remembering Pearl Harbor with a vengeance. When Halsey captured the Solomons and MacArthur New Guinea, Rabaul became isolated. On Rabaul, 100,000 Japanese soldiers waited for an invasion that never came.

New Guinea and the Solomons gave Americans the experience they needed to contend with a skillful, durable, and wily enemy. GIs eventually became better conditioned to the intense heat, the bugs, the snakes, and the foul stench of rotting jungle vegetation. They learned to distinguish between the natural noises of the jungle and the squawking signals produced by the enemy. When the shooting ended, the stage was set for the joint forces to begin an island-hopping campaign that would end on the island of Okinawa, three hundred miles from the coast of Japan.

Once the Japanese lost their foothold in the Solomons and New Guinea, MacArthur and Halsey discovered that by keeping Imperial forces committed to the defense of strongholds such as Rabaul, Allied casualties could be minimized by capturing the lightly defended outer islands. There, air bases could be established to deprive the enemy of supplies at their bastions of strength.

By mid-1943, MacArthur still had only four American divisions and six Australian divisions, and Halsey had neither battleships nor heavy cruisers. In the Central Pacific, Nimitz had only nine Army and Marine divisions to operate against the Gilberts, Marshalls, and Marianas.

Every American commander had been schooled in traditional tactical concepts, but the island-hopping strategy MacArthur and Nimitz designed and perfected for fighting in the Pacific transcended anything in textbooks. It isolated 135,000 Japanese in strongholds where they gradually became flanked, bypassed, and buried without any hope of rescue far behind the fighting front.

On November 20, 1943, the Central and South Pacific commands – the largest flotilla in history – came together and pounded the shores of Makin and Tarawa in the Gilberts. A few days later a series

Below: On October 25, 1944, during a *kamikaze* attack on the U.S.S. *White Plains*, a Japanese Mitsubishi Zeke crashes into the water off the ship's quarter.

Above: During the Battle of Philippine Sea in June, 1944, a Japanese bomb scores a near-miss on the U.S.S. *Bunker Hill* and pays the price by having its tail shot off (at left).

of amphibious attacks subdued the fanatical defenders of Makin, most of whom had been fortified with rice wine. Hollywood liked the story, put Randolph Scott into a Marine uniform, and produced the film "Gung Ho," starring the 2nd Marine Raider Battalion. The quirky film impressed the public much better than it did the Marine Corps.

On Tarawa, more than 4,000 crack Imperial Marines held the principal island of Betio, a stronghold comprised of connecting pillboxes made of concrete, coral, steel beams, and coconut logs. Tokyo boasted that the island could never be taken by assault. Though bombarded by naval guns and bombed by carrier planes, the pillboxes and their occupants survived. When the U.S. Marines waded ashore, they were hit hard with machine gun, mortar, and artillery fire.

Naval guns continued to shell the island defenses with little effect. Marines

faced a stubborn and bloody battle, storming every position with grenades and flame throwers. During three days of intense fighting, the Marines suffered 3,000 casualties – 40 percent of the assault force – with 1,000 dead. Japan lost 4,500 men, all on an island of less than three square miles.

Marines going ashore observed an enemy tactic that senior officers had overlooked. The Japanese let the first wave come ashore, intending to entrap it after pulverizing the second wave. "I know," said one Marine. "I could see them. Those poor guys were dropping in bunches." The casualties were atrocious. "I was on that small piece of hell known as Tarawa for seventy-six hours, but it seemed like seventy-six days to me. My memories are mainly one of fear."

Though lessons learned at Tarawa were applied to subsequent landings, assaulting strongholds would continue to be bloody work despite all efforts to soften enemy defenses. The Navy could find no alternative to frontal attacks on strongly defended islands, and the worst was yet to come. When in November, 1943, the American and British Combined Chiefs of Staff (CCS) forged ahead with an "Overall Plan for the Defeat of Japan," it called for more assaults of fortified islands. Nimitz received a schedule to take the Marshalls in January, the Carolines and Truks in July, and the Marianas in October. MacArthur, Nimitz, and Halsey did not like the plan, and had the CCS listened to them there may never have been another

Right: A selection of technical manuals and training equipment issued to U.S. troops in the Pacific theater. The largest item is a carrying box of War Dept. training aid set on Japanese mines and hand grenades. The little red book (upper, left of center) is a War Dept. Japanese language phrase book, though the average GI didn't really want to talk to the enemy!

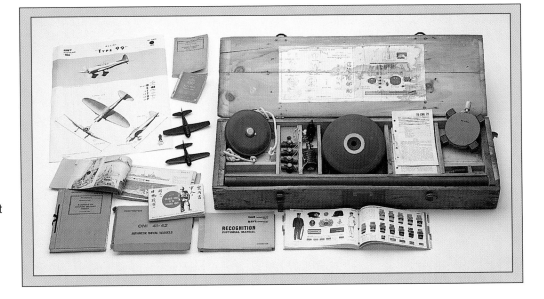

Left: In the Battle of the Philippine Sea, American fighters fly above Task Force 58 during the "Marianas Turkey Shoot," on June 19, 1944. Japanese aircraft losses during the day amounted to 218.

blood bath like the one on Tarawa.

As soon as the smoke cleared on Betio, the Seabees moved equipment onto the island and began building the airstrip needed for planes to reach Kwajalein in the Marshalls. In civilian life, Seabees had been professional men, steam-shovel operators, mining engineers, quarriers, or road builders. Almost overnight, using bulldozers and earth movers, they turned the pock-marked coral landscape into an airfield.

Before Nimitz assaulted Kwajalein, the largest atoll in the world, his ships and planes dropped fifteen thousand tons of explosives on the island. On Kwajalein, the first prewar territory of Japan to be assaulted, Imperial defenders hunkered down in the rubble and fought savagely. Marines took heavy casualties as they struggled to establish a beachhead. Every

pillbox, every fortification, and every foxhole had to be blown or burned out to rid the atoll of the enemy.

By March, Nimitz was ahead of schedule. He had retaken the Gilberts and Marshalls, and, using carrier-borne fighter-bombers, had leveled the enemy's huge base a Truk, rendering it useless.

By 1944 Japan began to feel the squeeze from China and Great Britain in the west, Russia in the north, and the United States everywhere else. America's industrial power astonished Japan. Since Pearl Harbor, the United States had built the largest fleet – 4,700 vessels and 613 warships – and the greatest air force – 18,000 aircraft – on the planet. Even more disturbing, the American high command had developed a strategy for island-hopping that left some of the Imperial Army's veteran fighting units

Below: A selection of U.S. Army armor crew (left-hand group) and aviator's (right-hand group) uniforms and equipment. The herringbone twill one-piece overalls (far left) were worn by tank crews and maintenance personnel; the helmet was lightweight and pierced for ventilation. The aviator's leather jacket features the insignia of the 90th Bombardment Group, nicknamed "Jolly Rogers". At bottom right are silk escape and evasion maps.

Above: In February, 1944, Army tanks of the 7th Division smash through the beachhead on Kwajelein, followed by infantrymen armed with machine guns and Browning Automatic Rifles (BARs).

trapped behind the front. And while Japan continued to turn out Zeros, Grumman developed F6F Hellcat planes that could outfly Mitsubishi's best fighter aircraft.

After recapturing thousands of square miles of enemy occupied territory, the Joint Chiefs of Staff began formulating plans for invading Japan. This meant getting much closer to Japan than the Marianas or the Philippines. Each island along the way formed an important stepping stone to Iwo Jima and Okinawa. Admiral King, Chief of Naval Operations, at first hoped to bypass places like the Philippines by building airstrips in eastern China but changed his mind. In March, 1944, he decided to take back the Philippines and give MacArthur an opportunity to wipe out the stain of 1942's humiliating defeat.

The route to the Philippines led through Netherlands New Guinea to the south and the Marianas to the east. While MacArthur's army pushed up from the south, Spruance hit the Marianas – Saipan, Tinian, and Guam – with 535 ships and 127,000 men. The Navy needed the islands as a submarine and supply base, the Army Air Force needed them for

airstrips from which B-29s could operate against Japan.

Some of the fiercest fighting of the war occurred on Saipan. The hilly island, filled with rock formations and caves, withstood the naval bombardment, suffering little damage to its natural fortifications. Soldiers hitting the beach were met by successive *banzai* attacks. More than three weeks of ferocious fighting – burning and blowing the enemy out of caves – occurred before the island came under American control. Tinian and Guam fell with light loss. The Seabees went to work on the rocky turf, and on November 24 the first B-29s took off from Saipan to bomb Japan.

On June 19-20, during the fight for Saipan, another battle took place at sea and in the air. Americans called it the "Great Marianas Turkey Shoot." The Imperial Fleet made a desperate attack with carriers and fought furiously. One sailor wrote, "When the air was filled with Zeros and other Japanese planes the slaughter began." At one point, Zeros "fell like flaming torches, fifteen burning simultaneously in the sky." The enemy lost more than 450 planes; the United

States 130. Having sacrificed most of its air cover, the Japanese fleet limped toward the Philippines, losing thirty ships, among them three carriers.

With the Marianas cleared of the enemy in the air and on the sea, Americans mopped up isolated pockets of resistance. Private George Ruckman remembered Saipan as "an orgy of death." He recalled firing blindly into some brush at fifty yards and killing eighteen of the enemy. When the fighting finally ended, 23,811 Japanese lay dead on Saipan, among them civilians who had committed suicide. On August 10

Guam fell, giving the Seabees another airstrip to build.

The loss of Saipan, followed by the first B-29 bombing raids, caused great consternation in Tokyo. Tojo's Government fell, replaced by a cabinet under aged General Kuniaki Koiso, whose attitude toward the war had turned to thoughts of securing an honorable peace. While the new cabinet contemplated its predicament and more bombs fell, Halsey's Third Fleet side-stepped the heavily fortified island of Truk and on September 15, 1944, hurled 1,350 tons of shells and 9,000 rockets into the Palau

Below: One of the important duties of submarines was to rescue downed pilots. Here the U.S.S. *Sea Devil* rescues a crew from a Navy plane downed in the East China Sea.

"*We'll lick 'em—* **JUST GIVE US THE STUFF!**"

Above: One of many posters produced by the U.S. Government Printing Office urging greater wartime productivity of military equipment. Others included the "Enlist Now!" and "We Couldn't Have Done it Without You!" variety.

Islands of Peleliu and Angaur. As the smoke cleared, 45,000 Marines and soldiers waded ashore. The 1st Marine Division swept over reefs, through barbed wire, and established a two-mile beachhead along the southwest coast of Peleliu.

The island, but twelve square miles, contained a valuable airstrip. Marines secured the field the day after landing, but it took another month to rid the island of Japanese. Defenders holed-up on "Bloody Nose Ridge," a mountainous mass of clefts and crags perforated by hundreds of caves. Veteran Marines called the fighting "the worst yet encountered in the long history of the First Division." In the end, 11,000 Japanese lay dead, but the Marines paid dearly, losing 1,800 killed and another 8,000 wounded. Another gateway to the Philippines and Japan now lay open.

Imperial Headquarters assumed that what MacArthur had said in 1942 about returning to the Philippines was a pledge the general intended to keep. They made elaborate preparations to bring on a decisive battle that would smash the Allied offensive. Using their intelligence network, lodged mainly in Moscow, they concluded that MacArthur would strike

Leyte sometime during the latter days of October and that the attack would be preceded by heavy bombing strikes from the 14th and 20th Air Forces. Tokyo had the American strategy analyzed almost to the letter, but Admiral Soemu Toyoda refused to commit his vessels until he had positive proof that MacArthur was on the move. By hesitating, Toyoda lost the initiative, and during the interregnum, Admiral Mitscher's Task Force 38 attacked Japanese airfields and destroyed 3,000 aircraft.

On October 20, 1944, when MacArthur's army of liberation landed on Leyte, Admiral Toyoda's Imperial Fleet was nowhere to be found. The general waded ashore on the beach at Palo, trundled in wet trousers to a microphone on a radio truck, and issued his first broadcast: "This is the Voice of Freedom, General MacArthur speaking. I have returned!"

Three days later the greatest naval battle on the planet began in Leyte Gulf. Toyoda split his force into three separate commands, using one to decoy Halsey's Third Fleet away from the Gulf, intending to destroy it later. Halsey took the bait and made off after a squadron of carriers having few planes. This left Vice-Admiral Thomas C. Kincaid's Seventh Fleet to deal with the larger part of the Imperial Navy's 70 warships and 716 aircraft, the latter joining the fight for the first time as *kamikazes*, or suicide planes. Each *kamikaze* carried a 550-pound bomb, the purpose being to crash-dive onto a carrier deck.

When Halsey discovered that he had been duped, he sank four carriers, a cruiser, and two destroyers before turning around. Had Halsey blocked the San Bernardino Strait instead of falling for Toyoda's deception, the entire Japanese fleet might have been destroyed. As it was, Kincaid mangled the Japanese fleet to such an extent that Toyoda saved only four capital ships, and the Imperial Navy never again became a factor in the war.

While Kincaid and Halsey battled at sea, MacArthur encountered far less resistance on Leyte than expected. Supported by organized guerrilla attacks that disrupted Japanese supply lines, MacArthur's forces swept across Leyte

Left: In preparation for future operations, American troops of the 160th Infantry, 40th Division, rush ashore from a landing boat during amphibious training on Guadacanal.

and Samar. By the time the struggle ended, the Japanese had lost 125,000 men, the Americans, 2,888 dead and 8,500 wounded or missing. When the enemy attempted to withdraw from the island on warships, American aircraft sent the crowded vessels to the bottom. MacArthur moved up the line of islands, first to Mindoro and then to Luzon and the capital Manila.

On January 6, 1945, President Roosevelt spoke for tens of thousands of American soldiers, sailors, and marines when he informed Congress that, "We

have driven the enemy back more than 3,000 miles across the central Pacific.... The people of this nation have a right to be proud of the courage and fighting ability of the men in the armed forces — on all fronts." And so they were, but in January, 1945, Japan had not surrendered, nor had Germany. There was still a war to fight.

On January 29, MacArthur put General Eichelberger, the most experienced jungle fighter in the Army, ashore at San Narcisco with the 24th and 38th Army Divisions. The force drove inland and reached the town of Subic the same day it landed. When snipers' bullets began whizzing about the general's ears, Eichelberger grabbed a tommy gun from a soldier and fired back. A staff officer suggested that the general would be safer if he removed his stars, to which the latter replied, "What the devil's the use of being up here if nobody's going to know about it. I want all my boys to know I'm here going through it with them." Four days later Eichelberger led his divisions into Manila.

At nightfall, January 30, thirty green-clad Rangers and Filipino guerrillas initiated the first of a series of mass rescues of prisoners deep behind enemy lines. They crept noiselessly through the hills of Nueve Ecija Province and overwhelmed the guard at Cabanatuan prison camp. When the shooting began,

Left: Merrill's Marauders, fighting behind enemy lines in Burma with General Joseph Stilwell, receive an air drop of supplies and carry them off the field for distribution.

prisoners dropped to the floor, expecting their moment of execution had come. Rangers broke through the barbed wire and burst into the barracks, and their eyes fell upon 513 gaunt and ragged survivors from Corregidor and Bataan. "Take it easy, fellows," a Ranger said, "the Yanks are here! We got this place, pals!"

On February 7, MacArthur arrived. He spoke briefly to the cheering citizens of Manila. "I'm a little late," he said, "but we finally came."

After that, Japan lay exposed. She no longer had a navy, and 450,000 of the Emperor's best troops were annihilated on the Philippines. The only Imperial force that could still qualify as an organized army operated in southeastern Asia. When in October Stalin branded Japan as an aggressor nation, the announcement compelled the Imperial high command to retain a force of 2,500,000 men in Manchuria. With regards to China, MacArthur knew exactly what to do. Like the enemy island fortresses of the Pacific, he would "hop" it.

Admiral Spruance talked the high command out of attacking Formosa – a potentially costly and unnecessary conquest when the islands of Iwo Jima and Okinawa could serve the purpose of supplying air bases for B-29s. Iwo already had three airfields and a radar station. From there, P-51s could escort B-29s right into Honshu and back. The immediate problem was to shut down Iwo's airfields because Superfortresses bombing Japan from Saipan passed near the island and were harassed by Zeros.

The only problem was the eight-square-mile island itself. Twenty thousand Japanese defended it under Lieutenant General Tadamichi Kuribayashi, a courageous and ingenious commander who had fortified the island with minefields, concrete artillery embrasures for 115 heavy guns mounted on Mount Suribachi, interlocking underground tunnels forty feet deep, and two-story pillboxes. He had also removed all cover from the only two beaches on which an invading amphibious force could land. The Japanese considered the island impregnable. Kuribayashi had told them so.

Left: In February, 1945, members of the 503rd Parachute Infantry Regiment land on a knoll on the island of Corregidor, in the Philippines.

Since August, 1944, Iwo had been bombed by aircraft, shelled by naval vessels, and as each month passed into 1945, the bombardments intensified. At 9:00 a.m. on February 19, battleships, cruisers, and destroyers circled the island, jarring it with devastating fire. Two Marine divisions hit the beach. The 4th Division cut across the narrow tip of the island while the 5th Division captured the two main airfields in the island's center. The 3rd Division remained in reserve. Before long, all three divisions found themselves in the Marines' "toughest fight of its long career." "We took Iwo inch by inch," one Marine declared, "by crawling forward on our stomachs or behind tanks that bogged down in volcanic ash."

After three days of furious combat, Joe Rosenthal of the Associated Press took one of the most famous photographs of the war – five Marines planting a staff bearing the American flag on the rocky crest of Mount Suribachi. But the fighting continued for almost a month. Organized resistance ended on March 16 with a costly Butcher's Bill – 4,189 American officers and men killed in action, 441 missing, and 15,308 wounded. More than 20,000 Japanese died in the twenty-six day blood bath.

During the fight for Iwo, Admiral Mitscher's carrier planes, followed by 200 Superfortresses, hit Tokyo's industrial heart, burning out 29,000,000 square feet of the city and destroying airfields and shipping docks. As one pilot said, "Hell was breaking loose on Japan."

By March, the combined commands operating in the Pacific needed to tackle one more island before setting their sights entirely on Japan – the capture of the Ryukyu chain and its principal island of Okinawa, a perfect launching site 350 miles from the heart of the Rising Sun. Neither the Joint Chiefs of Staff nor the American soldiers who fought for the Okinawa beachhead knew that the

Below: After hitting the ground, this paratrooper quickly shed his 'chute and readied his .30 caliber M1 carbine. With binoculars slung around his neck and two spare clips in a pouch on the carbine's stock, he awaits orders to advance. As was common practice in combat zones, no insignia is worn.

campaign would be the last great battle of the war. Nor did the Japanese, who had massed more than 100,000 men and 3,000 aircraft for the island's defense.

The landing began on Easter Sunday at 8:30 a.m., April 1, 1945, under the experienced hand of Admiral Spruance. He put Vice-Admiral Richmond Turner in charge of amphibious landings. Turner arranged simultaneous attacks at four different points – one under himself, the others under Spruance, Mitscher, and Lieutenant General Simon Bolivar Buckner. They expected strong resistance but found little opposition on the beach. Five hours after the first wave of Major General John R. Hodges's XXIV Army Corps and Marine Major General Roy S. Geiger's III Amphibious Corps waded ashore along an eight-mile stretch on

Okinawa's west coast, they captured the first important airstrip without a shot being fired.

Sergeant Fred A. Myers, of Maybrook, New York, who jumped ashore on the islet of Aka at 8:04 a.m., earned the distinction of being the first American soldier to set foot on Japanese soil. A step behind him came Lieutenant Robert Berr, of Decatur, Illinois, commanding Company K of the 3rd Battalion, 305th Infantry Regiment. They met no resistance, but Japanese propaganda had half-convinced the natives that Americans would violate the women and slaughter the inhabitants, advocating mass suicide as a preferable fate. One soldier observed, "When the inhabitants saw they had nothing to fear, they came out of hiding and willingly did what they were told."

Not until six days later did the quietude end. Lieutenant General Mitsuru Ushijima, Okinawa's commander, had pulled his troops to the southern side of the island, waiting for an invasion that came from a different direction.

On April 6 and 7, the "maddest sea-air battle of the war" began. Seven hundred Japanese aircraft – half *kamikazes* – pounded the American beachheads and attacked the fleet offshore. The attack sent six American vessels to the bottom, but the Japanese lost its superbattleship, *Yamato*, two cruisers, four to six destroyers, 135 *kamikaze* aircraft, and 265 fighter-bombers.

After that, the island fight became a war of attrition. Nimitz described it best

when he reported, "Our troops are now striking at a fortified line which is organized in great depth and developed to exploit the defensive value of the terrain, which is dissected by ravines and terraced by escarpments....They include interlocking trench and pillbox systems, blockhouses, caves, and the conventional Japanese dug-in positions." Flame-throwing tanks turned defensive works into cinders, but most of the fighting on the ground became stubborn, scored daily in yards gained.

Eighty-one days later, June 21, the battle ended. General Ushijima and his executive officer ate their last great meal. Before it could digest, they knelt in full dress uniform and cut out their entrails. The Japanese lost 110,000 soldiers. Only on the Philippines had the Imperial Army lost more men than on Okinawa. The same could be said for 50,000 American casualties, 12,500 being those killed and missing. But, by then, 300,000 American troops had massed on the island, setting the stage for the invasion of Japan.

For the next forty days, B-29s plastered Tokyo, Nagoya, Kobe, and Osaka with devastation so horrible that fire-winds sweeping the streets tossed gushes of flame high into the sky. Ten days of successive bombing flattened twelve square miles of Japan's four greatest cities and reduced them to charred ruins. Yet the Japanese held on, gathering their forces to face an American invasion.

Instead, at 8:15 a.m. on August 6, the first uranium bomb created an inferno

over Hiroshima, turning the city into a gigantic fireball, killing and injuring 150,000 people. Still Japan held out. Three days later the first plutonium bomb blossomed over Nagasaki, incinerating 100,000 more.

Taking advantage of an injured enemy, Russian minister Vyacheslav Molotov advised the Japanese minister that the Soviet Union would declare war. With the words barely out of his mouth, Soviet troops invaded Manchuria. On August 10, Tokyo sued for peace, and the war in the east ended.

For the United States, war with Japan had been an island-hopping success. For the American soldier, it had been a nightmare. For the Japanese, it had been a disaster. For the world, it had been another war to end all wars but failed.

Above: On February 23, 1945, Pvt. Bob Campbell shot this photo of Marines raising a large American flag on Mount Suribachi, Iwo Jima.

Left: A scene of devastation at Hiroshima, after the B-29 *Enola Gay* dropped a "Little Boy" atomic bomb which exploded 2,000 feet above the city on August 6, 1945. It still took another atomic strike, on Nagasaki on August 9, to force the Japanese government, paralyzed by indecision, to surrender.

THE AIRMEN IN EUROPE AND THE PACIFIC

The first hint of what lay in store for Germany began on the night of August 4, 1940, when a small number of RAF planes did what in the mind of Hitler was unthinkable. They bombed Berlin. Damage was slight, but the wail of sirens, the piercing shafts of searchlights, and the thump of anti-aircraft guns gave the *Wehrmacht* a small dosage of the air war they had inflicted upon Britain. After that, the raids became more frequent and more devastating.

When the United States entered the war in Europe in 1942, they concentrated on destroying Germany before Japan. The initial burden fell upon the U.S. Eighth Air Force, organized on January 28, 1942, and in May placed under the command of Major General Carl Spaatz. Spaatz brought a staff to Bushy Park, near London, and sent his crews off to bases in Britain. But Spaatz had no aircraft, so the first missions flown by the Eighth Air Force were in British bombers attacking German submarine pens in France, and

the first fighter aircraft flown by Americans were Spitfires. Spitfires, however, did not have much range, and the first bitter comments came from bomber crews, who said, "Hell, we've got it now: Spitfires to the German border and Focke-Wulf 190s and Messerschmitt 109s the rest of the way."

After Spaatz received his first shipment of B-17 "Flying Fortresses," he insisted on using them for daylight bombing. The remarkable high-flying bomber came equipped with thirteen .50-caliber Browning machine guns mounted on the top, along the side, on the bottom, in the tail, and in the nose, with pairs fitted in rotating turrets. By flying in close formation, Spaatz believed the bombers could look after themselves by spraying enemy fighter aircraft with a hail of concentrated fire. The British attempted in vain to discourage Spaatz from daylight bombing. When the Germans had tried it over London in 1940, British Spitfires had knocked the bombers from the skies.

Spaatz's insistence upon daylight precision bombing had more to do with the B-17's Norden bombsight, which could drop, some said, a missile "in a pickle barrel." To achieve such accuracy, the target had to be pinpointed – something that could not be done at night. But dropping a bomb "in a pickle barrel" from 10,000 to 25,000 feet simply did not work. Free-falling bombs descending from such altitudes could drop anywhere within a five mile radius, and did.

The British argument against daylight raids continued until September 8, 1942, the day when the high commands in Washington and London reached an agreement – Spaatz would do the daylight raids, and the RAF's Sir Arthur "Bomber"

Below: "Mary Ruth – Memories of Mobile" B-17F Flying Fortress of 401st Bomb Squadron, 91st Bomb Group, leads a formation of bombers bound for German targets.

Harris would perform the nighttime raids. The arrangement gave rise to Hitler's worst nightmare – "around the clock bombing." As one news correspondent recalled, "When the sun went down over Hitler's *Festung Europa*, Royal Air Force Stirlings and Lancasters rumbled through the Rhineland mists and on to Saxony and Brandenburg. And when, through the swirling smoke, the sun arose in the East again, American Liberators and Flying Fortresses came roaring down the aerial avenues." With so many sorties coming and going, aircraft controllers on the ground ran a complicated timetable to prevent incoming and outgoing aircraft from occupying the same skies.

During World War I, the public fancied an airman as a handsome, romantic sort of chap wearing a colorful silk scarf who fought war more like a gentlemen's tournament than a deadly business. The home front impression carried into the first months of World War II, stimulated by motion picture idols like Jimmy Stewart, who flew twenty missions over Germany for the Eighth Air Force. The officers of a B-17 bomber – being the pilot, copilot, bombardier, and navigator – and their six crewmen never enjoyed the individualistic distinction of the fighter pilot because they operated as a team.

And, for every man in a bomber, there

were seven unglamorous guys on the ground maintaining the aircraft and repairing battle damage. They were mechanics and weathermen, ordnance and supply personnel, clerks, cooks, staff personnel, radio operators, and ground crews that had to load each B-17 with from 5,000 to 17,600 pounds of bombs depending upon the distance to the target.

In May, 1943, when the first American B-17 bombing raids began, there were

Above: A groundcrewman issues "Chocks away" signal to the cockpit of a B-17 at its base in England. Almost 8,700 Flying Fortresses were built for use over Germany and Occupied Europe, and for operations in the Far East and Pacific.

Left: B-17s undertook bombing missions over Europe by day, often operating beyond the range of their fighter escorts, until North American P-51 Mustangs became available.

Above: Pilots got all the credit, but ground crews did most of the work. After every flight they checked the engines, sometimes removing one and replacing it with another in less than a day.

Right: Close formations gave B-17s concentrated fire against enemy fighters but led to other problems. Here a bomb from an upper B-17 shaved off a tail section from the lower aircraft.

many problems. One member of the 335th Squadron, 95th Bomb Group, vividly recalled what it was like flying over hostile territory without fighter escort cover. After crash-landing at the airfield, he inspected the B-17, writing that it "was literally riddled with holes of varying size from flak and fighters, which we encountered over Nazi-occupied Europe. It was an absolute miracle that not one of our crew was killed or even injured from that sort of withering firepower. Little did we realize that this was only the beginning."

Every mission became a protracted ordeal where ten men spent five to ten hours jammed into a cramped duty station weighted down with sixty pounds of gear in freezing temperatures. They wore parachutes, steel reinforced flak vests, bulky flight suits, and oxygen masks that one B-24 airman declared "felt like a clammy hand clutching the lower part of your face." Nobody drank much liquid because the ordeal and discomfort of relieving oneself in the frigid altitudes was too much trouble.

Hours of grinding tedium added to the crews' discomfort. Pilots had to hold formation; navigators, from a cramped corner near the nose, reported the ship's position every few minutes; radio operators sat for hours listening to static; gunners stared into the skies searching for enemy aircraft; and everyone tried to stay awake and alert after a night on the town and three hours' sleep.

Planning and executing a mission involved more than the aircrew. For a routine raid, tens of thousands of men and women toiled for hundreds of thousands of hours to put several hundred B-17s, B-24s, or in the Pacific, B-29s, over an enemy target for five or ten minutes.

Americans were still trying to perfect daylight flying when the Eighth Air Force decided to strike the Kiel shipyards on the northwestern coast of Germany. This created a scurry of activity on the paved areas where the bombers parked. Thousands of specialists attached to the ground crew hurried to complete any servicing or repairs of the bombers' metal sheathing, the oxygen apparatus, instruments, guns, and other equipment. But each plane had three or four ground crewmen permanently assigned to her, and they took special pride in keeping her fit. When she returned, they lovingly painted another bombing mission on her fuselage, and when she failed to return, they wept.

For the Kiel raid, Brigadier General Nathan Bedford Forrest III, grandson of the famous Civil War Confederate cavalry leader, wanted to try a new flattened formation that brought all aircraft to the same altitude and literally flew wing-tip to wing-tip, the purpose being to bring a greater concentration of fire to bear on attacking enemy fighters.

Before the lead squadron crossed the enemy coast, Fw 190s and Bf 109s, with noses painted bright colors – red, yellow, and black-and-white checkerboard –

descended in a swarm on the bombers. B-17 pilots called them "Goering's Flying Circus," and, as one nose gunner observed, they quickly became "thicker than gnats around the rear end of a camel."

First came flak bursting off the wingtips and then came the fighters. Captain Grif Mumford remembered one of his pilots looking out the window and saying, "Boy, are we in a heap of trouble." Bursting flak shook the ship, "but the Fw 190s and the Bf 109s would put the fear of God into anyone."

Fighters attacked head-on from twelve o'clock, their wings flaring and smoking with machine-gun fire. Cannon fire burst from the noses of Bf 109s. It is "frightful," one first-time pilot recalled, "particularly when [I] realized that they were firing at us. For the next fifteen minutes I was in a state of absolute and incredulous shock." He spent half of his time watching burning aircraft go down, and the other half ducking under the instrument panel with his head in a steel helmet while the aircraft droned forward on automatic flight control.

General Forrest's flattened flying formation lasted one mission. As German fighters massed for a diving frontal attack, B-17s flying behind and under Forrest's wing could not fire without hitting his aircraft. As a consequence, the lead vessel absorbed a tremendous raking from the enemy and fell out of formation. It was the last anyone saw of Forrest or his B-17.

During the Kiel raid, German fighters followed the B-17s out over the sea. With engines feathered, some of the bombers dropped down to 500 feet and became sitting ducks for Fw 190s swooping down for the kill. One B-17, with all engines smoking, suddenly pitched nose first and plummeted into the North Sea. After surviving aircraft touched down safely at Framlingham, Suffolk, one pilot vowed "never to let the German fighters scare me again," and, he recalled later, "They never did."

Twenty-six B-17s from the 95th Bomb Group flew on the mission to Kiel. Two aborted the flight before reaching the target, ten of the aircraft never returned. After no more planes reached the field,

Above: Over Oranienburg, eighteen miles north of Berlin, cannon fire from an Me 262 twin-jet propelled fighter chops off the wing of this B-17 from the U.S. Army 8th Air Force.

Colonel Kessler called his fliers into the debriefing room. As he listened to their accounts, his eyes filled with tears, repeating over and over again, and to no one in particular, "What's happened to my boys? What's happened to my boys?" The war was yet young, and the Colonel Kesslers of the U.S. Army Air Force would have much to lament before it ended.

When the bombers returned to base,

SELECTIVE CHRONOLOGY OF WAR: 1941

June 20: U.S. Army establishes Army Air Forces, combining Air Corps with Air Force Combat Command.

Aug 18: The U.S. announces that Pan American Airways is ferrying warplanes to Britain from the Middle East via Brazil and West Africa in an attempt to speed up delivery to the hard-pressed British.

Dec 7: Following Japan's attack on Pearl Harbor, aircraft from the carrier U.S.S. *Enterprise* engage enemy aircraft in the first aerial combat by the Navy in the war; *Enterprise* is about 200 miles from Pearl Harbor, returning from delivering a Marine fighter squadron to Wake Island. Credit for the destruction of the first Japanese Zeros by the U.S. Army Air Corps is shared by 4 pilots, each of whom registers kills near Oahu, Hawaii.

Dec 9: B-17s bomb shipping in the Philippines in the first U.S. bombing mission of the war, as the heavy bombers, in consort with P-40s and P-35s, attack a Japanese convoy landing troops and equipment at Vigan and Aparri in North Luzon.

Dec 16: Flying a P-40 Warhawk, Lt. Boyd D "Buzz" Wagner becomes the first American ace of the war when he shoots down his fifth enemy warplane in succession in the Philippines.

Dec 20: Claire Chennault's "Flying Tigers" enter combat against Japanese in China, shooting down 4 of 10 enemy warplanes at Kunming, without loss.

Above: Ground crew members of the U.S. Air Force refuel and rearm an American P-47 Thunderbolt at a new Allied airfield in France, preparing it for another mission against the enemy.

mechanics swarmed over their plane. They tested the controls, inspected the brakes and landing gear, checked tire and the rubber-lined fuels tanks for leaks. They listened to the bombers' four engines, and if any had been damaged they pulled it off and replaced it with another. Many of the planes making it back to base were too badly damaged to

ever fly again, but their parts became a rich source for the ships that could still fly. Mechanics for the 398th Bomb Group changed 140 engines on B-17s, using salvaged or rebuilt engines from other aircraft.

After every raid, there were always B-17s that almost made it back. Unless someone actually saw a plane crash, it was presumed missing in action. Having aborted during the Kiel mission, Lieutenant Robert Bender was back in the air a few days later and headed with a load of bombs for the submarine pens at St. Nazaire. When he was over the target, enemy fire shot out one engine, so Bender stepped up the power on the other three engines in an effort to get home.

On rare occasions, a ground crew might miss an important item on their checklists. Early on the morning of a mission, a three-man crew drove fuel trucks to the aircraft and topped off the tanks while another crew loaded the plane with bombs and ammunition. For each mission, the exact amount of fuel and weight of bombs was carefully calculated, taking into consideration factors such as the distance to the target, the expected wind speed, and the planned cruising altitude. Fuel made up half the load. And all bombers – B-17s, B-24s, and B-29s – consumed fuel at a voracious rate, using nine tons for a mission deep into Germany or from a base in the Marianas to mainland Japan. Any miscalculation, a worsening of weather or if an aircraft failed to drop its bombs and tried to return with a full load, the fuel situation could become critical.

When Bender's aircraft headed over the English Channel, he discovered that the ground crew had failed to fill the long-range wing tanks with fuel. After jettisoning excess equipment overboard to lighten the load, the B-17 finally ran out of gas. Sixty miles south of the English coast, Bender ditched the 26-ton aircraft into a choppy sea at ninety miles an hour.

Everything went according to training. Two inflatable life rafts popped opened and everyone clambered on board – all except a major who had crawled out on a wing of the sinking aircraft and hollered that he could not swim. Two men stripped

SELECTIVE CHRONOLOGY OF WAR: 1942

Jan 6: President Roosevelt calls for 600,000 warplanes to be built by the end of the year, 10,000 more than goal set in 1940.

Apr 18: Lt. Col. Doolittle's 16 B-25 bombers take part in first U.S. air raid on Japanese homeland.

May 7: Battle of Coral Sea, the first naval encounter in history in which opponents fight each other with air power alone; Japanese lose 1 light carrier with 2 others damaged, but sink U.S.S. *Lexington*.

June 3: U.S. air power sinks 4 Japanese carriers during Battle of Midway, the decisive battle of the Pacific War, in which Japanese also lose 258 warplanes; U.S. loses 1 carrier and 132 warplanes.

July 7: U.S.A.A.F. achieves first certain "kill" of the war off Atlantic coast as a B-18 of 396th Bombardment Squadron sinks German U-boat near Cherry Point, N. Carolina.

Aug 7: Eighth Air Force conducts first U.S. strategic bombing of the war, attacking German-controlled Rouen, France.

Sep 10: Women's Auxiliary Ferrying Squadron (WAFS) is announced; later known as "WASPS" or "Ferry Pilots", the women perform back-of-the-line flying duties to free male pilots for combat duty.

Dec 5: U.S. warplanes make their first raid on Italy, bombing Naples.

Left: P-47 Thunderbolt pilots listen intently as intelligence officers brief them before starting for a mission over France.

off their clothes and scissors-kicked the officer over to one of the rafts. As the major climbed on board, his knife came through the bottom of its sheath and punctured the raft. The training manual did not cover such contingencies, but the hole received a patch from the repair kit and the major a verbal harangue from Bender, who was in no mood for any more problems.

Life rafts came with ropes, oars, cans of fresh water, big bars of unsweetened chocolate, and a small hand-operated, hand-generated radio transmitter that worked off a thin wire antenna elevated by a box kite. As both rafts drifted towards the German-occupied coast of France, the radio operator worked through the night tapping out distress signals. About midday two British motor torpedo boats hove into view and brought the crew on board.

Bob Bender, the pilot, never fully recovered from the experience. Like many men who risked their lives day after day in the face of enemy fire, he became

among the number who suffered a nervous breakdown. The Air Force sent him home where, at the age of twenty-five, he died from a heart attack, another casualty of war. During the same month, seventy-five fliers suffered mental breakdowns.

Men in aircraft shot down over Germany had no life rafts, only parachutes to carry them to the ground. A week after the Kiel raid the 88th Bomb Group headed for a synthetic rubber producing plant in the Ruhr Valley. After dropping its bombs over the western German town of Huls, one B-17 suffered heavy flak and aircraft fire and dropped out of formation. The Group Operations Officer hit the bail-out bell. All the men except for the navigator survived the drop, and all but one were rapidly scooped up by German patrols.

Joel Bunch came down on "a lofty

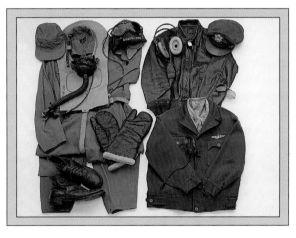

tree" and was "slammed to the ground." Having injured his back, he crawled away from his 'chute and lay hidden in a nearby woods. After an hour's rest, he started

Below: U.S. A.A.F. uniforms and equipment, including (left) summer flying suit Type A-4 and Type B-4 "Mae West" life jacket; and (right) leather Type A-2 flying jacket with emergency whistle at throat, and Type F-2 flying jacket.

Left: Major Glenn Eagleston's P-47D shows eighteen kills painted under the cockpit. Pilots frequently added a little individuality to their fighters by having a variety of images painted on the noses of their aircraft.

Right: U.S. Navy VCS-7 pilots are briefed before flying a gun-spotting mission over the Normandy beachheads in 1944. Instead of seaplanes, VCS-7 units preferred using the British Spitfires.

through the woods and came to a wide river – one he could not swim because of his ailing back. He crept through brush along the bank of the river until reaching a bridge, which he watched for a while from the distance. Seeing no guard, he crossed, only to be met by a German sentinel who searched him, stripped him, beat him up, and hustled him over to the city jail at Wesel. On June 22, 1943, the war ended for Joel Bunch. He spent the next twenty-two months in German prison camps.

In planning and conducting bombing raids little details made a big difference. Mistakes were few but always costly, and operations personnel made every effort to prevent them. Early on the day of a mission, usually before daybreak, runners aroused the crew, alerting them to get to the briefing room by a designated hour. Crews hurriedly dressed, downed a quick breakfast, and with a last cup of coffee gripped in their hands, took their seats in a sealed room. If the target was Schweinfurt, the officer in charge would go to a large map and, stretch a piece of yarn from the airfield to the city. A staff meteorologist would talk about the weather, a reconnaissance officer would discuss the target, and others would outline the best approach to a difficult objective where heavy flak and enemy fighters would be present in number.

For the big raid on Schweinfurt and Regensburg, where several bombing groups were to be involved and the resistance heavy, similar meetings would be held at other airfields. Crews would

Below: Even the B-3 and A-3 Shearing jacket and trousers were at times insufficient at keeping out the cold as American fliers conducted longer high-altitude raids. Gloves had to be worn at all times to prevent hands from sticking to the aircraft. The body armor (right) was devised in 1942 and made of manganese steel plate; by 1944, over 13,000 were protecting aircrew of the 8th Air Force.

groan or crack jokes to try and relieve the tension. At the designated hour, they dispersed to their aircraft, pilots and co-pilots ran through their lengthy checklists, bombers got into line along the taxiways, and at thirty-second intervals, thundered down the runways and lumbered into the air.

One reason for American losses stemmed from the flawed doctrine that Flying Fortresses could take care of themselves by concentrating their firepower. In the early months of long-range daylight bombing, there were only short-range fighter aircraft to serve as escorts. When the escorts reached the point of no return, they turned back to base. German fighters simply waited until the escorts withdrew before attacking the bombers. On missions deep into German territory the bombers had to fight Fw 190s and Bf 109s across Europe and back again. B-17s, however, proved to be more humane than RAF night bombers because their bombs fell mostly on military targets and not on civilians.

At Schweinfurt and Regensburg, German air defenses were much stronger than either Major General Spaatz or General Henry H. "Hap" Arnold, chief of the U.S. Army Air Forces, first envisioned. The enemy used 88mm cannon, a highly accurate, fast shooting anti-aircraft weapon that wrought devastation when scoring a hit. Over Schweinfurt, flak and enemy fighters brought down 36 of 230 bombers. Twenty-seven more were so badly damaged they would never fly again. Of 146 B-17s bombing

Regensburg, 84 never returned. The double mission cost the Americans more than 550 crewmen and left the Eighth Air Force crippled for weeks.

Spaatz and Arnold expected the raid to destroy Germany's ability to wage war and sue for peace. When nothing happened, they went back to the drawing board. The mission damaged but did not destroy either the Schweinfurt works or the Messerschmitt plant. In less than a month, both were fully operational. The Germans had so many bearings in the pipeline that they never had to shut down their aircraft assembly lines. Americans accepted their losses, but something had to be done.

Curtis LeMay, who had led the attack on Regensburg, concluded that homes as well as factories made good targets, and if airmen "put down enough bombs to destroy the town," factories would be disabled enough to preclude further attacks on the city. If so, daylight attacks could be suspended, but Spaatz continued them without cessation.

When airborne radar became available, American bombers used it in bad weather. Radar attacks had a modest impact on Germany's production, but it had a very frightening effect on civilians because the bombs landed all over the area and seldom struck the intended target. When in 1943 the Germans learned to use radar for directing their anti-aircraft fire and fighter attacks, British and American planes took countermeasures. As planes came over the target, they dropped enormous batches of tinfoil, befuddling the enemy's

ground radar receptors.

Four months later, a fuel container known as the "drop tank" became available, giving P-47 Thunderbolts and P-51 Mustangs built with Rolls Royce (Packard) engines half again the range, enough to follow beside the lumbering B-17s and B-24 Liberators into eastern Germany. The P-47 became one of the heaviest long-range fighters in World War II, its 2,000-horsepower engine generating a top speed of 412mph. Bomber crews preferred to be escorted by the longer-range P-51s, which could fly at 42,000 feet (10,000 feet higher than the Thunderbolt) and provide fighter escort all the way to Berlin. They called the speedy Mustang (487mph) their "little friend" and were always comforted by its presence.

As long-range fighters became available, bomber formations began meeting their air cover over France with clockwork precision. Bf 109s and Fw

Above: American pilots spent their money having colored pictures stitched on their flight jackets, and the same image could also be often found painted on the noses of their aircraft.

Left: Even before America entered the war, Maj. Gen. Claire Chennault had brought P-40s into western China and formed the first fighting squadron of "Flying Tigers."

Right: With the Curtiss P-40s came a small ground crew. The sergeant (pictured left) is there to train Chinese in the intricate work of keeping the *Rose Marie* in the air.

190s hauled off as the bombers crossed through flak defenses but returned in a fury. As German aircraft attacked the bombers, American fighters attacked the *Luftwaffe*. Unless disabled, bombers maintained their formation, following the lead plane. The autopilot went into the

SELECTIVE CHRONOLOGY OF WAR: 1943

Jan 13: U.S. 13th Air Force is established in New Hebrides; known as "Jungle Air Force," it concentrates its first efforts against Japanese strongholds in Solomons, and by war's end destroys 1,439 enemy warplanes and sinks 1,349,130 tons of Japanese shipping.

Jan 27: Eighth Air Force makes first U.S. air attack on Germany, bombing docks in Wilhemshaven.

Mar 2: In the Battle of the Bismarck Sea U.S. and Australian medium bombers fly low-level attacks under cloud cover and destroy 8 Japanese transports and 4 destroyers, killing 3,000 men; they demonstrate the "skip-bombing" method of attack adopted by the Allies.

Apr 18: American P-38s from Henderson Field shoot down Japanese transport plane over Bougainville, killing Admiral Yamamoto.

July 17: U.S.A.A.F. bombers attack marshalling yards in Rome.

July 25: While the RAF operates by night, U.S.A.A.F. bombers attack Hamburg by day for a week.

Aug 1: U.S.A.A.F. bombers based in Libya carry out successful raid on Ploesti oil refineries, Rumania; it is a record-breaking low-altitude, long-distance flight by 177 B-24s; 164 reach the target; 56 are destroyed in the mission.

Dec 24: U.S.A.A.F. bombers carry out first major raid on German secret weapon targets as 670 B-17s bomb V-weapon sites near France's northern coast.

control of the bombardier, who would make minor corrections in the aircraft's position and altitude by turning two knobs on his Norden bombsight. When the lead plane dropped its bombs, it was the cue for the bombardiers in the other planes to release theirs. Then, as the bombers circled about to head for home, the German fighters would come in a swarm, and the American aircraft would find themselves in a furious dogfight in the clouds.

The new arrangement of using long-range American and British fighters changed the complexion of the air war. In Europe, the combination of daylight bombing and superior aircraft won the battle of the skies. In the South Pacific, the Japanese Zeros could not contend with the Grumman F6F carrier planes.

Fighters became equipped with advanced radar that could spot German aircraft in the foggy dark. With fighter escorts, the bombers could now go anywhere in Germany. Between February 19-24, 1944, they did. The RAF sent 2,300 bombers over Germany at night, and the USAF sent 3,800 during the day. The *Luftwaffe* lost 450 fighter aircraft in an effort to stem the bombing raids – a rate of loss it could not sustain.

By late spring, Goering's air fleet had been severely crippled, enabling Eisenhower to ensure his D-Day troops that, "If you see fighting aircraft over you, they will be ours." From then on, the skies over Germany became untenable to the *Luftwaffe*, and the Allied bomber offensive began to crumble the great cities of the Third Reich into mounds of rubble.

Planes returning from a raid with wounded crewmen shot off red flares as they approached the base. Ambulances, better known as "meat wagons," rushed onto the field to meet them. After medics removed the wounded, the crew piled out and went to the debriefing room for coffee, greasy spam sandwiches, and a shot of whiskey. For the men who returned, there would be another night of celebration and one less mission to complete their tour. For the men missing, there would be a moment of grief. For maintenance crews, followed by an officer who determined whether the shot-

Left Center: Early in the war, sergeants flew fighter planes right along with officers. Here a lieutenant of a pursuit squadron discusses an assignment with his flying sergeants.

Left: At Daniel Field in Georgia, a 1st Sergeant from the Air Service Command runs a class in aircraft identification, using models arranged on a table.

up bomber could be made to fly again, there would be a mountain of work.

During the last months of the war in Europe, Germany's once mighty *Luftwaffe* could no longer defend the Third Reich. On February 13-14, 1945, British and American bombers flew over Dresden, killing 135,000 people in what was probably the most barbaric air raid of the war in Europe. The death toll eclipsed that of Hiroshima, where the civilian population suffered the ravages of the first atomic bomb. German fighter aircraft that once swept out of the clouds in swarms were no longer present to distract the lumbering bombers.

German engineers attempted to compensate for losses by developing the jet engine. During the latter months of the war, an impressive number of Messerschmitt Me 262 jets – flying at 540 miles and hour – outmatched the propeller-driven aircraft of the Allies. Hitler's obsession to punish the civilian population of Great Britain by building bombers, V-1, and V-2 rockets robbed resources from manufacturing the jets. Instead, he built more than 8,000 "Buzz Bombs" and targeted them on London. Most of rockets went astray or were shot down, but nearly 2,500 landed on the city, causing extensive damage. After Allied espionage and reconnaissance efforts identified Peenemünde as the source of the experiments and located the rockets' launching sites, bombing raids eliminated the V-weapons as a counteroffensive threat.

Though great innovators, once Germany lost control of the skies, they lost the war. After V-E Day, *Luftwaffe*

officers agreed that "the Americans harmed us most. The Russians were negligible as far as the home front was concerned, and we could have stood the British attacks on our cities. But the American devastation of our airfields, factories, and oil depots made it impossible for us to keep going." Daylight raids made the difference, a costly but effective strategy for speeding the war in Europe to its final climax.

Aerial warfare in the Pacific started and ended much differently from the air war in Europe. The United States unofficially entered the war months before Pearl Harbor when Claire L. Chennault, a retired air corps officer, went to China to help Chiang Kai-shek fight the Japanese. The Chinese general bought one hundred Curtiss P-40 Tomahawks with money borrowed from the United States, and Chennault used some of the money to hire American pilots to fly the planes. The so-called American Volunteer Group (AVG) booked passage to Burma and arrived in small groups using fictitious names.

Below: Capt. Marc A. Mitscher, commanding the U.S.S. *Hornet*, chats with Col. James Doolittle (left), who stands before the crew of the B-25s who made the historic bombing raid on Tokyo on April 18, 1942.

Above: Six hundred miles off the coast of Japan, Jimmie Doolittle's B-25 takes off from the deck of the *Hornet* to lead the first air raid on Tojo's Imperial homeland.

They had just finished their training when the Japanese bombed Pearl Harbor. Fliers wore the insignia of a winged tiger and painted a shark's mouth around the noses of their Tomahawks and Warhawks. Chennault called them his "Flying Tigers."

On December 19, 1941, Chennault set up his main airbase at Kunming, China, capital of the Yunnan province in western China. With him came two AVG squadrons looking for their first fight. The following day, Chennault received a radio message from his Panda Bear squadron that a large formation of Mitsubishi "Sallys," twin-engine bombers, had been spotted about sixty miles from Kunming. He sent Squadron Leader Robert J. Sandell into the air with fourteen P-40s to intercept the enemy. The Japanese airmen, having never encountered any resistance during their bombing runs over Kunming, flew without a fighter escort. Cruising in a perfect flat V-formation, the Japanese pilots expected no trouble and looked for none.

At Sandell's signal, Fritz E. Wolf pounced upon the bomber on the wing. "Diving below him," said Wolf, "I came up underneath, guns ready for the minute I could get in range. At 500 yards I let go with a quick burst... [four .30-caliber in the wings and two .50s in the upper nose]. I could see my bullets rip into the rear gunner. My plane bore in closer. At 100 yards I let go with a burst into the bomber's gas tanks and engine. The wing folded and a motor tore loose. Then the bomber exploded. I yanked back on the stick to get out of the way and went upstairs...."

Minutes later, Wolf fell in behind a second bomber and at fifty yards opened with his full battery on one of the Mitsubishi's engines. "Flame and smoke wisped into the slipstream, followed by a blossom of fire and the Japanese bomber was ripped to pieces in a violent orange-red explosion." Wolf kicked the rudder and barely escaped the inferno.

In the first American air battle in the Far East, the "Flying Tigers" lost one Tomahawk, but the Japanese lost six bombers, the other four beating back to Hanoi and trailing smoke. The encounter with Japanese aircraft ended in almost complete victory, but Chennault warned that the next bombing raid would be accompanied by fighters.

The words were hardly out of his mouth when a Tiger squadron based at

Right: Among the targets selected for the Doolittle raid was the Yokosuka Naval Base. Each of the B-25s carried five 500-pound bombs, and each pilot had a specific target when over Japan.

Left: During the Navy's attack on Rabaul, New Britain, a constant procession of Douglas SBD dive-bombers landing and taking back off for another strike leaves everybody on the carrier *Saratoga* watchful and busy.

Rangoon, supported by a squadron of RAF Buffaloes, attacked forty-eight Japanese bombers escorted by a swarm of twenty Zeros. For the first time, P-40 pilots witnessed the nimbleness of the speedy Zero. The Tigers lost four planes and two men over Rangoon, the RAF five Buffaloes. This time the score ended about even, the Japanese losing six bombers and four fighters.

After that, dogfights between Tomahawks and Zeros occurred almost daily. Guns on a P-40 had a nasty habit of jamming, but other than that, the fighter proved to be a rugged and durable aircraft. Flying out of Mingaladon, Parker Dupouy spotted a Zero on his tail. His guns had jammed so he kicked the Tomahawk around and collided with Zero. The Japanese plane collapsed and fell. Dupouy made it back to base with four feet nipped off his wing. In an attack on 108 Japanese bombers and fighters, Robert Smith dove through one wave and into another, firing into a Nakajima that blew up in his face, pockmarking his P-40 with pieces from the engine. The Tomahawk shuddered, but Smith got it under control and swung back into the action. Had the opposite occurred, pieces flying off a Tomahawk would probably have disabled the Zero.

For those back home, it was some comfort to know that American pilots were already shooting down Japanese aircraft. Probably no unit fighting in Asia stirred the hearts of Americans more than Chennault's "Flying Tigers." Every flier became a national hero. With war formally declared, the "Flying Tigers" eventually became the 23rd Fighter Group of the Fourteenth Air Force, and

Left: The U.S. Navy pilot wears a one-piece flying suit and life preserver, together with a lightweight flying helmet. In a shoulder holster he carries a .45 caliber semi-automatic pistol, and on his belt, spare ammunition and a knife.

for months to come they were the Army's only planes in east Asia. Chennault's aircraft were the first to use wing-mounted rockets, and one of his units became the internationally integrated Chinese-American Combat Wing.

Unlike during the war in Europe, heavy bombers did not reached the Pacific theater until 1944. Aircraft like Curtiss P-40s had to pick up the slack by swooping in over enemy positions, dropping bombs, and strafing with wing and nose-mounted machine guns. The "Flying Tigers" made romantic heroes, but in battle they could not outfly the lighter, more maneuverable Zeros. When engaged in a dogfight, the durability of P-40s and the added armoring helped to offset the aircraft's early disadvantages against the faster but flimsier Zeros. They could harass the enemy, but they could not stop him.

Following Pearl Harbor, President Roosevelt wanted to strike back at Japan

Keep him flying!

BUY WAR BONDS

with a vengeance, and he could not do it with P-40s. Roosevelt wanted bombs dropped on Tokyo. The mission called for aircraft that could take off in 500 feet from a carrier with a 2,000lb bomb load and fly 2,000 miles. The aircraft selected was a modified twin-engined North American B-25 Mitchell, and Lieutenant Colonel James H. Doolittle was chosen to lead the mission.

On February 2, 1942, cranes hoisted two B-25s onto the carrier *Hornet* at Norfolk, Virginia. Two young lieutenants, John E. Fitzgerald and James F. McCarthy, flew the bombers off the carrier and returned to base, mystified as to the purpose of the experiment. *Hornet*, commanded by Captain Donald W. Duncan, then headed for San Francisco. Vice Admiral William Halsey would be there to join him with the carrier *Enterprise*. Before leaving for San Francisco, Duncan wired General "Hap" Arnold, "Tell Jimmy to Get on His Horse" – the signal for Doolittle to bring his crews to California.

Twenty-six crews volunteered for the undisclosed mission. When they climbed on board the modified B-25s, the bombers looked unlike anything they had ever seen. The interior of the fuselage had been stripped away and filled with gas tanks. All the machine guns had been removed except for the twin .50s in the upper turret and a .30 in the nose. A pair

SELECTIVE CHRONOLOGY OF WAR: 1944

Jan 11: In the U.S. Eighth Army Air Force offensive against German aircraft industry, about 800 bombers with P-51 Mustang escorts attack factories at Halberstadt, Brunswick, and Oscherleben, losing 55 bombers and 5 fighters while shooting down several enemy fighters.

Feb 20: Operation "Big Week" begins 6 days of attacks by U.S. Eighth and Fifteenth Air Forces against German aircraft factories. U.S. bombers attack by day, and RAF by night, both against heavy *Luftwaffe* opposition. *Luftwaffe* loses 692 aircraft in the aerial battles, while the U.S. loses 244 bombers and 33 fighter escorts.

May 9: U.S.A.A.F. and RAF begin attacks on French airfields in preparation for D-Day.

May 11: Operation Strangle ends: U.S.A.A.F. have been heavily involved in Mediterranean Allied Air Forces' dropping of 26,000 tons of bombs on enemy lines of communication.

June 19: U.S. Naval warplanes shoot down 476 Japanese aircraft in "Marianas Turkey Shoot" in 2-day Battle of Philippine Sea; 130 U.S. warplanes are lost.

June 21: U.S.A.A.F. carries out 1,000-bomber raid on Berlin.

June 22: U.S.A.A.F. is involved in 1,000-bomber raid on Cherbourg, France, supporting U.S. drive into suburbs and liberation of Cherbourg by June 29.

Nov 24: U.S. undertakes first bombing mission against Japan from Marianas as 9 B-29 Superfortresses of 21st Bomber Command strike Mushashima aircraft factory and other targets in Tokyo.

Dec 14: U.S. warplanes strike Japanese airfields on Luzon.

Left: In November, 1943, after the raid on Rabaul, a crewman lifts rear gunner Kenneth Bratton, who has a shattered knee, out of the turret of a TBF for treatment on the U.S.S. *Saratoga*.

of Quaker guns, two broomsticks painted black, protruded from the tail turret to scare away nosy Zeros. Captain Charles R. Greening, unwilling to have a Norden bombsight fall into the hands of the enemy, designed what he called the "Mark Twain," a simple device using twenty cents of metal that proved more effective at fifteen hundred feet than the highly touted Norden.

By mid-April, Navy Captain Henry L. Miller had Doolittle's crews yanking fully loaded B-25s into the air from a 500-foot track, though at the time none of the pilots knew why. In late March, twenty-four B-25s flew to McClellan Field, near Sacramento. A few days later Doolittle flew them to Alameda and put sixteen on the deck of the

Hornet. On April 2, Captain Marc A. Mitscher ordered *Hornet* out to sea. Only Doolittle, Mitscher, and Miller knew the details of the mission.

Doolittle planned to lead the bombers, hitting Tokyo's industrial center at dusk and laying down fires to act as beacons for the aircraft in the rear echelon. Lieutenant Travis Hoover would follow, bombing factories, gas, and chemical plants in northern Tokyo. Captain David M. Jones's squad would concentrate on oil storage tanks and power plants. Captain Edward J. York's wing would hit the southern section of Tokyo. Greening would strike the navy yard at Yokohama, while Major John A. Hilger's section went after targets in Nagoya, Kobe, and Osaka.

Left: To support the Guadacanal landings in August, 1942, ordnancemen of Scouting Squadron Six load a 500-pound demolition bomb on a Douglas SBD on board the U.S.S. *Enterprise*.

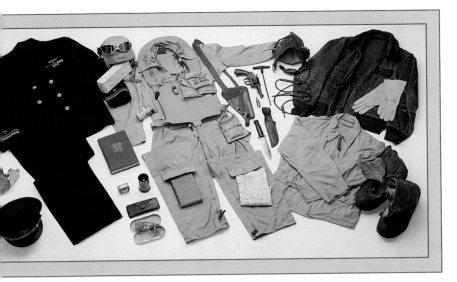

Above: A selection of U.S. naval aviators' uniforms and equipment, including (left) naval officer's service jacket and trousers, with aviator's wings; (center) lightweight cotton flying suit and inflatable buoyancy vest with dye markers; (top right) A-2 flight jacket; (bottom right) lightweight windbreaker.

Each B-25 carried four 500-pound bombs, three demolition and one incendiary. Doolittle cautioned his crews, "You are to look for and aim at military targets only, such as war industries, shipbuilding facilities, power plants and the like." How much damage sixteen planes carrying a total of sixty-four bombs could do to the Japanese war machine never became a larger part of the strategy. Roosevelt wanted to send a message to Prime Minister Tojo, and Doolitle intended to deliver it.

Knowing that B-25s would not be able to land back on the carriers, elaborate arrangements were made to have sites prepared for landing the bombers in unoccupied China. Chiang Kai-shek halfheartedly agreed to provide a number of forward bases with radios and directional beams so the planes could land, refuel, and fly to Chungking. Thinking that all the details had been worked out between Washington and Chaing, Doolittle waited to reach the takeoff point, 400 miles east of the Japanese mainland. *Hornet* was still 670 miles short of the island when sighted by a Japanese patrol boat. Halsey flashed a hurried message to *Hornet*: "Launch Planes. To Colonel Doolittle and his gallant command Good Luck and God bless you."

On April 18, 1942, one day earlier than planned, Doolittle's squadron thundered down the deck of *Hornet* in a stiff headwind that helped lift the aircraft off the short deck. When the last plane disappeared in the clouds, Halsey turned the carriers around, and Task Force 16 vanished into the Pacific. As the B-25s

Right: A 7th Air Force bomber crewman in 1945 carrying his B-3 fleece-lined flying jacket and wearing A-6 fur-line boots, both necessary even though he was operating in tropical locations; at high altitude the conditions were freezing.

thundered toward Tokyo, bombers and fighters from the Kisarazu Air Base in the city took to the skies in search of Halsey's fleet. The Japanese patrol planes found only bad weather. A solitary report of a twin engined plane sighted 600 miles from Japan drew no curiosity because no American plane could have reached that point from any American base.

At 12:30 p.m. on April 18, the residents of Tokyo had just relaxed from a practice air raid – which most ignored – when Jimmy Doolittle's B-25 dropped its bombs over the western outskirts of the city. Hoover came in next and dropped his just to the east of downtown Tokyo. Few, if any bombs, fell on industrial centers, and after dropping their payloads the B-25s headed around the southern tip of Japan and into China. The raid lasted six minutes.

Doolittle lost contact with his squadron, except for Hoover, and began looking for Chaing Kai-shek's landing fields. Weather worsened, and no directional signals came from Chaing. Doolittle bailed out, as did Hoover's crew. Days passed before Doolittle learned that of sixteen B-25s, only one made a safe, down-wheels landing, not in China but in Vladivostok, Russia. Eleven of the crews bailed out and four attempted crash landings. Eight men fell into Japanese hands and received merciless torture. Three were executed and a fourth died of

maltreatment and disease. Of eighty flyers, seventy-one eventually returned to the United States.

Japanese intelligence fished about to learn where the bombers had come from. Roosevelt told the public it was Shangri-la, a fictitious haven in the Himalayas made famous by novelist James Hilton in *Lost Horizon*. There is no record of whether the Japanese ever found the place.

In the United States, the news of the bombing flashed across the airways, and a wave of jubilation swept the country and gave a boost to morale. Despite the Japanese propaganda machine intimating that the bombing of Tokyo amounted to a "Do Nothing Raid," morale in Japan suffered. The war had come to the land of the Rising Sun, implanting an uneasy air of doubt where once there had been only optimism.

The air war with Japan had begun, and Jimmy Doolittle's raid served up only a small dose of what was to come. Two months later at Midway, aircraft of the U. S. Navy upset Admiral Isoroku Yamamoto's strategy in the South Pacific and destroyed the greater portion of Vice Admiral Chuichi Nagumo's First Carrier Striking Force. Four Japanese carriers went to the bottom, along with one cruiser, 322 planes, and 3,500 men. The United States lost the carrier *Yorktown*, a destroyer, 150 planes, and 307 lives. The Imperial Navy learned a lesson it never

forgot. As one high-ranking Japanese official remarked, "the Americans have avenged Pearl Harbor."

When the Pacific conflict roared into gear in early 1942, the combined forces of Japan had more than 3,000 aircraft and twice as many pilots, most of them veterans of the war with China. Of 900 American planes on station in the Pacific, most of them were lost at Pearl Harbor or destroyed weeks later in the Philippines. And while the United States tried to mobilize its industry to produce aircraft, Japanese factories turned out 425 planes a month. Japan's strength in the air peaked at 4,000 aircraft. But, by 1944, the United States had 10,000 warplanes and 8,000 transports at its disposal for operations in the Pacific. When Tojo decided to attack

Right: On October 5, 1942, B-17 bombers operating out of Henderson Field on Guadacanal hit the island of Gizo in New Georgia Sound, known as "the Slot".

Pearl Harbor, the one equation he dismissed was America's engineering and industrial might. He also misled himself in thinking that Americans had grown too soft for war.

SELECTIVE CHRONOLOGY OF WAR: 1945

Feb 3: U.S.A.A.F. bombs Berlin with 1,000 B-17s supported by 900 fighters.

Feb 14: U.S. Eighth Air Force bombs Dresden, Chemnitz, and Magdeburg, Germany. Together with RAF attacks a day earlier, the bombings cause fires in Dresden which kill an estimated 100,000 people, more destructive than the bombing of Hiroshima and Nagasaki.

Feb 16: Over 1,000 carrier aircraft from U.S. Navy Task Force 58 raid Tokyo and Yokohama, and repeat this on Feb 17.

Mar 9: Beginning a campaign of low-level attacks against Japan, 279 Superfortresses drop incendiary bombs on Tokyo, killing 84,000 and destroying a quarter of the city; 14 Superfortresses are shot down.

Mar 18: Carrier-borne planes from U.S. Navy T.F. 58 attack Kyushu, Japan, in advance of U.S. invasion of Okinawa; 528 Japanese aircraft are destroyed by fighters and AA guns, while *kamikazes* damage *Enterprise, Yorktown, Intrepid, Wasp, Halsey Powell,* and *Franklin.*

July 10: 1,000-aircraft raid on Tokyo is launched from U.S. Task Force 38 carriers.

July 28: U.S. carriers launch raids by 2,000 aircraft against Kure, Kobe, and other targets around Inlnd Sea.

Aug 6: B-29 drops atomic bomb on Hiroshima, killing estimated 80,000 and injuring 80,000 more.

Aug 9: Second atomic bomb dropped on Nagasaki by B-29, killing 40,000 and injuring 60,000.

Aug 15: Day after Japanese surrender, aircraft from U.S. Third Fleet bomb Tokyo against heavy Japanese air resistance; first of three strikes is carried out before reports of surrender are received; 2nd and 3rd strikes cancelled.

Airmen went to war either because they wanted to fight or because they were called to fight. Marine pilot Lieutenant Samuel Hynes, stationed in the Pacific, belonged to those who wanted to fight and his crew belonged to the latter. His was a strange relationship with the two enlisted men on a Grumman TBM torpedo plane. A few years after the war he could no longer remember their full names, only that one was Edwards and the other Campbell. In his logbook he listed them as passengers, though Edwards was his radio and radar man and Campbell his turret gunner who rode in a glass bowl on the backbone of the plane with a .50 caliber machine gun. During flight, they were Hynes's best friends. On the ground, they separated at once, each to their own segregated quarters, "two areas," said Hynes, "that were as remote and isolated from each other as two countries that have cut off diplomatic relations. I never saw where my crew lived, and they never came to my tent. We never ate a single meal together. We never discussed any human problem. They simply rode at my back...." There may have been a reason that had nothing to do with officer/enlisted man relationships. Edwards was a Reservist, and Hynes concluded that, "It wasn't his war, and it wasn't his Marine Corps. He did his job well when it needed doing, but he did it for Edwards, not for glory."

Perhaps the reason why enlisted airmen remained cloaked in obscurity was because the spotlight always centered on the pilots. Yet it took dozens of men to keep a big bomber in the air and dozens

more to plan its missions. It took fewer men to keep fighters in the air, but, like Edwards, they did it "not for glory" but for their own self-respect and a great contempt for the enemy. For every pilot that became an ace, there were a bunch of mechanics, electricians, hydraulics experts, and arms personnel who knew more the plane than the pilot and did more to keep him safe than he ever truly appreciated.

In the South Pacific, General Arnold recognized that he could not win the war with three-man torpedo bombers, or with B-17s, so important to the war in Europe, because the latter did not have the range to reach Japan from the islands of the Pacific. He wanted a superbomber that could fly farther with a heavier payload than any airship ever built. What he got was the B-29, a sixty-ton aircraft that could fly for sixteen hours fully loaded without refueling. In April, 1944, the first B-29s landed on enormous airfields built in eastern India and western China, but as the Navy and the Marines began hopping the islands to Japan, they came to bases in the Marshalls, Marianas, and eventually to Iwo Jima and Okinawa.

The first bombing raids were relatively short excursions – a railroad center in Bankok, a steel-producing center on Kyusu Island. Not until General LeMay took command of the XX Bomber Command and adapted it to the same close-formation daylight raids as in Europe did the B-29s begin to inflict the heaviest damage upon the enemy.

In 1945 enormous amounts of explosives made of jellied gasoline and magnesium turned cities like Tokyo, Kobe, and Nagoya into blazing infernos. On August 2, four days before "Enola Gay" dropped the first of two war-ending atomic bombs on Japan, 855 Superfortresses obliterated six cities in a single raid. Even without nuclear bombs, the devastation caused by the new explosives had brought the Japanese to the brink of surrender. The old axiom that air power alone could not end wars no longer applied. The bombers ruled the skies, and those who lived beneath their wings could no longer find a place to hide.

THE SAILOR'S WAR

Politicians called it a "Two-Ocean War," but the sailors who fought it found service at sea much different in the Pacific than on the Atlantic. Fierce naval battles were fought in the Pacific, while in the Atlantic Britain's Royal Navy had rid the ocean of enemy surface vessels months before America entered the war. The danger lay beneath the waves from German U-boats. For the American sailor, the Atlantic battle became a dirty, cold, nerve-racking business of hunting down submarines while being hunted themselves. And when amphibious landings began in North Africa and the European continent, the Navy had to be there with battleships and cruisers to help get the troops ashore. But, for the United States, the real fighting for the dominance of the seas did not begin or end in the Atlantic. It began on December 7, 1941, in the center of the Pacific Ocean at Pearl Harbor.

No event indoctrinated the American sailor to the catastrophes of war with more stark reality than the Japanese attack on Honolulu. Strangely enough, the United States Navy drew first blood. At 6:30 a.m., December 7, 1941, a sailor on watch on the auxiliary ship U.S.S. *Antares* sighted a suspicious object rippling the water in the early morning light. *Antares* signaled the destroyer U.S.S. *Ward*, Lieutenant Commander W. W. Outerbridge, that a periscope had been sighted in Pearl Harbor's channel. Outerbridge closed on the target and at fifty yards ordered a shell fired that struck the periscope. The mysterious vessel proved to be a Japanese midget two-man submarine. *Ward* dropped depth charges on the vessel and sent it to the bottom. At 7:12 a.m. Outerbridge reported the action to the base staff officer. Nobody thought to close the torpedo net obstructing the channel. Forty minutes later all hell broke loose. For the sailors in Pearl Harbor, the "date which will live in infamy" had begun.

At 7:55 a.m. the first wave of Japanese dive bombers struck the airfields, depriving the island of its air cover. Behind the mustard-colored planes with the rising sun painted on their wings came the torpedo planes. They leveled off over the waters of the Naval Basin and dropped shallow-running torpedoes. Contrary to popular belief, 96 percent of the ships' crews were on board their vessels, as were 60 percent of the officers. When bombs began falling on the 88 naval craft in the harbor, sailors on shore rushed back to their ships, many to join the growing number of those killed or maimed in the holocaust.

At 9:45 a.m. the raid ended. Black smoke smothered the sky, and one-half of the United States Navy's Pacific Fleet lay in ruins. Nineteen ships – battleships, cruisers, and destroyers – had been sunk

Bottom Right: A salvage crew works on board the captured submarine *U-505*, while observers watch from the U.S.S. *Guadacanal*. The Navy renamed the submarine *Nemo*. It is now preserved in Chicago.

Below: Troops and supplies reached Europe by convoys plowing through heavy seas of the North Atlantic. Sailors on board the U.S.S. *Greer* stand watch, always in search of unfriendly periscopes.

or badly damaged and 250 planes destroyed. Of 2,383 men killed, 1,842 wounded, and another 960 missing, most were sailors. Japan's one short, swift blow had inflicted more damage on the U.S. Navy than had been suffered during all of World War I.

Typically American were the sailors' reactions to the sneak attack. Forty-two-year-old Samuel Fuqua had been knocked senseless by explosions on the blazing *Arizona*. Regaining consciousness, he fought his way through bombs and bullets to the quarterdeck, directed fire-fighting operations, and organized details to look after the dead and wounded. Dorriss Miller, a black mess attendant assigned to *Arizona*'s galley, had never fired a weapon during his career in the Navy. He came topside, wound his way through fires and wreckage, located an unmanned anti-aircraft gun, spun it about to find a target, and kept shooting until the ammunition ran out.

When *Arizona*'s magazines exploded, the blast blew Cassin Young off the bridge of the repair ship *Vestal*. Cassin landed in blazing oil-covered water, but he swam back to his ship, climbed on board, and moved the flaming vessel to a safer anchorage. Nearby, Thomas E. Bailey helped rescue his mates from a sinking ship. After Bailey reached shore, an officer sent him to the Marine air base at Ewa to go up in a search plane. Bailey took a jeep to the airfield and jumped on the aircraft, clad only in his underwear.

Not all sailors went to sea. Over a period of sixteen hours, navy doctors and nurses treated 960 casualties, most of

them from burns. Mechanics and ground personnel at Ford Field salvaged weapons from burning planes, braced them against their shoulders, and fired at the enemy. One man used a garbage can as a mount. Lieutenant Clarence E. Dickinson, flying in from a carrier 200 miles away, found himself right in the middle of the attack. Shot down by a Zero, he parachuted to the ground and hitch-hiked back to the airfield. He jumped into the cockpit of another plane and went hunting, shooting down a Zero before being shot down for the second time. "I got mad," Dickinson said, but by then the enemy had vanished.

The Japanese believed that the United States Navy would never recover from the "day of infamy." Little did they realize that American sailors would raise and restore all but three of the capital ships damaged at Pearl Harbor. What they did note with consternation was the absence of three Pacific Fleet carriers thought to be at Pearl Harbor but which were at the time away on maneuvers. For

Above: From the naval air base at Pearl Harbor, sailors look on in despair as smoke from burning cruisers and battleships smother the sky with clouds of black smoke.

Left: By July, 1942, training at the U. S. Navy Academy at Annapolis, Maryland, intensified. Pictured here are midshipmen receiving a course in gunnery.

Above: EMS Herman W. Kreis directs James L. Garnet and Robert T. Craig in the process of sending the U.S.S. *Batfish* into a dive. Garnet mans the stern planes, Craig the forward planes.

Top Right: A selection of Navy uniforms and equipment, including (left) enlisted man's wool pullover blouse, (center, bottom) emergency/survival all-purpose fishing pack carried in rafts and by flight personnel, and (right) naval aviator's jacket.

Right: In August, 1943, a sailor aboard the U.S.S. *Capelin* at the submarine base in New London, Conn., reads in his bunk while surrounded by his favorite pin-up girls.

the Imperial Navy, the three absent American carriers would lead to dire consequences six months later.

On December 17, U. S. Secretary of the Navy Frank Knox recalled Admiral Husband Kimmel, Commander in Chief of the Pacific Fleet at Pearl Harbor, and replaced him with Admiral Chester W. Nimitz. On December 11, Knox elevated Admiral Ernest J. King from Commander in Chief of the Atlantic Fleet to Commander in Chief of the U.S. Fleet. Together, King and Nimitz possessed two of the keenest strategic minds in the service, but to contend with the Imperial Navy, they needed ships and sailors, and they needed them fast.

The Japanese wasted no time extending the war after bombing Pearl Harbor. On December 7 they attacked Guam, Wake, and Midway, and on the following day they put a force ashore at Bataan in the Philippines. On December 10 they occupied Tarawa and Makin in the Gilbert Islands and mounted air attacks against the naval base at Cavite in the Philippines. On December 22, Wake Island fell after a stubborn resistance, and two days later, Japan landed 7,000 troops on Luzon.

On March 11, President Roosevelt ordered MacArthur to leave the Philippines and make his way to Australia. Six days later, March 17, he arrived at Darwin, where he made his famous statement, promising to return.

Another scene of vital importance occurred on the same date, March 17, as Secretary of War Henry L. Stimson, in Washington, D.C., dipped his hand into a fishbowl and drew the numbers to start the wartime draft. But the Navy had already swung into action with voluntary enlistments. The first convoy was already at sea, zig-zagging the 10,000 mile route from the United States to Australia. Nimitz had wisely established bases for the protection of convoys in the central and south Pacific, and none to soon, since the Japanese rapidly closed in on the Marshalls, the Carolines, New Britain, and New Guinea. On May 7 Imperial forces controlled the western Pacific from the outer Aleutians to the Solomon Islands, but there the expansion of the Rising Sun stopped.

The first convoy to Australia, like all those to come, contained remodeled liners, fast freighters, and naval vessels. Effective antisubmarine protection brought the convoy through without loss. Ships communicated with each other using dim-spot blinkers and flags.

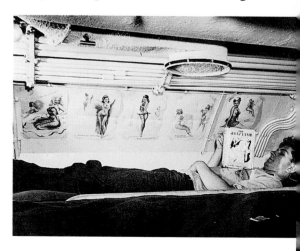

Garbage went overboard only at dusk, to be dispersed by currents. Details smashed bottles and punctured tins before dumping them over the sides, and not a speck of paper left the deck. The first, record-breaking trip, the longest non-stop voyage ever made by a United States convoy, took twenty-four days.

American submarines operating in the Pacific began cutting heavily into Japanese shipping. They carried the war to the doorstep of the enemy's home seaports, torpedoing Imperial ships within sight of their lookouts. Attacks were quickly pursued by enemy destroyers and an interminable nerve-racking pounding from 600-pound depth-charges. Most missions took the submarines on long, perilous voyages during which they were cut off from all

communication with the outside world. In their cramped and stuffy quarters, sailors risked the combined total of all the hazards of war, because rescue from a submarine was rare.

The first turning point in the war in the Pacific occurred on May 8, 1942, in the Coral Sea. When on May 3 eight Zeros appeared over Port Moresby looking for the South Pacific Fleet, MacArthur knew the aircraft had come from carriers. He dispatched U.S. Army Air Force bombers to search for the vessels. The planes returned, having destroyed one warship, but they brought back a wealth of information. MacArthur flashed the intelligence to Rear Admiral Frank J. Fletcher, who was operating in the Coral Sea with the carrier *Yorktown*, three cruisers, and six destroyers. Certain that the Japanese did not know of his

Above: On May 8, 1942, the carrier U.S.S. *Lexington* is badly damaged and burning. The crew eventually saved the vessel, while the wounded were evacuated to a destroyer coming through the smoke.

presence, Fletcher boldly slipped into position 100 miles southwest of Guadacanal and sent his carrier planes swooping at tree-top level toward the mass of shipping anchored in the harbor. In a furious action lasting fifteen minutes, twelve of fifteen Japanese vessels went to the bottom and the other three fled to sea.

The enemy now knew that an American carrier was in the area and concentrated their forces to bring on a conclusive battle. Fletcher withdrew to refuel, and while doing so rendezvoused with the carrier *Lexington*, commanded by Captain Frank C. Sherman, the heavy cruisers *Minneapolis*, *New Orleans*, and *Chicago*, and eleven destroyers. *Lexington*, converted from a battle cruiser, was a rugged ship. Also joining the combined squadron were two Australian cruisers commanded by Rear Admiral J. G. Grace of the

Left: In addition to the wounded, a number of uninjured survivors were also removed from the *Lexington*, as some doubt existed regarding the carrier's ability to remain afloat.

SELECTIVE CHRONOLOGY OF WAR: 1941

Apr 10: U.S.S. *Niblack* becomes first U.S. Navy ship to depth-charge a U-boat after a Dutch freighter is sunk off Iceland.

Sep 11: Following attack on U.S.S. *Greer* by German U-boat on Sep 4, President Roosevelt orders "shoot-on-sight" order to warships in U.S. defensive waters.

Oct 17: The destroyer U.S.S. *Kearney* is torpedoed and damaged south west of Iceland while on escort duty; 11 Navy personnel are killed and 22 injured, considered to be the first U.S. casualties of the war.

Oct 31: The destroyer U.S.S. *Reuben James* is torpedoed and sunk by German submarine U-562 while on patrol off Iceland, the first loss of a Navy ship in the war.

Nov 10: U.S. Navy escorts its first troop convoy of the war.

Dec 8: River gunboat *Wake* becomes first and only U.S. warship to surrender during World War II as her crew try unsuccessfully to scuttle her near Shanghai.

Above: Men on board the U.S.S. *Yorktown* attempt to clear away the wreckage caused by Japanese dive-bombers. A few hours later, a Japanese submarine sank the damaged carrier with a spread of torpedoes.

Bottom Right: As *Yorktown* began to list, all hope of saving her vanished. Sailors donned their life preservers, waiting for the order to abandon ship.

Royal Australian Navy.

During the next two days Fletcher moved across the Coral Sea and deployed his forces. Being heavily outnumbered by the enemy worried him, but the desperate situation in the Solomons and New Guinea made it imperative that he gamble the remnants of the South Pacific Fleet to keep the Imperial Army from landing near Port Moresby. Fletcher dispatched three cruisers to the Jomard Passage to hold off a Japanese amphibious force rounding New Guinea and led his two American carriers and

their supporting vessels toward Tulagi.

Before daylight on May 7, Fletcher decided to pass up the transports and to attack Japan's fighting fleet. Scouting aircraft left the decks of the carriers at dawn. At eight o'clock a reconnaissance plane spotted part of Vice-Admiral Shigeyoshi Inouye's Japanese fleet: one carrier, three cruisers, and six destroyers north of Misima Island and steaming southeast. MacArthur found the transports and sent in his bombers.

At 8:15 Fletcher launched 76 aircraft: 24 torpedo planes, 36 dive-bombers, and 16 fighters. They located the big new Japanese carrier *Ryukaku* just as she began turning into the wind to launch her planes. In less than two minutes, fifteen bombs landed on the carrier's deck and fifteen torpedoes ripped open her hull. A few minutes later she slid under the water with all her planes and 1,600 men. Commander Bob Dixon opened his radio long enough to report, "Scratch one flattop!" Another pilot, in the midst of a dive, saw the carrier go under and banked just enough to drop his load on a cruiser's fantail, sending her to the bottom.

When Fletcher learned that to the east one American destroyer had been sunk and the tanker *Neosha* crippled, he realized that the Japanese had another battle fleet swinging into the Coral Sea from around the Solomons. At 8:30 on the morning of May 8, an American scout flying through a heavy cloud belt broke into the clear long enough to spot two carriers, four cruisers, and a number of destroyers 175 miles northeast of *Lexington* and *Yorktown*. In less than an hour, 73 planes took to the air and set a heading for the Japanese squadron.

SELECTIVE CHRONOLOGY OF WAR: 1942

Jan 27: First contingent of U.S. Navy Seabees leave U.S., arriving at Bora Bora, Society Islands, on Feb 17. U.S.S. *Gudgeon* becomes first U.S. Navy submarine to sink an enemy submarine, a Japanese I-173 type in central Pacific.

Feb 25: U.S. Coast Guard assumes responsibility for security of U.S. ports.

Aug 17: U.S. Marines land from U.S. submarine to raid Makin Island.

Sep 1: Seabees are used in combat zone for first time, as they continue work begun by Japanese to develop what became Henderson Field, Guadalcanal.

Oct 11: Navy Task Force 64 (4 cruisers, 5 destroyers) prevents Japanese force from bombarding Guadalcanal in Battle of Cape Esperance.

Oct 26: In Battle of Santa Cruz Islands, U.S. Navy loses U.S.S. *Hornet*, 78 aircraft, 3 destroyers, with 2 battleships severely damaged, but shoot down 100 Japanese warplanes and seriously damage 2 carriers and a cruiser which are attempting to attack Guadalcanal.

Nov 12: Naval battle of Guadalcanal begins in earnest, resulting in end of Japanese naval action in the Solomons, and helping to turn the tide of the war in the Pacific.

Left: On October 26, 1942, aircraft from two American cruisers engage a Japanese task force off Santa Cruz Islands. A bomb barely misses the *Enterprise*, pictured here; she is later struck but survives.

During the same timeframe, an enemy scout sighted Fletcher's squadron and escaped to report the position to Inouye. Five minutes later 108 Japanese planes took off from carriers and headed for Fletcher, half bearing toward *Lexington*, the other half toward *Yorktown*. By eleven o'clock, opposing aircraft filled the skies, swooping over each other's carriers.

Lexington dodged nine out of eleven torpedoes launched at her in as many seconds, but a 1,000-pound bomb wrecked her forward 5-inch battery and killed its crew. *Yorktown* took a bomb square through the deck; it blew out a compartment, killing 44 men. Before the day ended, the Japanese lost its greatest carrier, *Shoho*, and fourteen warships. Inouye's other carrier limped away damaged, along with two cruisers, three destroyers, and fourteen other vessels. Fletcher lost *Lexington*, the destroyer *Sims*, the tanker *Neosho*, 66 planes, and 543 airmen and sailors.

The Battle of the Coral Sea marked the first major engagement in naval warfare where surface ships never exchanged a shot, the action being entirely between carrier fleets. The engagement stopped the Japanese advance and saved Australia from the threat of invasion. It also weakened the Imperial Navy and opened the door for amphibious landings in the Solomons.

Fletcher's action in the Coral Sea set the stage for an even bigger surprise. Admiral King gave much thought to where the Imperial Navy would strike next. Among the obvious outposts was the island of Midway, 1,000 miles northwest of Hawaii, which had survived earlier Japanese attacks, and Dutch Harbor in the Aleutians.

Having broken the Japanese code, King knew the intentions of Admiral Yamamoto, who looked upon Midway as a springboard to Hawaii and the occupation of the Aleutians as a base from which the Imperial Army could invade the American continent. Yamamoto, the architect of the Pearl Harbor attack, would not tolerate any more repulses like the disaster in the Coral Sea. He planned well and took command of the combined fleet himself. He ordered a diversionary attack against the Aleutians while his main force struck Midway. He marshaled an armada of more than one hundred warships, including eight carriers and eleven battleships, plus transports and supply ships for the knockout blow. He placed the vital Carrier Striking Force under

Below: During the battle of Santa Cruz Islands, plane handling crews working the deck of *Enterprise* shove a Grumman F4F Wildcat to the side as four incoming planes circle to land.

Vice-Admiral Chuici Nagumo, who had led the sneak attack on Pearl Harbor. As May passed into June, the Imperial Navy deployed for another great campaign based upon surprise, but this time the American Navy was not to be caught napping.

Yorktown, patched up after the Coral Sea affair, rushed through 5,000 miles of sea to join the carriers *Enterprise* and *Hornet* near Hawaii. Along with the three carriers, King sent all the ships he could spare to Nimitz at Honolulu-seven heavy cruisers, one light cruiser, fourteen destroyers, twenty submarines, but not a single battleship.

To operate an aircraft carrier required about 3,000 men, enough to populate a small town. It contained all the facilities of a city – a huge power plant to keep it running, a dial telephone system connecting all rooms, and enormous

facilities for housing and feeding its crew. The carrier existed for one purpose – to launch aircraft and get them back down safely. Most days passed uneventfully, even boringly. Men occupied their time exercising, playing cards, maintaining aircraft, and waiting for something to happen, which was rare.

Nimitz, however, did not want his floating airfields to be idle. He broke the fleet into two task forces, one under Spruance and the other under Fletcher. As a battle fleet, the two commands were too weak to compete with the Yamamoto's huge flotilla, but as an equalizer, Nimitz relied upon land-based aircraft from Midway and Honolulu.

Ensign Jewell Reid, flying a navy patrol bomber, spotted the Imperial fleet 2,600 miles west of Midway and reported "eleven big ships in the water beneath him." The enemy vessels were far beyond the range of carrier bombers, but not the nine Flying Fortresses sent into Midway from Honolulu. Behind the bombers came Lieutenant William Richards with four slow and ponderous flying boats (PBYs), hastily fitted with improvised gadgets that enabled the aircraft to release torpedoes from under the wings. The early action set the stage for the morning of June 4, 1942, when Lieutenant William A. Chase, patrolling beyond Midway, sighted more than one hundred enemy bombers, heavily escorted, flying in tight formation toward the island.

The furious fight in the air over Midway involved American land-based planes. Not until 11:00 a.m., after being attacked by B-26s and Flying Fortresses, did Yamamoto discover the presence of American carrier planes – *Hornet*'s "Torpedo Squadron 8," led by Lieutenant Commander John C. Waldron. Waldron

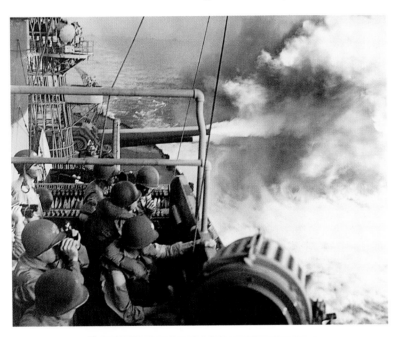

reported his planes low on fuel, but Spruance ordered him to attack the four carriers, even if the entire squadron had to ditch on their way back. All fifteen planes were lost. The only survivor, Ensign George Gay, scored a direct hit on a carrier before being hit himself. His plane crashed into the sea, but he came up from under the water, grabbed a floating cushion, and witnessed the most spectacular sight "human eyes had ever seen.... The enemy line was strung back for ten miles, with the air full of Zeros and tremendous anti-aircraft fire."

From his ringside cushion in the Pacific, Gay saw two squadrons from American carriers hove in sight under fighter cover. "The torpedo planes kept the enemy's fighters and anti-aircraft so busy that the dive bombers were able to drop bomb after bomb. He watched as the carrier *Kaga* tried to get off her refueled Zeros but was pounded with bombs and finally blew up. Two other carriers, *Akagi* and *Soryu*, were struck repeatedly by bombs and torpedoes; two battleships were hit and burning; a destroyer sank.

Nagumo's aircraft finally spotted the American carriers, but most of the attacking bombers and torpedo planes from *Hiryu* were shot down by anti-aircraft weapons on the flattops. Of four surviving aircraft, three dropped bombs on the *Yorktown*, disabling her. At 5:00 p.m. *Hiryu* sent another swarm of torpedo planes supported by fighters and attacked again. Two torpedoes got through and penetrated *Yorktown*'s vitals. She listed heavily, but bombers from her deck and the deck of *Enterprise* set *Hiryu* ablaze from stem to stern. In the end, the Imperial Navy lost four of its finest

carriers, a heavy cruiser, and countless numbers of damaged vessels. Planes that could fly off the crippled Japanese carriers had no place to land and splashed into the Pacific.

During the three-day Battle of Midway, Americans lost *Yorktown*, one destroyer, and a hundred aircraft. Yamamoto had forced a showdown using decisive strength, and lost. Instead of threatening the West Coast of America, Yamamoto put Japan on the defensive. He now began to understand the fighting qualities of the American sailor.

As in the battle in the Coral Sea, sailors in the sky, augmented by the Air Force, did the fighting. Not one warship fired upon another. Once Yamamoto became aware of the presence of American carriers, he never deployed his twelve battleships.

Because Roosevelt placed priority on whipping the Germans, most of America's destroyers remained in the Atlantic to escort convoys and to chase U-boats. The Japanese soon discovered

Above: A "Kingfisher" OS2U lands in Truk Lagoon and rescues nine navy fliers downed during an air strike on Truk in April 1944. The rescued fliers hug the wings as the aircraft nears a friendly submarine.

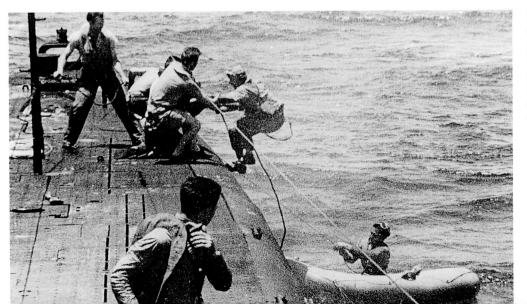

Left: The fliers are helped aboard the submarine U.S.S. *Tang*. The operation is hurried because enemy aircraft are in the area and both the sub and the fliers are vulnerable to attack while on the surface.

Above: From the battle-torn invasion beaches of Eniwetok Atoll, Coast Guardsmen prepare to hoist a wounded fighter pilot aboard their assault transport.

that carriers in the South Pacific roamed the seas with little destroyer protection, giving them freedom to boldly attack America's big ships.

During a period of time spanning a few days, *Hornet* dodged twenty-two torpedoes, and aircraft from her flight deck sent six prowling submarines to the bottom. The carrier *Wasp* was not so lucky. While escorting a convoy to Guadacanal, two torpedoes caught her amidships and a third hit her aft. The convoy reached Guadacanal safely, but *Wasp*'s magazines exploded and she sank.

On occasion, battle fleets without carriers made contact off Guadacanal. Just before midnight on October 11, 1942, Rear Admiral Norman Scott surprised a Japanese squadron in "the Slot" between Choisel and New Georgia. With two heavy cruisers, two light

cruisers, and five destroyers, he attacked a superior enemy force attempting to land reinforcements on Guadacanal's Cape Esperance. In the darkness the battle became confused, with friendly fire taking its toll among the combatants.

When the smoke cleared at dawn, Scott's mini-battle fleet, in a purely naval engagement, had destroyed four Japanese cruisers, four destroyers, and left another destroyer and four cruisers damaged. Scott lost one destroyer. When daylight flooded the sea on the morning of October 12, dive-bombers took off from Henderson Field, sank another cruiser, and severely hobbled two more vessels. To the sailors in the American Navy, it was becoming distinctly apparent that the warships of the United States were much more durable and better protected than the thin-skinned vessels of the Imperial Navy.

On October 18, 1942, Admiral William "Bull" Halsey took command of the South Pacific Fleet. Seven days later patrol planes spotted three Japanese battle squadrons north of Santa Cruz Island. With only two carriers – *Hornet* and *Enterprise* – and a handful of cruisers and destroyers, Halsey went into battle against overwhelming odds.

Japanese bombers went after *Hornet* with a vengeance, perhaps because she had been the carrier responsible for carrying the B-25s that had bombed Tokyo. Struck by two torpedoes and three high-altitude bombs, *Hornet* lay dead in the water when a suicide plane, loaded with bombs, dove into the carrier's stack. A second fully loaded suicide bomber crashed onto her deck. On the afternoon of October 26, *Hornet* sank off Santa Cruz Island, leaving Halsey with only one superficially damaged carrier, *Enterprise*.

But the fight had not been in vain. The Imperial Navy limped away from the battle with one battleship, three carriers, and five cruisers so badly damaged they may never have made port. Four Japanese air groups had been cut to pieces, forcing the Imperial Army to delay their next large-scale effort to reinforce Guadacanal.

On November 12 patrol planes spotted another large Japanese force descending

SELECTIVE CHRONOLOGY OF WAR: 1943

Jan 2: Allies capture Buna Mission, New Guinea, the first time the Allies defeat the enemy in an offensive operation.

July 6: In the Battle of Kula Gulf the U.S. Navy wins the first victory in South Pacific offensive, sinking 2 destroyers for the loss of 1 light cruiser, and preventing the Japanese from reinforcing their Munda, New Georgia, base.

July 13: U.S. Navy hunter-killer groups operate against German submarines in the Atlantic, sinking 12 U-boats over the next month.

Nov 25: Five U.S. destroyers sink 3 Japanese destroyers and severely damage 2 more in Battle of Cape St. George. The U.S. vessels suffer no damage as they catch the Japanese returning from reinforcing Bougainville.

down "the Slot" for Guadacanal. *Enterprise* was out of the area for repairs, and Rear Admiral D. J. Callaghan was left to face the enemy with only five cruisers and eight destroyers. His mission – to fight a delaying action while Vice Admiral Thomas C. Kincaid intercepted the Japanese transports with a heavier force.

On the night of November 13, two Japanese battleships, two cruisers, and fourteen destroyers opened on Henderson Field as another squadron of destroyers with eleven transports carrying 11,000 soldiers moved toward Cape Esperance. Callaghan surprised the heavier force off Fort Henderson, blowing up one vessel and setting two enemy cruisers on fire. After that, the fight began to stabilize with both sides taking heavy casualties. Callaghan got on the radio and hollered, "We want the big ones!" meaning the battleships *South Dakota* and *Washington*, which had just been repaired at Pearl Harbor and delivered to the South Pacific Fleet.

While Callaghan fought an unequal battle with the enemy, Kincaid turned

back the transports attempting to reinforce Guadacanal. But on November 14, twelve transports returned, this time supported by a battleship, two heavy cruisers, and ten destroyers. Just to the west another column of two light cruisers and five destroyers steamed toward the Japanese squadron. Kincaid could not get there in time and radioed Henderson Field with orders to "hit the transports." When the last flight returned at dusk, every Japanese warship had fled. Five transports had been sunk, three were burning and dead in the water, and two of the remaining four were nursing bomb damage.

The carrier Enterprise and the battleships *Washington* and *South Dakota* never got into the battle. Admiral Callaghan lost his life fighting an enemy battleship. Kincaid repulsed the Japanese squadron attempting to reinforce Guadacanal. Army and Navy aircraft did the rest.

The hard-fought American victory came at a cost of two light cruisers and seven destroyers. Of several ships damaged, all were repaired. Not counting those damaged, the Japanese lost twenty-eight vessels: two battleships, eight cruisers, six destroyers, eight transports, and four cargo ships. More than 5,000 Japanese troops died on their way to Guadacanal. Though the fight for the island continued, the crisis had ended. So many vessels had been sunk off the north coast of Guadacanal that the thirty-mile stretch of water became known as "Ironbottom Bay."

Among the island fortresses bypassed during amphibious operations in early 1944 was the huge Japanese base at Truk

Left: As the escort carrier U.S.S. *Princetown* is set afire by a Japanese bomber in the Leyte Gulf, the U.S.S. *Birmingham* pulls alongside to render assistance.

Bottom Left: A PT boat, working through the Surigao Strait in the Philippines, takes time out from spotting Japanese naval vessels to hook onto an enemy pilot and pull him to safety.

Below: In the Leyte Gulf on October 25, 1944, Grumman Wildcat fighters rev their engines on the U.S.S. *Kitkun Bay* as they prepare to join the fight off Samar Island.

Above: On April 28, 1945, a *kamikaze* pilot attempts to maneuver his "Zeke" onto the deck of the U.S.S. *Missouri*, but he misses and splashes into the sea.

Below Right: Above the dungaree work uniforms are earphones, microphone and (right) steel talker's helmet used by guncrew, while the M1 helmet (top left) is adorned with folk art. The leggings (below left) are M1938 pattern issued to Seabees.

in the Carolines. On February 16 Admiral Spruance brought Task Force 58 close to the island. While Grumman Hellcats launched from carriers destroyed the enemy's air cover, more than forty enemy ships began pouring through the North Pass in an effort to get to sea.

Sixty miles to the northeast, Spruance waited with two battleships, a pair of cruisers, and an escort of destroyers. By noon on February 17, twenty-three enemy vessels lay on the bottom of the ocean. Thirteen others struggled to stay afloat, many having gone aground to keep from sinking. The myth of Truk's invincibility

had been shattered in thirty hours. Admiral Nimitz proudly announced, "The Pacific fleet has returned at Truk the visit made by the Japanese at Pearl harbor on December 7, 1941, and effected a partial settlement of the debt."

In most naval engagements like the action at Truk, submarines played a dual role. The submarine *Tang*, under the command of Lieutenant Commander Richard H. O'Kane, lay offshore during the attack. By pre-arrangement, O'Kane would torpedo any enemy vessels that put in a sudden appearance, but he also fulfilled a dual role – rescuing American fliers who had been shot down.

Small planes equipped with pontoons also participated in the rescue process. Lieutenant John A. Burns, flying a single-seater, picked up so many men that they over-weighted his aircraft. Burns motored over to *Tang* and put them on the sub. Throughout the day, the sub and the rescue plane worked in concert. Late in the action, Burns delivered three airmen on each wing and one on his lap in the cockpit. Under fire from shore, O'Kane hustled them all below. Burns came on board and dropped through the hatch for a breather. When he returned topside, his plane had been sunk by gunfire.

When the raid on Truk ended, O'Kane had rescued twenty-two pilots, most of them injured. On the cramped submarine he could barely find space to put them, but he kept them alive and

SELECTIVE CHRONOLOGY OF WAR: 1944

Feb 16: U.S. Navy task force begins assault on Truk; by the 18th it has destroyed the Japanese airfield and harbor, 400,000 tons of shipping, and 270 warplanes.

Mar 29: U.S. Navy task force begins attack in Carolines.

June 15: Battle of Philippine Sea begins; U.S. warplanes achieve great aerial successes during "Marianas Turkey Shoot", and 3 Japanese carriers are destroyed with support of submarines; 3 U.S. warships are damaged.

July 8: U.S. Navy battleships, destroyers, and cruisers bombard Guam in action that lasts until July 19, by when almost 29,000 5- and 6-inch rounds have softened up Japanese defenses in preparation for Marine landings.

Sep 3: U.S. Navy bombards Japanese targets in Palau Islands and Carolines, sinking 13 warships.

Oct 23: Battle of Leyte Gulf begins; it lasts 3 days during which U.S. Navy destroys 4 Japanese carriers, 3 battleships, 10 cruisers, 9 destroyers, for the loss of 1 light carrier, 2 escort carriers, 2 destroyers, 1 destroyer escort; U.S. land- and carrier-based warplanes pursue what remains of Japanese Navy, which ceases to be an effective force in the Pacific.

Nov 11: U.S. Navy bombards Japanese positions on Iwo Jima.

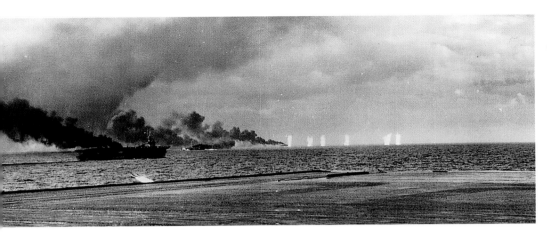

Left: On October 25, 1944, off San Bernandino Strait, two American escort carriers with the U.S.S. *St. Lo* in the foreground, are bracketed by shell fire from the Japanese fleet.

carried them all safely to Hawaii.

Admiral Spruance continued to press westward through the Gilberts, Marshalls, and Marianas while MacArthur hopped through Netherlands New Guinea to the island of Morotai, edging ever closer to the Philippines. Vice-Admiral Jisaburo Ozawa sought to block the Navy's advance by catching Mitscher's Task Force 58 in a pincers and pounding it "until not a United States ship remained afloat." Ozawa overlooked one important element. Once he launched his carrier planes, they might not have any place to land and refuel but Saipan, Rota, or Guam. Spruance took care of that by invading Saipan on June 15 and by sending air coverage over Guam.

On June 18, 1944, Spruance and Mitscher held the fleet near Guam and destroyed Ozawa's carrier planes. Mitscher then hurried Task Force 58 west in an effort to overhaul the enemy fleet. On June 19 patrol planes spotted Ozawa's carriers in the Philippine Sea and, with only two hours of daylight remaining, Mitscher turned his carriers into the wind and launched hundreds of planes at extreme ranges to catch the foe.

At 6:30 p.m., the lead aircraft caught sight of Shimada's most rearward vessels. Despite low fuel and the prospect of never making it back to the carriers, the Navy pilots flew straight on until they sighted six Japanese flattops – all with empty flight decks – midway between the Marianas and the Philippines. The furious attack consumed fifteen minutes – the toll, one large carrier and one heavy cruiser sunk; two light carriers, a battleship, three cruisers, and a destroyer damaged, along with several other vessels. In the confusion that followed,

American submarines sank two more carriers. Seventy-five percent of the planes reached Mitscher's carriers safely, and aircraft rescued most of the eighty pilots ditching into the ocean.

The Battle of the Philippine Sea all but wiped out the Imperial carrier force. It would never again be a serious threat. Combined with the invasion of the Marianas, Imperial forces lost 757 planes and thirty ships. The so-called "Great Marianas Turkey Shoot" was the worst Japanese disaster since Midway and gave the United States its first bases for bombing Japan.

MacArthur's landing on Leyte on October 23, 1944, induced the Japanese Navy to make one last all-out bid to halt the American advance. In scope, the plan was gigantic. Admiral Toyoda split every ship and plane he could muster into three commands. While Vice-Admiral Jisaburo Ozawa's Northern Force, made up mostly of carriers without planes, lured Halsey's Third Fleet away from Leyte, Vice-Admiral Takeo Kurita would bring his Central Fleet over from Singapore and take it into the Leyte Gulf from the northeast, using San Bernardino Strait. At

Below: On April 1, 1945, the California-class battleship U.S.S. *Tennessee*, one of those thought by the Japanese as having been destroyed at Pearl Harbor, takes her revenge on the shores of Okinawa.

Above: On February 16, 1945, Task Force 58 with the new U.S.S. *Hornet* send planes on a bombing mission to Tokyo while men on board the carrier exercise the 40mm guns in anticipation of an attack.

warships and 716 planes for his three commands. Halsey and Kincaid shared 166 warships and 1,280 planes. Even if Toyoda's strategy to decoy Halsey worked, Kincaid still had enough ships and aircraft to contend with Vice-Admirals Kurita and Nishimura.

On October 23, Toyoda's plan got off to a bad start. Halsey's aircraft spotted Kurita's Central Force and sank two cruisers. American submarines, *Darter* and *Dace*, sank two more and damaged a third. On the 24th, planes from the Third Fleet sank one of Japan's great battleships, *Musashi*, and damaged a cruiser, but Halsey lost the use of the light carrier *Princeton*, which enemy land-based aircraft damaged. During the fight, the admiral's patrol planes spotted the decoy squadron under Ozawa, so off went Halsey on a wild goose chase, leaving the San Bernardino Strait unguarded.

But Admiral Kincaid suspected a ruse and steamed the Seventh Fleet into Surigao Strait. When Nishimura's Southern Force came in sight on the night of October 24-25, a squadron of PT-boats ambushed it. The attack attracted the attention of Rear Admiral Jesse B. Oldendorf, who brought down most of Kincaid's battleships and cruisers and all but blew Nishamura's flotilla out of the water. Five of Oldendorf's battleships were those the Japanese thought they had destroyed at Pearl Harbor. Now here they were back again, rebuilt, modernized, and with 14- and 16-inch guns more powerful than ever. When Nishamura attempted to turn and flee, he made the mistake of enabling Oldendorf to "cross the T" and rake every vessel in the two Japanese columns. "Every damned salvo," declared Oldendorf, "landed right on!" Oldendorf wiped out the entire Japanese force, pursuing it all the way into the Mindanao Sea.

the same time, Vice-Admiral Shoji Nishimura would bring a smaller Southern Force through Surigao Strait and enter Leyte Gulf from the south, thereby squeezing Admiral Kinkaid's Seventh Fleet in a pincers and trapping MacArthur on his beachhead. When Halsey returned, the victorious Imperial Navy could turn on the Third Fleet and put an end to American naval superiority in the Pacific.

Japanese planners overlooked one detail. Halsey's Third Fleet and Kincaid's Seventh Fleet covering MacArthur's landing had each grown in size, and either of them could operate on its own against the entire Japanese Navy. In the last days of October, Toyoda could muster only 70

Admiral Kurita brought his Central Force through San Bernardino Strait one day too late and found himself among sixteen American escort carriers and a flotilla of escort destroyers in the Samar Sea. Planes from all sixteen carriers descended on Kurita's ships, quickly sinking three cruisers. With the battleships and cruisers of the Seventh Fleet chasing the remnants of Nishamura's command, Kurita passed

---

SELECTIVE CHRONOLOGY OF WAR: 1945

Jan 3: U.S. Navy's Task Force 38 begins 3-week heavy carrier strikes against Japanese bases in Western Pacific and South China Sea, destroying 600 enemy aircraft and sinking 325,000 tons of Japanese shipping in Formosa, the Ryukyus, Luzon, Pescadores, Saigon, Hong Kong.

Apr 6: U.S. Navy suffers first of 10 mass *kamikaze* attacks over 8 weeks off Okinawa, losing several ships.

Apr 7: U.S. Navy sinks battleship *Yamato*, plus a cruiser and 4 destroyers, and shoots down 58 aircraft.

Aug 15: Day after Japan surrenders, U.S. Navy begins location of Japanese PoW camps, dropping supplies and liberating Allied PoWs.

up a golden opportunity to cause extensive damage to MacArthur's defenseless beachhead. Instead, he retreated in haste, leaving for posterity a garbled explanation for his flight.

Though Kurita's force sank one escort carrier and three destroyers, the most serious damage was inflicted by land-based *kamikaze* aircraft carrying 550-pound bombs. By then, almost all of Japan's top pilots lay dead, and most of her best planes had been destroyed. Picked from more than one hundred Philippine airfields, youngster's flew the obsolete suicide planes, and while Kurita's force engaged the carriers and their destroyer escorts, *kamikazes* crashed into the flight decks of the carriers *Santee*, *Suwannee*, and *St. Lo*.

The battle in the Leyte Gulf became the testing ground for kamikaze attacks and gave the Japanese high command a new terrible weapon, one that would be used with tenacity and effectiveness at Iwo Jima and Okinawa. Before the conflict ended in August, 1945, suicide planes would sink thirty ships and damage 368, including carriers and battleships. Five thousand sailors would die from *kamikaze* attacks, and 10,000 more would be injured. As one sailor said, "It is a tough job to hold back this tidal wave of suicide planes." Another described his mixed emotions as he "watched a man about to die — a man determined to die in order that he might

destroy us in the process."

During the battle for Leyte, Halsey chased Ozawa far to the north, sinking four carriers, a cruiser, and two destroyers 200 miles off Cape Engano without suffering so much as a scratch on his ships, though he lost ten planes and eighteen men. Nimitz ordered him back to Leyte to protect MacArthur, but by then the remaining vessels of Kurita's Central Force had vanished.

Because Halsey believed he had to locate the Japanese carriers, he always justified his pursuit of the decoys, but in the end, it made little difference. The Imperial Navy no longer had a force deserving the distinction of being called a fleet. Admiral Mitscher declared that "Japan had been left wide open by reduction of her navy to the status of a fifth-rate power."

There would never be another battle with a Japanese squadron. After Leyte, the American sailor fought *kamikaze* planes, not enemy ships. The battles continued, first at Mindoro and then at Luzon, while in the Pacific, forces under Spruance faced *kamikaze* attacks at Iwo Jima and Okinawa.

Naval engagements between American and Japanese warships became a thing of the past. As one noted historian observed, "The Japs...lost more than a thousand ships; their navy was a vanishing ghost; their air fleet was but a stalking skeleton." What the Imperial Army still had was 5,000,000 troops and a sinking desperation to save face. In early August, 1945, B-29s dropped two atomic bombs on Japan, settling the issue once and for all, and for the American sailor, World War II came to a horrible but honorable end.

Left: On May 11, 1945, men on board the carrier U.S.S. *Bunker Hill* run along the deck in an effort to quench a fire started by a *kamikaze* flying off an airfield on Okinawa.

Below: Ordinary seamen crane their necks to watch as formal ceremonies of the Japanese surrender take place on board the U.S.S. *Missouri* in Tokyo Bay.

THE MARINES IN THE PACIFIC

The U.S. Marine Corps functioned as a separate service within the Navy Department, but it had a distinct advantage over any other marine force in the world because it operated with its own air arm. No military entity other than the Marines could have been better suited to cope with an enemy on the fortified islands of the South Pacific.

In 1933 the Marines numbered only 20,000 men – two brigades and one aviation group. Though years passed without much military spending, the Marines worked at techniques for amphibious landings which led to the development of specialized landing craft. By 1941, the two original brigades

became the 1st and 2nd Marine Divisions. The air group split into thirteen squadrons with 641 pilots. During the war, the Corps never grew beyond six infantry divisions, roughly 500,000 strong at its peak.

Fighting on the islands of the Pacific bore no similarity to the fighting in Europe. After D-Day, an infantryman in combat for eleven months in Europe could expect to be wounded. In the Pacific, it was unusual for a Marine to go through a single campaign without being injured.

After bombing Pearl Harbor, the Imperial Navy set its sights on three strategically important islands west of Hawaii – Midway, Wake, and Guam. To control the Pacific, Japan needed these islands. Guam maintained a token garrison of 674 defenders, mostly Navy personnel. Because of the proximity of the island to Japan, Congress had wished to avoid diplomatic hostilities and failed to provide funds to fortify it. The Japanese bombed the island on December 8, 1941, and captured it two days later. A Navy captain surrendered Guam to a Japanese officer who demanded that he strip to his shorts as a gesture of submission. To the Imperial high command, wresting American islands in the Pacific from pants-dropping naval officers promised to provide lots of amusement. But then the Japanese came to Wake.

In 1941, the typical American did not know very much about the Marines. The stubborn defense of the island by 378 Marine infantrymen, 62 Marine pilots, and 74 officers and men of the Navy and the Army Signal Corps changed all that.

A week earlier, twelve slow, clumsy, Grumman F4F3 Wildcat fighter planes reached Wake from the carrier *Enterprise*. Aside from that, Major James P. S. Devereux, the garrison commander, had no scouts, no bombers, and no

Below: The Japanese enjoyed taking photographs of the American troops who on May 6, 1942, finally surrendered on Corregidor and were hauled into prison camps on the mainland.

warships. He did have one cumbersome Clipper, rifles and side-arms, six 5-inch naval guns, twelve 3-inch anti-aircraft guns, and eighteen .50-caliber and thirty .30 caliber machine guns. Wake had no aircraft warning system, and at 11:58 a.m., December 8, when 24 twin-engine Japanese bombers swooped out of the sun and leveled off at 3,000 feet to strike the airfield, it was only by an accident of good fortune that Devereux had four of his Wildcats in the air and away from the field. The raid destroyed seven of the planes on the ground and rendered the eighth temporarily useless.

On December 9 the Japanese returned, this time with 27 bombers. Tokyo radio had already announced Wake captured, putting extreme pressure on the Imperial Navy's airmen to pound the island into submission. Four Wildcats took to the skies, shot down a bomber, but could not drive the enemy away. More bombs fell, flattening every building in proximity to the airfield.

On December 11, two transports supported by three cruisers, six destroyers, and two gunboats appeared off the island and laid down a heavy bombardment. Devereux waited until the warships came in range before opening with his artillery. As the first shells began crashing into the transports, the Wildcats took off loaded with 100-pound bombs fitted in emergency racks. Artillery sank one destroyer and a gunboat. The Wildcats sank a second destroyer. The pilots turned their attention to a light cruiser, struck her with eight bombs, strafed her decks with 20,000 rounds of

ammunition, and watched her sink. Two other destroyers and a cruiser limped away with heavy damage. As the Imperial Navy withdrew to the Marshall Islands for repairs, Tokyo radio again announced the capture of Wake. One Japanese naval authority called it "one of the most humiliating defeats our Navy ever suffered."

By using typical Marine ingenuity, mechanics got one of the Wildcats damaged during the first bombing raid back in the air. On December 12, when the enemy bombers returned, up went the Grummans. Pilots shot down two of the bombers but lost one of their fighters when it crash-landed on the beach.

Later that day the enemy tried again,

Above: In April, 1942, American prisoners of Japanese on the Philippines use improvised litters to carry comrades who, from lack of food or water on the march from Bataan, fell along the road.

Left: A selection of Marine Corps equipment, including hats (left to right): World War I style campaign hat, Model 1917 A1 steel helmet, lightweight tropical helmet, and (below these) collapsible field hat. The weapons are (center) M1 Garand with M7 grenade launcher and (bottom) M1 carbine with grenade launcher attachment on muzzle.

Above: On November 20, 1943, after several days of naval bombardment, Marines disembark from transports and begin to approach the shore of Tarawa in landing craft.

supplies, a war of attrition began on Wake Island. As each day passed, Japanese bombers intensified their attacks, losing an average of two per day. By December 15, the daily skirmishes had cost the Marines all but two Grummans. Heavy bombing continued, taking out anti-aircraft and artillery positions. Naval Commander Winfield S. Cunningham reported, "The planes are full of bullet holes…and ammunition is running low." The Japanese, however, had not been able to knock out the 5-inch guns, so they brought up carriers whose aircraft could dive bomb the sites.

On the night of December 21-22, Imperial forces attacked in overwhelming numbers. One of the last messages from Devereux read, "Attacked middle of night by…carrier bombers and fighters. Our two remaining fighters aloft. Several enemy accounted for." Then, during the dark hours of December 23, a Japanese amphibious force of 2,000 elite marines, supported by six cruisers and two aircraft carriers, landed on Wake. "Urgent!" radioed Devereux, "Enemy on island. The issue is in doubt." On one of Wake's three atolls, 70 Marines wiped out a landing force of 100 enemy.

To save 1,000 island inhabitants, Devereux, with a white rag lashed to a mop handle, surrendered the survivors. The Imperial Navy, in a war barely two

this time with 27 bombers, a flying boat, and a submarine. Second Lieutenant David D. Kliewer dropped a bomb on the sub and sank it. The other fighters knocked down the flying boat. The Navy, perhaps to give national morale a boost, advised the American public that a call had been made to Devereux asking if he needed anything, to which the major had replied, "Send us more Japs."

Unable to obtain reinforcements or

Right: On September 15, 1944, Marines assault the beaches at Peleliu in the Palau Islands and soon find themselves immersed in the jungle and under fire from snipers.

weeks old, had finally met the American Marine. The Japanese might hope that the stubborn defense of Wake Island was merely an anomaly, but they had touched swords with some of the toughest fighting men in the nation. The motion picture industry promptly produced "Wake Island," and suddenly every young man in America wanted to be a Marine.

Another small garrison of Marines held the tiny island of Midway, 1,300 miles northwest of Hawaii. Five miles long and five miles wide, the United States used the island as a cable station and a refueling base for trans-Pacific flights. At 9:50 p.m., December 7, 1941, a pair of Imperial warships and a flock of planes bombed and strafed the island. Much to the enemy's surprise, they found their ships in range of shore batteries. Searchlights from the island silhouetted a destroyer and a cruiser. Soon 5-inch

Above: On November 1, 1943, Marines landed on Bougainville in the Solomons. Here a mortar team slogs through mud and swamps filled daily by fresh rains.

Left: On December 26, 1943, Marines meet little resistance at Cape Gloucester, New Britain, but as they leave their LST, they are hit by waves three feet high when they approach the beach.

Above: Cautiously advancing through the jungle while on patrol off the Numa-Numa Trail, this GI of the 93rd Infantry Division is among the first African-American foot soldiers to go into action in the South Pacific.

shells began slamming into both vessels.

Marine Lieutenant George H. Cannon directed the fire until an enemy shell shattered the lower part of his body and mortally wounded him. The same shell broke the leg of Corporal Harold R. Hazelwood, the switchboard operator, but Hazelwood set the board back up and continued to direct the artillery fire.

For the next three months, the Japanese made weak attempts to capture the island but never did. As Colonel Harold D. Shannon, Midway's Marine commander said, "The Marines will hold it until hell freezes over." Hell never froze over, and Japan's failure to capture the island led in early June to one of the Imperial Navy's greatest naval disasters – the carrier battle at Midway.

In November, 1941, a veteran regiment under Colonel Sam Howard of the 4th Marines moved from China to the Philippines and joined MacArthur's force. MacArthur had 100,000 men, but most of them were raw, inadequately armed Filipino reservists. After being pushed up the Bataan Peninsula, Major General Edward King surrendered the force under his command, but Howard hunkered down on Corregidor with General Wainwright's remnants. For a month the Japanese pounded the rocky island day-and-night with more than 100 guns. On May 6, 1942, Wainwright surrendered his entire force, including the 4th Marines. "My God," grumbled Howard in despair, "I'm the first Marine officer to surrender a regiment." Howard no longer had anything left with which to fight. Though deeply troubled, he had to agree with his wireless operator, whose last message read, "The jig's up."

By then the fighting had moved to the Solomon Islands, where Japanese forces continued to make small advances against Australian troops. After capturing Tulagi, a small island with a fine natural harbor, the Japanese set their sights on Guadalcanal, twenty-five miles to the south. Strategically situated as a stepping stone to northern Australia, the island also provided an ideal site for building an airstrip. In June the Imperial Navy put a force ashore and construction crews went to work carving an airfield out of the jungle.

Right: Edged weapons played an important role for American forces, particularly in the Pacific theater, where they had to fight their way through jungle wilderness. Machetes were used to clear undergrowth, and fighting knives were found to have important advantages, being silent and needing little maintenance.

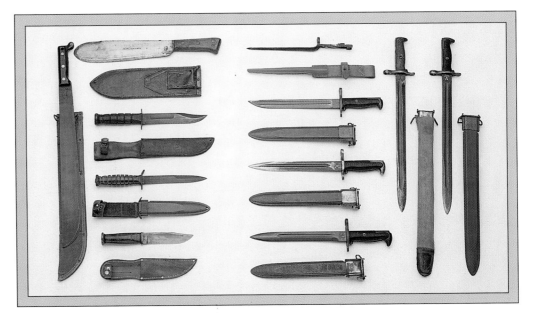

Left: During the November, 1943, landing on Red Beach No. 3 on Tarawa, the 2nd Marine Division make their way through the rubble towards Burns Phillips Pier.

At daybreak on August 7, 1942, the 1st Marine Division under the command of General Alexander A. Vandergrift scrambled into landing craft and pushed ashore. Ten thousand Marines swarmed across the beach unopposed and set up a perimeter inland. The first American offensive of World War II was underway. Only one casualty came to the attention of a medic. A Marine cut his hand opening a coconut.

The next morning Marines pressed through the jungle against scattered resistance and reached the nearly completed airfield. The surprise had been complete. The few enemy soldiers guarding the runway fled into the jungle. Construction crews set to work and in thirteen days had the newly named Henderson Field ready to receive its first aircraft.

The Japanese quickly recovered from their setback. Waves of bombers from Rabaul began hitting the airbase. Japanese warships poured down what became known as the "Slot" and ripped into American warships and transports off Savo Island. Vice Admiral Frank J. Fletcher took his carriers temporarily out of harm's way, exposing the Marines on Guadacanal and Tulagi to counterattacks. And then the real fight began.

The first attack came from 1,000 troops under Colonel Kiyono Ichiki, who landed at night on the coast east of Henderson Field. Marines at the airfield had heard the wash of passing destroyers

Below: On November 20, 1943, after being brought by landing boats and barges to within 500 yards of the beach, Marines are forced to wade through the surf off Tarawa because the coral bottom prevented the vessels from getting closer.

Above: Marines on Tarawa Atoll wore camouflage combat fatigues and were armed mostly with MI Garand rifles (shown right) and .30 caliber carbines (not shown). The GI on the left carries a Browning Automatic Rifle (BAR).

"Little Chuck." The battalion commander sent a platoon to picket the river and Chuck went with it. Everyone expected trouble, especially Chuck, who dug a deep foxhole, crawled inside of it, snapped on his bayonet, and then braced his rifle so the blade projected at a forty-five degree angle above his foxhole. When the fighting started, Chuck huddled in his hole, firmly holding the rifle so the blade pointed upwards. At 3:00 a.m. on August 3, Ichiki's soldiers waded across the Ilu with bayonets fixed. The Marines cut them down with rifle and machine gun fire. Wave after wave of Japanese charged like screaming devils, one suicide attack followed by another.

At dawn the Marine squad leader observed a dead Japanese soldier impaled on Chuck's bayonet. He crawled over to the private's foxhole and found the lad transfixed, staring at the dead Jap. There was a bad smell. The squad leader noted with amusement that "Chuck had...crapped his pants." The lad got up, sighed, and cleaned himself up. Dead enemy soldiers lay all about him, half buried in the sand where they fell. Chuck's baptism under fire came with a reward. He survived his first engagement and never became "petrified again."

Colonel Ichiki was not so lucky. After losing 800 men, he burned his regimental flag and, on a peaceful spot on the beach, committed hara-kiri. As time passed, the Japanese would lose their best officers to the same practice.

The Imperial High Command had

and reported the incident up the chain of command to General Vandergrift, who detailed a reconnaissance in force. The Marines crossed the Tenaru River and dug in on the west bank of the Ilu.

The Marines were mostly greenhorns, as was one young private known only as

Right: A selection of Marine Airborne uniforms and equipment, including (left) herringbone jump smock with padded elbows and pockets, (center) reversible camouflaged jump smock, and (bottom right) non-issue parachutist's fleece-lined vest. The weapons are (center) Johnson Model 1941 semi-automatic rifle and (right) Johnson Model 1941 light machine gun.

underestimated the number of Marines on Guadacanal and in September sent 6,000 men to recapture the airfield. The plan called for a three-pronged attack from three equally divided forces. One would attack the airfield from the west, another from across the Ilu River, and a third from a heavily jungled area having a rise named Bloody Ridge. Marines repulsed the two coastal assaults without much trouble, but the jungle fighting in the rain, mud, and miasma near Bloody Ridge became fierce and hand-to-hand. Some Marines discovered that the best weapon to carry in the jungle was a 12-guage shotgun loaded with buckshot. For quick, reactive combat, a shotgun did not have to be aimed, but its booming discharge sometimes drew unwanted attention from the enemy.

Jungles produced casualties unlike anything experienced in Europe. New species of venomous insects were everywhere. One Marine got bitten between the eyes, and his head swelled like a melon. For five days a corpsman drained the bite before the terrible pain began to subside. Whatever bit the man drained his immune system. A month later, when hit by a shrapnel splinter no bigger than a toothpick, blood poisoning killed him. Yet other men survived the most devastating wounds one can imagine.

In the jungle, fighting became both an

art and a skill. Marines learned to become good trackers and good sniffers. If the enemy was in the area, a good nose could smell him, despite the foul, rank stench of rotting jungle vegetation. Unless the enemy was on the move, he could not be seen, but as time passed, Marines became more adept at locating snipers concealed behind trees and ledges.

On occasion, Japanese snipers climbed trees when they could draw a bead on a clearing along the edge of a jungle. Locating them required patience because snipers were small and hid themselves well. A rifleman shot one who had been sniping into a perimeter. Standard operating procedure called for a body search to identify the enemy's unit.

Above: Marine Raider fighting knives and machetes and Raider shoulder patch (top right). The first two Raider battalions were activated in January and February 1942 to undertake amphibious, commando-style raids. The Raiders took part in the Guadalcanal landings, the defense of Midway, the raid on Makin Island, operations in the northern Solomons, Bougainville, New Georgia, and elsewhere.

Left: Japanese on Tarawa stacked coconut logs as obstructions, which Marines hurdled as they moved out from the beachhead and toward the valuable smoke-smothered enemy airstrip.

Above: In February, 1944, weary and begrimed Marines get a respite on board a troopship after two days and nights of intense fighting at Eniwetok Atoll in the Marshall Islands.

Right: On February 22, 1944, Marines on Parry Island, Eniwetok Atoll, are constantly on the alert for enemy snipers hidden in holes among the rubble created by an earlier naval bombardment, while two Navy hospital corpsmen administer first aid to a fallen Marine.

to the veterans lived; too many of those who learned the hard way died. There were plenty of veterans around to help neophytes. One private took his new platoon sergeant aside and said, "When a Jap fires at you from concealment, especially at night, don't have your men open up on him. He may be a suicidal decoy. There are probably several other Japs watching and ready. They'll saturate the area where they see [your] fire...."

Another Marine warned that the enemy, knowing that soldiers had discarded their gas masks, would send over a screen of harmless smoke and shout "Gas attack."

"Don't panic," the veteran warned. "Hold your position and give them hell if they start charging through the smoke." And, he added, "never go by a bunch of so-called dead ones without spraying the lot. There might be some of them playing possum who will open up on you when you've walked by." Above all, he warned, "if they capture one of your men, write the poor guy off. They'll tie him to a tree and go to work on him. They're experts at this. They want your men to come running in to rescue the guy. They'll be waiting for you and not one of your men will survive." Most importantly, he cautioned, watch for wires. "Those guys can set wires up in the jungle that can wipe out half a platoon."

After the first Japanese infantry division failed to recapture Guadacanal, an Imperial task force arrived off the island with another division. In what the Navy called the Battle of Guadacanal,

When going through a fallen enemy's shirt, the soldier's hand ran across a pair of breasts. There is no record of the number of women serving as Japanese snipers, but there was at least one on Guadacanal.

In October, after 6,000 veteran troops could not dislodge the Marines from Guadacanal, the Japanese sent a full division. This time they stayed off the beaches and attacked east and west through the jungles. By then, new Marine units and Army troops had reinforced the exhausted defenders of the airbase.

For the young Americans entering the steaming jungle for the first time, it was a learning experience. Those who listened

thirteen Japanese vessels, including two battleships and a heavy cruiser, joined the hulks resting in the depths of "Ironbottom Bay." With the invasion force all but annihilated, the Japanese began evacuating 13,000 sick, wounded, and starving survivors, having lost 36,000 men and at least one woman sniper on what the retreating enemy called the Island of Death.

While MacArthur's army struck New Guinea, the Marines began moving up the Solomons. Island by island, they created room for the Seabees to bring in their equipment and build new airstrips.

When the high command decided to invade New Georgia, they made the mistake of sending in the Army's inexperienced 43rd National Guard Division. New to combat, the GIs entered an endless tangle of jungle heavily defended by a well-conditioned enemy. Banyan trees blocked mortars, and grenades hurled at enemy defensive positions bounced off trees and rebounded among the Guard. At night, Japanese crawled through the perimeter and slit the throats of drowsing sentinels. A week into the jungle, men began to crack-up. One man went berserk after jumping into an old foxhole dug by its dead and bloated former occupant. Finally, Halsey sent in the 4th Marines.

Raider battalions began landing on New Georgia and pushing through the jungles. The typical battalion carried, M1s, BARs, machine guns, Thompson's, mortars, and antitank guns. After tripping

over snarls of vines covering every foot of the jungle floor, the men tossed away the antitank guns. No tank could possibly penetrate such dense vegetation. During a three-day march, the command averaged a half mile an hour.

The Raiders developed tactics that worked well when moving through a jungle. They put a man with an M1 on each flank with a BAR man in the center. First one rifleman would move up, start firing, and be followed by the other. Then the BAR man would move up, plant his weapon, and lay down a covering fire as the two riflemen advanced. The plodding process, though arduous and slow, worked well in the jungle.

By August 5 Halsey's force had taken Munda, but doing it required four divisions – 40,000 men – to oust 10,000 Japanese. But by early September, Marines had planes flying from the first of two airfields built on the islands of New Georgia.

On November 1, 1943, the 3rd Marine Division landed on Bougainville. Halsey wanted the airfields, which would put bombers in easy reach of the enormous enemy base on Rabaul. He sent Marines ashore with Army units at a spot on Bougainville where the enemy least expected a landing to be made, thereby forcing the Japanese to slog through the jungle, and not the Americans.

When a lieutenant colonel who had just taken command of the 2nd Marine Raider Battalion waded ashore, a sniper's

Left: A combat Coast Guard photographer caught this shot of Marines advancing across the beachhead on Parry Island moments before a Japanese mortar shell blew him into a nearby foxhole and destroyed his camera.

Below: Though civilians on Saipan had been urged by the Japanese to kill their children and then themselves, this Marine located a mother and four children who had wisely ignored the injunction and taken refuge in a foxhole.

Above: In July, 1944, after Marines captured this mountain gun from Japanese troops on Saipan, they put it into service during the attack on Garapan, the capital of the island.

Right: On September 14, 1944, Marine PFC Douglas Lightstreet (right) cradles his .30 caliber machine gun while he and his buddy, PFC Gerald Churchby take time out for a cigarette while mopping up the enemy on Peleliu Island.

bullet killed him instantly. Death always affected the fighting man in curious ways. After the unit's executive officer took charge of the battalion, he paused to reflect on the colonel's bad luck, lamenting how a man "could go through some extremely hot action and never get touched and then, bang! One sniper's bullet could kill you right off the top of the barrel."

Raiders who fought in the jungle on Guadacanal found Bougainville even worse. "All the physical disorders you can imagine were here, and there was constant rainfall. The next time someone wants to start a war they should make him spend a week or so fighting in a tropical jungle. He'll change his mind quickly enough." But Halsey had done his Marines a favor. They reached the area where Halsey wanted his airstrip and set up a strong perimeter, leaving thousands of Japanese to die slowly from the tortures of the deep jungle.

Marines who survived conditions on Bougainville remembered that it rained every day, usually at four o'clock in the afternoon, and because everyone was in or near the jungle, nothing ever dried. One Marine corporal recalled conditions being "hotter than hell during the day and colder than a witch's tit at night."

The humidity and the night chill made life unbearable. Marines on the perimeter laid on a wet poncho in a hole and tried to pass the night. "You'd be soaked and you'd get so goddamn cold that you thought you were going to die. It was so bad that you'd try to keep your teeth from chattering because you wanted complete silence." Almost any noise on the perimeter drew fire, and if a Marine caused it, his buddies might toss a grenade in his direction. Huge land crabs made disconcerting noises as they scuffled about the jungle at night. "They scared the hell out of greenhorns," one Marine recalled, "and for a week or two on the perimeter, greenhorns scared the hell out of us."

Marines did more than fight in jungles. Many years had passed since a white man had stepped foot on Japan's fortress in the Carolines – the islands of Truk. All that was known was what old maps showed – many volcanic islands set within a lagoon thirty-three miles in diameter and surrounded by a fringe of coral reef having only a few entrances from the ocean. Each channel contained mines, underwater obstructions, interlocking gun positions, and submarines.

Nimitz believed he could isolate the island without invading it, so on the morning of February 4, 1944, two marine pilots, Major James R. Christenson and Captain James Q. Yahn, took off on an historic 2,000 mile flight in two unarmed Liberators to photograph it.

Flying over enemy-controlled waters, the two Liberators passed through tropical storms and, when crossing the Equator, freakish weather that coated their wings with ice. At seven degrees north latitude they broke through the clouds. Pilots spotted the island and began shooting pictures. Fifteen minutes

passed before the Japanese recovered from their shock of seeing two B-24s swooping over their island fortress. Flak began to fly, and for twenty minutes Christenson and Yahn let the cameras roll as they bumped between the clouds from one island to another, but the Japanese never got a plane in the air.

The photographs were the first on record of Truk and showed twenty-five ships in the harbor, most of them warships. Admiral Spruance took a quick look at the pictures and promptly headed for Truk with every carrier, battleship, cruiser and destroyer he could put at his disposal. Early on the morning of February 16, Grumman Hellcats swooped over the islands and in a battle that lasted hours, destroyed 204 Japanese planes and opened the way to the Gilbert and Marshall Islands.

The jungles of the South Pacific had taxed the physical endurance of the Marine. Now the flat, rocky atolls of Tarawa and Makin with their jagged coral reefs would tax his sanity. Tiny coral islets blocked access to the beaches, and once on land there were few trees and no ridges to provide cover. On both islands the enemy fortifications were well concealed, heavily protected, and firmly dug into the coral.

In November, 1943, two hundred American ships appeared off the two atolls. For several days, B-24s from bases in the Ellice Islands had been plastering Makin and Betio. Then at dawn on the 20th, just before the first wave of men started ashore, naval guns laid down a bombardment that would seemed to have killed every living creature on the two atolls. Yet on Makin, the first wave of 6,500 infantrymen from the 27th Infantry Division found themselves pinned down by 300 Japanese who refused to be dislodged.

Several miles away, waves from the 2nd and 8th Marines flooded ashore on Betio Island, Tarawa's main airstrip in the atoll's southwest corner. Three U.S. battleships, five cruisers, and nine destroyers had dumped ten tons of high explosives per acre on an island no larger than New York's Central Park. One Marine, waiting in an amtrac (LVT, landing vehicle, tracked) to go ashore,

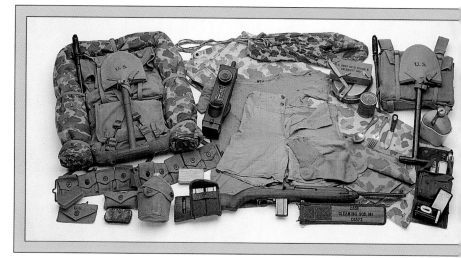

expected to see "the whole goddam island...fall apart and sink." A day later he admitted that, "This tiny chunk of real estate had been turned into the most heavily fortified bastion for its size in the world."

The defensive works were so strong that shells could not penetrate, and forty pieces of artillery had been emplaced in such a way that every gun could bear upon every beach. One first-time Marine moving through the lagoon entrance in an amtrac turned to his buddy and said euphorically, "Ain't we givin' those Japs hell!" The veteran beside him said nothing because he knew that all the artillery fire was coming from the enemy's shore batteries and killing Marines in the wave behind them. Then, at two miles, the Japanese artillery opened on the amtracs. Closer in, machine gun fire began spattering off the LVTs' armor. Moments later, the amtracs were on the beach, crawling through a wall of fire.

Men in rubber Higgins boats (LCVP,

Above: Marine Corps equipment, including (left) Model 1941 field transport pack, and (top right) 1941 marching pack with trenching tool fastened to back of knapsack. At center are undershirt and shorts. The weapon is an M1 carbine, while at bottom right is a personal medical kit.

Below: In November, 1944, landing craft loaded mainly with equipment and supplies head for the beaches at Jacquinot Bay, New Britain.

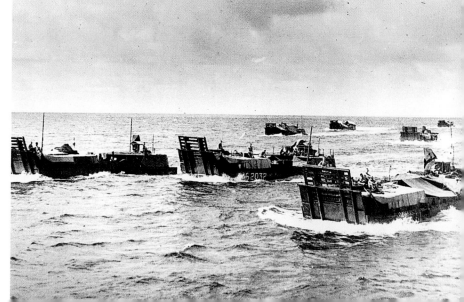

Above: On February 19, 1945, Marines land on Iwo Jima, establish a beachhead among the island's black sands, and begin the slow advance to capture the airfield. Mount Suribachi rises in the rear.

landing craft, vehicle and personnel) in the wave behind the LVTs dropped into neck-deep water as soon as they reached the shallows and began to spread out. When men began to fall, the others began slogging toward the protection of a coconut-log sea wall. As one Marine recalled, "I looked back and all I could see was wreckage all around me. On the beach, the Japs were laying down one hell of a fire from concealed positions. I thought about swimming back to California, but knew I couldn't make it, so I stayed behind the seawall until a sergeant came along and prodded us all ashore, yelling at the top of his lungs that we had better shoot some of those bastards unless we all wanted to die right there on the beach. So we all started firing, and then the lieutenant came along and screamed at us to aim. It was all like a crazy war movie, but people were really dying."

The Betio beachfront had been divided into three sectors of assault. With entire companies decimated during the assault, and with water saturating the

radio equipment, communications within and between units broke down. One battalion commander believed he had lost his entire force, only to learn later that most of his men had gone ashore and overrun pillbox and artillery positions.

For four days, the fight raged unabated. On November 24, it ended. Of 4,700 Japanese troops and construction workers, only seventeen surrendered. The rest died in bombproofs and pillboxes, roasted by flame throwers or blasted by demolition devices. Betio became the bloodiest four days in the Pacific, taking the lives of 1,027 Marines and 27 sailors.

The bloodiest campaigns were just beginning. On January 31, 1944, the Marines hit the Marshall Islands and secured airbases at Kwajalein and Eniwetok. They went ashore preceded by a more effective bombardment and with more heavily armored amtracs. On June 15, the 2nd and 4th Marine divisions – 20,000 strong – tackled Saipan. Compared with Betio, getting ashore proved to be easy, but the 29,000 Japanese defending the island fought to the last man, battling for every yard as one *banzai* attack was followed by another. As one Marine recalled, "Some of the Japs didn't have guns. They came at us with grenades or with a bayonet tied to the end of a stick. They'd crawl over the dead piled up in front of them and come at you screaming their heads off. They all seemed to be drunk. I had to keep moving my machine gun around because the pile of dead Japs blocked my view. They just kept coming and coming, and the gun got so damned hot I was afraid it would jam."

When the fighting on Saipan came to an end, the Marines witnessed another

Right: On March 3, 1945, as Marines prepare to advance on Mount Suribachi, rockets are fired from portable carriers on Japanese positions dug into the side of the mountain.

horror. Civilians joined the Imperial Army in mass suicide. One Marine described a horrifying scene on a cliff near the northern tip of the island. "The damned Japs had told the people that we would molest their women, so instead of believing us, they took their children to the cliff, threw them over the rim, and jumped after them. We tried to get to them, but most of us were too late. If we hadn't killed all the damn lying Japs, I think most of us would have gone after the rest and shot them."

While MacArthur led the Army back to the Philippines, the Marines captured other key bases in the Carolines. Then Nimitz took the Marines north to Iwo Jima and Okinawa. "Iwo Jima was a nightmare," said one Marine. "Every leatherneck on the island hoped for a 'Hollywood' wound that would get him out of that hellhole."

Only eight square miles of rock and ash, Iwo lay only 600 miles from the Japanese mainland and a lot closer than Saipan and Guam. Okinawa was half again as close. "Nimitz knew it would be a hell of a task to take those islands," Lieutenant General Holland M. Smith said, "but to put an army on Japan, we needed to have them." He predicted the attack on Iwo would cost 15,000 casualties.

To soften up Iwo's defenses, B-24s, B-29s, and carrier planes bombed it

seventy-four days in an row, and as D-Day approached, the largest fleet ever assembled in the Pacific, 485 vessels, added the weight of their heavy guns to flattening the island defenses.

General Tadamichi Kuribayashi had used Korean conscripts to bury Iwo's fortifications deep. They had dug sixteen miles of tunnels, connecting them to caves, underground command posts, and 800 concrete structures on the surface. If the Japanese could stand the intense volcanic heat in the tunnels, they had enough supplies and ammunition to hold out indefinitely. Unlike the beach defenses on Betio, Kuribayashi had set his into the rocky slopes and craggy ravines of Mount Suribachi where his guns could bear on the island's two airstrips.

As the 4th and 5th Marine Divisions prepared to assault Iwo's beaches, another full division, the Marine 3rd, waited in reserve. At 8:59a.m. on February 19, 1945, the first LVTs crawled ashore. The soft volcanic sand on the beaches made it nearly impossible for any tracked vehicle to climb the low slopes leading inland. Marines piled up on the beaches, but the only fire they encountered came mainly from the enemy's defensive positions on Suribachi. By the time the 3rd Battalion, 25th Marines, reached the edge of the airfield, it had lost 550 of its 700 men.

Marines fought for ten days before subduing the Japanese holed up in their mountain fortress, but it took another twenty-five days to clear the island of

Left: When Japanese who were holed-up in caves could not be dislodged, Marines burned them out using the M2-2 portable flame-thrower. This GI's only other weapons are the holstered .45 caliber automatic pistol and the knife fastened to his belt.

Below: Pvt. Bob Campbell sits by an American flag raised on Mount Suribachi and watches from the heights as landing craft nose onto the beach to deliver holds of fresh supplies.

resistance. "The only way to kill a Jap," said one Marine, "was to crawl around the blind side of a pillbox with a flame thrower, or when approaching a cave, to toss in a satchel charged with explosives." When Marines located ventilators used to exchange air in the tunnels, they would wait until they heard voices below before pouring a drum of gasoline down the duct and setting it on fire. One Marine recalled "roasting more Japs than I shot. I still hear their hellish screams."

Three Japanese lost their lives to every American, but Iwo Jima took the lives of 6,821 Marines – the highest death toll of any campaign in the Corps' long history. On March 26, 1945, the day that hostilities ended on Iwo, Nimitz never had time to count the casualties. He had Okinawa in his sights, an island sixty times the size of Iwo. He did not want the entire island, but he wanted its airstrips.

On Easter Sunday at 8:30 a.m., April 1, 1945, two Army and two Marine divisions encountered almost no opposition when they landed along a five-mile stretch of sandy beach fronting the village of Hagushi on Okinawa's west coast. Five hours later the Marines captured the first of the vital airfields.

Behind Hagushi, however, lay 300-foot ridges scalloped with ravines, caves, and ledges, much like the rocky formations on Iwo. There, with more than 100,000 men and 3,000 aircraft, Lieutenant General Mitsuru Ushijima planned to make his stand. He had already decided to concentrate his men in the south and to not defend the northern part of the island, so when the 1st and 6th Marine Divisions marched north and reached Hido Misaka on the tip of the island, there were few enemy forces in their front to stop them.

After five days of relative inaction, Ushijima struck the beachheads with 700 aircraft and tore into the fleet offshore with 350 *kamikazes*. On April 13, when Army divisions in the south found themselves in a pack of trouble, Lieutenant General Simon Bolivar Buckner, Jr., ordered the two Marine divisions in the north to fight their way back. Buckner's GIs had been moving forward at the rate of about 1,000 yards a day and taking heavy casualties. Nimitz became so upset over the situation that he flew into Okinawa from Guam and told Buckner to get the men moving or he would send in a general who could.

Ushijima knew that Buckner had split his force and hoped to delay the return of the two Marine divisions while he destroyed Buckner's Army divisions.

After the 2nd Marine Division landed on the southern end of Okinawa, the battle shifted to the ancient city of Shuri, where Ushijima concentrated his forces to organize a counterattack. He waited too long, enabling the two Marine divisions to return from the north and add their firepower to quelling what became the single largest suicide attack ever mounted by Japanese infantry.

After a ten-day struggle, Okinawa's annual monsoon struck and flooded the battlefield until June 5. By then, Ushijima had regrouped and prepared new defenses. Not until June 22 did the Marines overrun the enemy's last strongpoint, the Kiiyama Peninsula. During the final four days of battle, Buckner finally got the job done, but he lost his life doing it, adding his name to the 7,613 Americans killed or missing on Okinawa. General Ushijima paid his final respects to the emperor by disemboweling himself with a ceremonial knife, joining 110,000 Japanese soldiers killed in action.

Nimitz now had his airfields on what was strategically the last stop on the way to Japan. Three hundred thousand troops had come to the island in preparation for the invasion, and more were on the way. For the Marines, the war had come to an end, but they did not know it. At 2:45 a.m. on August 6, Colonel Paul Tibbetts took off in a B-29 named "Enola Gay" and dropped a device called "Little Boy"

Above: In May, 1945, two miles north of Naha, "A" Company of the 2nd Battalion, 5th Marine Division, battle for possession of an Okinawa ridge where strong enemy forces held up the advance for forty-eight hours.

on Hiroshima. It was 28 inches in diameter, 120 inches long, and weighed 9,000 pounds. When it exploded over Hiroshima, the first atomic bomb released the explosive power of 20,000 tons of TNT.

Marines fought and died in the jungles of the Solomons and the Philippines. They crawled the rocky slopes of Iwo Jima and Okinawa with flame throwers and satchel charges. They made their stand against the greatest army that had ever conquered the Pacific, and they won it back, island by island. They were a proud group of men, a unique group of men, and when it came to fighting, the toughest men on the planet.

Left: In the fight for Wana Ridge near the town of Shuri, Okinawa, S/Sgt. Walter F. Kleine of the 1st Marine Battalion draws a bead on a Japanese sniper with his tommy-gun as his buddy ducks for cover.

FIGHTING THEIR WAY TO BERLIN

Every amphibious operation had its D-Day, whether in North Africa, Sicily, or Salerno. But for the GIs that assaulted the Normandy beaches of France on June 6, 1944, the Allied campaign known by its planners as Operation Overlord would forever be condensed to just four letters, D-Day. After that, when a soldier spoke of D-Day, no one asked, "Which one?"

For two years Joseph Stalin had pressed the Allies to open a second front. In late 1943 Roosevelt promised Stalin that a cross-Channel invasion would take place during the spring of 1944. He placed General Eisenhower in command of Operation Overlord and told him to make it happen. By May, 1944, Eisenhower had herded nearly 3,500,000 men from Europe, Africa, Asia, North America, and Australia into Britain, along with ships, planes, tanks, trucks, ammunition, fuel, rations, medicines, and every other item needed for moving eight combat divisions into France.

As days passed, Eisenhower recalled that, "The mighty host was tense as a coiled spring, and indeed that is exactly as it was – a great human spring, coiled for the moment when its energy should be released and it would vault the English Channel in the greatest amphibious assault ever attempted."

As the day of embarkation drew near, GIs found themselves shoved into marshaling areas. From Southampton, Army Sergeant Henry Giles grumbled, "If we were prisoners of war we couldn't be more closely guarded. There's not only a barbed wire fence all around the camp but there are guards posted everywhere to keep civilians from coming anywhere near. By George, when you come through that gate and get behind this wire it really hits you that the only way out is through France and Germany. It's strictly a one-way road."

At 21:30 hours, June 5, 1944, Eisenhower received good news from SHAEF's Scottish meteorologist – a

Below: Army infantrymen practise assault on beach defense obstructions – barbed wire and pillboxes in background – on Slapton Sands Beach, southern England, in preparation for the Normandy invasion.

thirty-six hour break in the otherwise miserable weather. He asked all fourteen men on his staff for their opinions. The answers came back mixed. Eisenhower paced the floor, stopped, and asked, "The question is just how long can you hang this operation on the end of a limb and let it hang there?" No one answered, and the general resumed his pacing. Everyone could still hear strong winds rattling the doors.

At 21:45 hours Eisenhower stopped his pacing, turned to the staff, and said, "OK, we'll go." Two hours later, 5,000 ships put to sea. Eight allied combat divisions – five infantry and three airborne – departed from twelve British ports and two airfields shortly after midnight on June 6 and headed for France.

At 5:30 a.m., landing craft began their run, carrying the U.S. 1st, 4th, and 29th Infantry Divisions onto Utah and Omaha Beaches and British and Canadian troops onto Sword, Juno, and Gold Beaches. Hours earlier, American and British paratrooper and glider units landed behind German lines in Normandy to secure bridges, crossroads, and exits from the beachheads.

From the outset, sections of the 82nd and 101st Airborne Divisions landed in mass confusion because their flak-dodging transport aircraft either missed the drop zone by too wide a margin or sent the paratroopers floating into the very town they were supposed to surprise. At Sainte-Mere-Eglise, located behind Utah Beach, one paratrooper landed in the town square, another became entangled on the church steeple

and for more than two hours pretended to be dead. Two others plunged through the roof of a house, setting off mortars they carried and blowing themselves and the house to bits. Enough paratroopers landed outside the town to capture it before the vessels transporting the

Above: In May, 1944, Army forces board landing craft in preparation for the Normandy invasion. The vessel at left is an LCI; in center is an LCV from the U.S.S. *Thurston*.

Left: On June 6, paratroopers become airborne on a Douglas C-47 of the 9th Troop Carrier Command, as the aircraft form overhead and head across the English Channel to France.

SELECTIVE CHRONOLOGY OF WAR: 1944

Jun 6: Operation Overlord, D-Day invasion of Europe, begins as 2 American and 1 British airborne divisions begin dropping behind Normandy beaches at 2:00 a.m. At 6:30 a.m. Allied forces land on beaches in an amphibious operation carried out by over 4,000 invasion craft supported by 600 warships and 11,000 warplanes. American forces meet heavy German opposition, but by 1:30 p.m. have broken through Omaha Beach defenses.

July 17: U.S. troops enter St Lô, France, and break out of Normandy July 24, after overcoming heavy opposition with aid of strong air support.

July 19: U.S. forces liberate Cherbourg.

Aug 4: U.S. Eighth Army reaches Florence, Italy, while Third Army moves into Rennes, France.

Aug 7: U.S. forces reach outskirts of Brest, northwest France.

Aug 9: U.S. Third Army moves in toward Falaise, France, St Malo on northwest coast, and takes Le Mans inland.

Aug 15: U.S. Seventh Army begins Southern France Campaign with invasions of French seaports on Mediterranean.

Aug 20: 50,000 Germans captured and 10,000 killed as U.S. and British forces close on Falaise-Argentan pocket, west of Paris. American casualties total 29,000.

Aug 25: American and French forces secure surrender of Paris, ending German occupation which began in June, 1940.

Aug 28: Germans surrender Toulon and Marseilles, southern France, to Allied forces.

Aug 31: U.S. Third Army crosses Meuse River and reaches Verdun in pursuit of German forces.

Sep 7: U.S. forces cross Moselle.

Sep 10: U.S. forces enter Luxembourg; U.S. Fifth Army begins assault on Gothic Line, north of Rome, driving Germans back to North Apennine Mountains.

Sep 11: First U.S. patrols enter Germany, crossing border near Stalzenburg.

Sep 12: U.S. First Army crosses into Germany near Aachen.

Sep 15: Allied forces begin Rhineland Campaign, crossing Siegfried Line.

Oct 13: U.S. First Army enters Aachen.

Nov 9: Following heavy U.S.A.A.F. bomb attacks, U.S. Third Army moves on Metz, capturing it by Nov 22.

Nov 16: U.S. First and Ninth Armies moves toward Roer River in month-long drive during harsh winter conditions and against strong opposition.

Dec 16: After U.S. forces sweep into Germany on 30-mile front (Dec 1), Battle of Bulge begins, ending Dec 27, by which time Americans have suffered 77,000 casualties but have stopped German Army assault, leaving Germany on brink of disaster.

4th Infantry Division hove into view off Utah Beach.

First Lieutenant Elliott Johnson was one of 152,000 officers and men who waded ashore that morning. He remembered the short trip across the Channel – short, but just long enough for hundreds to get seasick. Nobody slept, he recalled, and to take their minds off the inevitable, "A lot of boys played poker all night. I wanted to take a bath. Don't ask me why, 'cause I can't explain it. It was against the rules, but I took a shower anyway." He knew it might be his last.

Like most of the infantry, Johnson went ashore shortly after 6:51 a.m. from a 300-foot landing ship tank (LST). Before the ramp splashed down, he climbed to the highest level on the upper deck and watched the panorama unfold off Utah Beach. What he witnessed was an enormous flotilla of amphibious personnel carriers and swimming tanks, the latter supported by an inflatable rubber skirt and driven by a propeller attached to the drive shaft. Then, said Johnson, "I s[aw] one of our ships take a direct hit and go up in a huge ball of flames. There were big geysers coming up where the shells were landing and there were bodies floating, face down, face up. The LST, as we vacated it, was to become a hospital ship. The boys who had gone first and been wounded were now being brought out. This continued my education: recognizing our body as finite."

In 1942 Timuel Black could not decide whether to enlist or wait for the draft. African Americans were not getting a good deal in the service, so Black waited. In 1943 the Selective Service sent him "Greetings" and shoved him into the Quartermaster Corps. It looked like a posh job until the morning of June 6, 1944, when he found himself on an LST and headed for the beach. "It was a weird experience," Black recalled, "young men cryin' for their mothers, wetting and defecating themselves. Others tellin'

jokes. Most of us were just solemn. I was thinking, Boy, if I get through this, it'll never happen to me again.... All you know is that you wade to the beach."

At Omaha, Allied aircraft were to have knocked out German batteries along the shore, but the pilots overflew their targets and dropped their bombs too far inland. As the 1st Infantry Division waded ashore, the Germans laid down a murderous fire. Some assault companies lost 90 percent of their men in the first minutes after hitting the water. Navy guns opened and laid down an accurate fire. By midday the Americans secured the beach, following tanks inland through mine fields and shore obstructions.

On June 7, as more soldiers headed for Omaha Beach, they passed dead bodies floating in the water. From the distance, they could see nothing moving on the beach but a single bulldozer and a flock of gulls. "The beach was covered with debris," one soldier observed, "sunken craft and wrecked vehicles....We jumped into chest high water and waded ashore. Then we saw that the beach was literally covered with the bodies of American soldiers wearing the blue and gray patches of the 29th Infantry Division."

A few days later Sergeant Giles arrived. When he had a moment to spare he wrote, "I don't feel as nervous as I thought I would. Not nearly as nervous as when we left the States. I'm not as cool as a cucumber – I notice I'm chain smoking – but I'm not as shaky as I thought I might be."

There had been hell to pay on the beaches. SHAEF (Supreme Headquarters,

Allied Expeditionary Force) predicted that 10,000 would die in the initial assault. In the event, no more than 2,500 men lost their lives. GIs had established their lodgment, but the hedgerow fighting had just begun.

Normandy developed into a soldier's battle. The fighting became head to head between riflemen, machine gunners, mortarmen, artillerymen, and tanks on the

Above: Shoulder insignia of various American units involved in the D-Day landings, Normandy, 1944, where the invaders encountered withering defensive fire and some soldiers had to struggle through high surf, encumbered by individual equipment loads that exceeded 60 pounds.

Far Left: On the morning of June 6, 1944, troops and crewmen aboard a Coast Guard manned LCVP (Landing Craft, Vehicle Personnel) peer over the beam as the craft approaches the beaches on D-Day.

Left: After making their landing in Normandy to disrupt enemy communications behind the lines, Army glider pilots relax and have a smoke in a LCVP that is taking them on the first leg back to England.

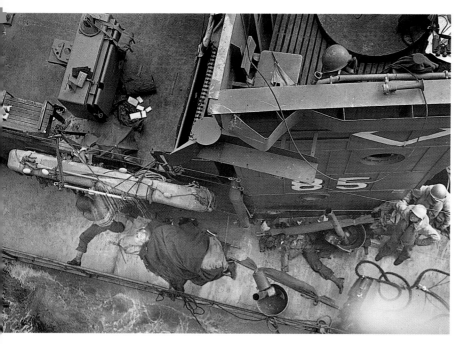

Above: A sinking LCI (Landing Craft, Infantry), manned by the Coast Guard and bearing casualties, comes alongside another landing craft to transfer her survivors after being hit by German shells off Omaha Beach.

front line, the Americans advancing and the Germans resisting. Every step became a new experience for the American soldier. When a group of infantrymen from the 49th Division found themselves pinned down by Germans in a farmhouse, Brigadier General Norman "Dutch" Cota came up to ask the captain in charge to explain the delay. "Sir," the captain replied, "the Germans are in there shooting at us."

"I'll tell you what," replied the general, removing two grenades from his pocket. "You and your men start shooting at them. I'll take a squad of men and you and your men watch carefully. I'll show you how to take a house with Germans in it."

Cota led the squad around a hedge close to the house. Giving a yell, he rushed forward, the squad screaming at his heels. They tossed grenades through the windows while Cota and another man kicked down the door and rolled a pair of grenades inside. After the explosion, they burst through the door, just in time to see the enemy streaming through the back entrance, running for their lives. The general returned to the captain and said, "You've seen how to take a house. Do you understand? Do you know how to do it?"

"Yes, sir," gasped the captain.

"Well, I won't be around to do it for you again," said Cota. "I can't do it for everybody."

As the fighting moved slowly inland, Eisenhower pushed toward phase two as rapidly as logistics permitted – the capture of Cherbourg, and the buildup of sufficient forces to break out across France. The road to Cherbourg led through Carentan, near where Lieutenant Colonel Robert Cole had gathered up 250 paratroopers from the 3rd Battalion, 502nd Infantry Regiment. Oblivious to what dangers lay in his path, he marched them down a causeway. Germans concealed behind a hedgerow watched them come. When the enemy opened on the American column, General Cota was not there to tell Cole what to do.

Instead of moving when under fire as veterans did, Cole jumped behind the far bank along the causeway and his men

Right: A variety of U.S. arms and equipment, including (rifles, left) M1903A3 .30-60-cal, and M1 Garand and grenade launcher below it; (rifles and smgs right, top to bottom) M1903A4 with weaver M73B1 sight, M1 carbine .30-cal, M1A1 carbine with folding wire "airborne" stock, Thompson M1928A1 smg, Thompson M1 smg, and M3 smg; revolvers (top to bottom), S&W "Victory," S&W M1917 Army, Colt M1917 Army; and (to the right of these) M1911A1 pistol and M3 shoulder holster.

tumbled after him. For the next half hour, Germans lobbed mortars at the position and sniped at anyone who peaked over the embankment. The GIs took casualties, and Cole, though a graduate of West Point, voiced an order rarely heard in World War II, "Fix bayonets!"

Had Private William Craft of the 314th Infantry Regiment been with Cole, he might have given some sage advice to the West Pointer. Craft had been fighting Germans in the hedgerows for several days and come to the conclusion that it made no sense to get "out of my hedgerow to run over and get the German out of his, not when there was artillery around to do that."

Cole's greenhorns, having received bayonet training, knew no better and began crawling over the embankment, yelling like fiends as they charged the hedgerow. Many fell, but the men who rushed through the brush and dove into the enemy rifle pits stampeded the enemy out of their hiding places. Those German soldiers not shot or bayoneted fled out the back and disappeared into another hedgerow.

Exhausted and shaking from their brush with death, Cole and his men gave a cheer of exultation and returned to the causeway, crossing over the Douve River to link-up with the divisions from Omaha and Utah Beaches. Even bad tactics sometimes worked. Cole's sophomoric charge would have made a marvelous scene for a movie, but not a single commanding officer in a hundred would have attempted it. The other ninety-nine would have called for artillery or aircraft support.

When Joseph Balkoski published the history of his infantry division, he paid tribute to the GI, writing, "The 29ers were humble men caught up in a war of

Right: On the northern coast of France, the yawning doors of an LST (Landing Ship, Tank), open onto the beach to pour forth jeeps, trucks, and tanks to waiting drivers.

immeasurable complexity. Most 29ers had done what they were told to do, even when orders made little sense. On the deadly battlefields from Omaha Beach to St Lô, these simple acts of obedience reflected astounding personal courage. Any soldier who could bring himself to leap over a hedgerow upon command and race, hunchbacked, across a grassy field with bullets snapped over his head like cracking whips, was a brave man indeed."

In the 29th Infantry, hedgerow fighting soon evolved into attack teams consisting of one Sherman tank, a team of engineers, a squad of riflemen, a light machine gun, and a 60mm mortar. The tank initiated the action by thrusting its cannon through a hedge and firing a round of phosphorous at an enemy machine gun pit lodged in a hedgerow across the way. American tankers discovered that one or two phosphorous shells fired into a pit sometimes failed to silence the machine gun. The tankers then sprayed the base of the hedgerow with

Below: After the breakout from St Lô, U.S. troops advance from Normandy into Brittany, 97 miles in ten days, passing a knocked-out German Panther as they pass up the road.

.50-caliber machine gun fire while the mortar team lobbed shells into the field directly behind the enemy. After the tank advanced, the riflemen fell in behind and used conventional methods of attack as they assaulted the enemy position. The tactics worked marvelously, the only weakness being the lightly armored underbelly of the Sherman tank, which could be easily penetrated by 88mm artillery.

GIs hated to be caught in a barrage of phosphorous shells, and they were fortunate that the Germans had so few. One soldier recalled being caught in "a snowstorm of small white particles that floated down upon us. We looked in amazement, and eyes filled with instant terror. Where the particles landed on shirts and trousers, they sizzled and burned. White phosphorous! We brushed our clothing frantically, pushed shirt collars up. If any of the stuff touched the skin, it could inflict a horrible burn, increasing in intensity as it burrowed a hole into a man's flesh....There was no place to hide, no place that was safe." Friend and enemy hated the stuff, but the tankers loved to use it.

By June 27 there were a million Allied troops in Normandy, but the average infantryman believed the invasion had reached a stalemate. "We were stuck," Corporal Bill Preston declared. "Something dreadful seemed to have happened in terms of the overall plan." He was certain that "The whole theory of mobility that we had been taught, of our racing across the battlefield, seemed to have gone up in smoke." Morale began to sag when small gains in the field resulted in heavy losses, but GIs like Preston could not see the big picture. The Allies needed Normandy to build up their forces, and the breakout was about to begin.

During the first week of August, Eisenhower sent General George S. Patton, Jr., and his Third Army to France. Patton put phase two into operation, plunging ahead, sweeping southward and eastward to envelop the main German Army. As he moved in his command jeep across fields of burning enemy vehicles and bloated German corpses, he turned to his driver, and said, "Compared to war, all

other forms of human endeavor shrink to insignificance. God, how I love it."

The words were barely out of his mouth when on August 7, the Germans counterattacked from the town of Mortain in an effort to stop Patton and drive him back to Avranches. Having broken the enemy code, the Allies expected the attack, and a combination of infantry, artillery, and air power stopped the German *Panzers* in their tracks.

On August 15, Lieutenant General Alexander Patch's Seventh Army came ashore between Cannes and Toulon on the French Riviera. Code-named Dragoon, the invasion force consisted of 1,500 ships, including nine aircraft carriers, and all the troops of General Jean de Lattre de Tassigny's First French

Above: In August, 1944, members of the 1st Airborne Division deploy along a road near La Motte, France, in support of the U.S. Seventh Army's invasion of southern France.

Below: On July 11, 1944, an American artillery crew responds to a call from the infantry and opens with a howitzer to shell German forces retreating near Carentan, France.

Above: On September 22, 1944, and backed up by a Sherman tank, an American sets up a machine gun on the sidewalk of a French town and waits for trouble from the enemy.

On September 3, the British Second Army liberated Brussels. On the 4th, the Canadian First Army marched into Antwerp, while the U.S. Ninth Army drove the Germans out of Liege and back to Aachen. By the end of September the battle line of the Allied forces extended from the Riviera to the North Sea.

For the American soldier, the breakout did not come easy. Without a massive bombardment on enemy positions from the air, it may not have come at all. On July 18, 7,700 tons of bombs delivered by 1,676 four-engine bombers and 343 mediums marked, according to SHAEF official historian Forrest Pogue, "the heaviest and most concentrated air attack in support of ground troops ever attempted."

It was still not enough. Field Marshall Bernard L. Montgomery, commanding the 21st Army Group, took possession of the ruins of Caen, gained a few miles, encountered stiff German resistance, and called a halt. So close were the lines that Allied artillery could not be ranged-in on the enemy without fear of hitting their own infantry. Planes bombed and strafed German positions, but there would be no breakthrough on Montgomery's flank, at least for the moment.

But, while Montgomery held down a large number of German troops west of Caen, Patton's Third Army moved so rapidly to the south and east that the Germans, fearing encirclement in what was called the "Falaise pocket," withdrew to escape entrapment.

By the end of July, the Ninth Tactical

Army. Preceded by a brilliantly executed airborne landing, and supported by air and sea bombardment, the Seventh Army waded ashore with little loss. The German Nineteenth Army, with the 11th Panzer Division, put up a hard fight around Toulon and Marseilles, but Patch's drive up the Rhone threatened to cut them off and forced the Germans north through Avignon.

While Patton's Third Army plowed across France, liberating Le Mans, Orleans, and Troyes, Patch's Seventh Army rolled up the Rhone Valley, passing through Lyons and into Bourg and Poligny. On September 11, spearheads from the two armies met north of Dijon and a few days later linked up at Epinal, north of Switzerland.

Right: White phosphorus shells explode dangerously close as American soldiers dash across a street in Brest, France, to drive German snipers from hideouts in strongly built stone houses.

Air Force had a dozen airfields operating in Normandy. From any one of them pilots could be over their target in minutes. They flew five sorties a day, some of them lasting no longer than twenty minutes. P-47s and B-17s dominated the sky, often coming within a few hundred yards of American lines, hitting the enemy with rockets, machine gun fire, and 500-pound bombs. While standing in the barnyard of a French farm, Ernie Pyle watched planes attack in groups, "diving from every direction, perfectly timed, one right after another. Everywhere you looked," he recalled, "separate groups of planes were on their way down, or on their way back up, or slanting over for a dive."

The breakout by the U.S. First Army came on July 27; on the opposite end of the Normandy peninsula, Cherbourg fell. American soldiers accomplished a feat they were not trained or equipped to do. They ignored their flanks and, with close air support, pushed through to block roads the Germans needed to bring up transport vehicles and heavy weapons. The breakout put the First Army's tanks into open country and exposed the Germans' left flank.

Patton sent a tank division from the Third Army toward Argentan. The Germans, caught in their stronghold at Falaise, took heavy casualties as they wriggled through a gap. The German withdrawal sprung Montgomery, and during the month of August Allied forces swept across France, Belgium, and Luxembourg. As the German front collapsed, a general retreat began, and with the *Wehrmacht* moving along roads and through open fields, American air power pulverized the fleeing columns, pressing them back to their homeland.

The Third Army, spearheaded by Patton's tanks, swirled up the roads to Paris. On August 25, General Jacques Leclerc, commanding the French 2nd Armored Division, led his American-built Sherman tanks into the city. To demonstrate a show of strength to the Communist-dominated resistance in the city, Eisenhower ordered the 4th and 28th Infantry Divisions to march right through Paris on their way to the battlefield east of the city. Sergeant Giles entered the city

Left: On October 9, 1944, German 88s burst near a squad of advancing paratroopers near Arnhem, Holland, as they dash through a field in an assault.

Below: On August 29, 1944, after the liberation of Paris, American troops of the 23rd Infantry Division march down the Champs Elysees during a "Victory parade." By nightfall they were back at the front.

Above: On November 22, 1944, members of a tank destroyer unit load their weapon along one of the approaches to Metz, the German fortress city which later fell before the American air and ground attack.

a day later, writing, "Much putting in for passes all at once, everybody excited, everybody happy. It has suddenly turned into a damned good war. The boys remind me of kids waiting to go to a circus."

The liberation of Paris also had a downside – it consumed a lot of fuel, which had become scarce, and delayed the pursuit of a disorganized German Army fleeing toward the safety of their defenses along the Rhine.

The Allied race for the Rhine encountered little resistance from the enemy but serious stoppages for want of fuel. East of Paris, artillery units outran the infantry, and infantry units outran the tanks. One GI in the 4th Infantry Division called it "A wild, mad, exciting race to see which army could gain the most ground in a single day," but the soldier on the front line could not understand the rapidly diminishing fuel supply.

The cause emanated from SHAEF headquarters, where Eisenhower believed that the Allies' best chance of getting across the Rhine and into Germany was through Holland. Field Marshall Montgomery had already lobbied for Patton's daily fuel allotment, promising to cross the Rhine north of the Ardennes and reach Berlin before winter. Eisenhower thought Montgomery had a good chance of keeping his promise and authorized the diversion of fuel. The British Second Army got off to a good start, almost achieved its objective, got repulsed with heavy losses at Arnhem, and

Right: On April 2, 1945, riflemen of Company K, 3rd battalion, 255th Regiment, 63rd Infantry Division, follow the 10th Armored Division into Sinsheim, Germany, and search for snipers as they move down the street.

Montgomery's effort ended in failure.

In the meantime, Patton battered his way through Metz and into Luxembourg, and on September 12, men of the 4th Division, First Army, penetrated the Siegfried Line. Lieutenant George Wilson, leading a reconnaissance platoon into the Ardennes, observed a German soldier emerge from a mound of earth less than a 100 yards away. "I got a slight chill," declared Wilson, "as I realized I might well be the first American to set eyes on a pillbox in the famous Siegfried Line."

He had brought his platoon east of Saint Vith, about twenty miles north of Bastogne. He hunkered down and looked about. Everywhere around him were more thick concrete encasements for machine guns, but he found them empty. Here, he thought, was a way for the 4th Infantry to drive right through the Siegfried Line. The 14th Infantry gave it try, plunging through with units from the First and Ninth Army. They captured Aachen and reached the Roer River. With flanks exposed, snow falling, and part of the First Army still pinned down in the Ardennes, the force paused at the Roer to solidify its position.

While the German Army beat off attacks against the Seigfried Line, Hitler planned a counteroffensive. He resented being on the defensive, and rightfully believed that only through a brilliant counterstroke could Germany win the war. He began consolidating his Army, bringing troops from the Eastern front. His plan – to break through the thinly held American line in the Ardennes, drive onto Antwerp, sever Eisenhower's supply

line, and thrust a wedge between the British in the north and the Americans in the south. He envisioned another Dunkirk, one so disabling to the Allies that he could shift resources to the east and fight the Soviets on a single front.

Bad weather and good secrecy cloaked the German buildup of two army groups opposite the Ardennes, twenty-four divisions supported with Tiger tanks. Intelligence operatives never saw trouble coming, lulling SHAEF headquarters into believing on December 16, 1944, that, "The enemy is at present fighting a defensive campaign on all fronts; his situation is such that he cannot stage offensive military operations."

Those in the Ardennes would agree. For two months the line had been stagnant, the guns quiet. The first indication of enemy activity came from a Belgian woman who had visited relatives on the German side of the line. She had seen bridging equipment, rubber boats, and more, but nobody seemed interested.

The Battle of the Bulge began on December 16th, but a full day passed before Americans awoke to the threat. On the night of the 15th, Lieutenant Lyle Bouck and his reconnaissance platoon of the 394th Regiment, 99th Division, occupied a listening post near Lanzerath. Bouck kept his men awake all night because he heard muffled noises beyond his front. Near dawn, the sky burst with flashes of light from 100 pieces of German artillery. Silhouetted against the backdrop of artillery fire, Bouck spotted dozens of tanks, self-propelled guns, and other vehicles outlined against the sky. He sent a patrol forward to investigate. They climbed to the second floor of a farmhouse, spied a column of enemy infantry approaching the village, and raced back to inform the lieutenant. Bouck got through on his radio, but the officer taking the call refused to believe that Germans were mounting an attack.

"Damn it," Bouck shouted into the phone. "Don't tell me what I don't see! I have twenty-twenty vision. Bring down some artillery, all the artillery you can, on the road south of Lanzerath. There's a Kraut column coming up from that direction."

No friendly artillery came, and the

two tanks supporting the platoon withdrew. Bouck put his men in foxholes, brought the BARs forward, and took on the entire enemy column. During the day, he watched for reinforcements, but none came. By mid-afternoon, more than 400 German bodies lay in the field in front of the platoon. During a lull, Bouck turned to Private William James and said, "I want you to take the men that want to go and get out."

"Are you coming?" James asked.

"No, I have orders to hold at all costs. I'm staying."

"Then," said James, "we'll all stay."

An hour later both James and Bouck lay wounded and out of ammunition. A German doctor dressed their wounds in a cafe set up as a first aid post. At midnight, the cuckoo clock in the café struck midnight, and Bouck turned twenty-one, mumbling to himself, "What a hell of a way to become a man."

He and his platoon had blocked the Lanzerath road against a full-strength German battalion for a day, inflicting

Above: Uniforms and equipment of U.S. assault troops who landed in Normandy and fought their way through Europe. They were probably the best armed and equipped forces ever to undertake an amphibious landing. The camouflaged uniform (right) was quickly withdrawn when it was found to be too similar to uniforms worn by the *Waffen-SS*.

Below: On March 26, 1945, Seventh Army riflemen of the 7th Infantry Regiment, 3rd Division, leave the assault boat used to cross the Rhine and begin the climb up the enemy-held east bank near Frankenthal.

Above: As riflemen from the Seventh Army's 45th Division pass through Bensheim, Germany, an elderly German woman stops in the street to stare in despair at the hopeless wreckage of her home.

Right: Infantrymen of Co. C, 62nd A.I. Bn., 14th Armored Division, XV Corps, on the alert for snipers, double-time past burning buildings after Gemenduen, Germany, was taken without armored support when a blown-up bridge prevented the use of tanks.

Below: On April 6, 1945, PFC Armand Rindone of the 378th Infantry Regiment, 95th Division, searches for enemy movement as he crouches with a carbine at the devastated railroad station at Hamm, Germany.

casualties of more than fifty percent. Had the officer on the other end of Bouck's phone reacted with promptitude, the German thrust into the Bulge might have been met with organized resistance.

Yet on Sunday, December 17, for most units in the Ardennes it was business as usual. Sergeant Giles got a pass and tried to go to Saint Vith. Roads usually quiet were inexplicably jammed with traffic. The driver of the jeep plunged onto a side road and, after encountering masses of snow, slush, and mud, he turned around and started back. "We came out a different place," Giles declared, "and an MP stopped us there and told us all hell had busted loose, the Krauts were attacking and the whole country was crawling with them.... He was shaking like a leaf and it was plain whether it was true or not he believed it." Little did anyone know, the Battle of the Bulge had already begun the previous day, and the German attack was moving into full swing.

When the magnitude of Hitler's

counteroffensive became clear, a stupefied General Bradley snorted, "Where in hell has this son-of-a-bitch gotten all his strength?" A few days later Bradley got his answer. Captured German soldiers turned out to be fifteen- and sixteen-year-olds.

At first, the surprise attack achieved enormous success, all but destroying one U.S. division. As the *Panzers* pressed westward, more divisions collapsed in confusion. Snow a foot deep, covered over by ice, and zero temperatures added to the plight of the Americans. Bad weather had cancelled out the Allies' most important advantage, command of the air. But in the field, groups of GIs organized small fighting teams and slowed the German assault, disrupting the *Wehrmacht*'s timetable.

To the south, two battalions of the

110th Infantry supported by two companies of tanks hunkered down and fought off four German regiments and never gave an inch of ground. "That was," said Charles B. McDonald, the U.S. Army's official historian, "around two thousand men versus at least ten thousand [Germans]....Considering the odds, nowhere on the first day of the German offensive was there a more remarkable achievement by the American soldier."

When Eisenhower learned of the attack, he reacted quickly. The Germans had come out of their defenses, now they were vulnerable. He began moving troops from the north and south into the Ardennes, and on December 19 he got the 101st Airborne Division into Bastogne. For four days, six German divisions – two of them armored – surrounded the

small island of resistance and demanded its surrender. To the Germans' persistent demands for surrender, General Anthony McAuliffe tersely replied, "Nuts," creating a small amount of consternation on the part of the enemy as they sought to translate the meaning of this odd American expression.

During the next two weeks, the entire German counteroffensive collapsed. North of Bastogne, the 82nd Airborne blocked the Germans at Saint Vith, smashing the enemy's efforts to strike at Antwerp. Patton came up from the south and rolled into Bastogne.

On December 24 the skies cleared and 10,000 aircraft pummeled the Germans on the ground. By January 3, 1945, Eisenhower had his army back on the offensive. Hitler paid an enormous price for his gamble – 30,000 killed, 40,000 wounded, 40,000 prisoners, thousands of his finest tanks destroyed.

Eisenhower had thrown 600,000 troops into the battle – the largest American engagement ever fought – and the GIs paid a heavy price, 20,000 killed, 40,000 wounded, and 20,000 captured.

But Hitler had squandered his army on the wrong front. The Soviet military machine sprang into action, and on January 12, the race for Berlin began.

Operations during the month of January opened in some of the coldest weather GIs ever experienced. The oil in engines hardened, and when weapons froze, GIs urinated on the working mechanisms, which only created other problems. To make matters worse, the Germans fought back in ice and snow, making Americans pay as they pressed toward the Seigfried Line.

Eisenhower did not want to give the enemy time to reorganize. The only troops available were those who had for three weeks fought to secure the Bulge. They were dead tired and expected to be relieved, but they were all that Eisenhower had at the front. When orders came down the line on January 3 to advance, Sergeant John Martin of the 101st Airborne gasped, "I could not believe that they were going to put us on the attack. I figured, Jesus, they'll take us out of here and give us some warm clothing or something." In another unit,

Right: Bombed and shelled severely before its capture, a large part of Magdeburg, Germany, had been razed to the ground before Company B, 117th Infantry, 30th Division, set foot in the desolated city.

SELECTIVE CHRONOLOGY OF WAR: 1945

Jan 3: U.S. First Army begins counteroffensive operations from the north to reduce stubborn opposition in Ardennes salient, coordinated with Allied counterthrusts from the south; in appalling weather, the German main northern supply route is cut, and the enemy withdraws, having suffered 120,000 casualties and exhausting Hitler's mobile reserves.

Jan 16: U.S. First and Third Armies meet at Houffalize, establishing tactical victory in Ardennes; German losses total 250,000, their supplies become stretched; British Field Marshal Montgomery cites "staunch fighting qualities of the American soldier" as reason for Allied victory.

Mar 7: U.S. First Army crosses Remagen bridge over Rhine.

Mar 8: U.S. troops move into Bonn.

Mar 17: U.S. Third Army captures Coblenz.

Mar 24: Operation Varsity begins, with first airborne landing of Allied troops across the Rhine.

Mar 25: U.S. Third Army captures Darmstadt, while 9th Army joins British forces east of the Rurh.

Mar 27: U.S. forces capture Wiesbaden.

Mar 29: U.S. Third Army moves into Frankfurt, while First Army moves north to Paderborn.

Apr 1: U.S. First and Ninth Armies encircle Rurh.

Apr 27: U.S. and Russian troops meet at Torgau, on Elbe River, setting groundwork for separate occupation of Germany at war's end.

May 2: German forces in Italy surrender to Allies; the Italian campaign has cost 114,000 American casualties, but has tied up German forces which would have been used against Allies in France.

May 7: Germany surrenders unconditionally to Allies.

May 8: VE Day, official end of war in Europe.

Captain Jay Prophet of the 333rd Infantry Division grumbled laconically to the battalion commander, "Colonel, there's nothing I'd like more right now than a nice warm court-martial."

The fighting during January became some of the fiercest, and sometimes the "weirdest," of the war. Because Hitler ordered "no retreat," house to house fighting became pervasive. During artillery barrages, both sides would seek shelter in a building, sometimes with Germans on a second floor while GIs occupied the first. When the shelling stopped, each departed by some mutually unspoken détente. Private Pat Reilly of the 79th recalled, "If they didn't make a move we left and if we didn't make a move they left."

Hitler seemed to ignore his best option – to withdraw to the Rhine and consolidate his forces. Instead, he exhorted his troops to stand fast. The advancing American infantry took advantage of the mistake by killing more Germans and destroying more tanks, thereby reducing the *Wehrmacht*'s ability to defend the Rhine in the weeks to come. By the end of February, Allied forces were converging on the river from its mouth to its source.

By the time the First Army reached Cologne – the fourth largest city in Germany and the largest on the Rhine – so many German units had been sopped up that the city's defenses had been reduced to a weak outer ring manned by survivors from the earlier fighting – police, firemen, and the *Volksstrum* (armed citizens). On March 5 the 3rd Armored Division entered the city, but retreating Germans had blown all of the bridges spanning the Rhine.

South of Cologne, the 9th Armored Division closed rapidly on the Ludendorff Bridge at Remagen. The Germans were setting their charges when Lieutenant Karl Timmerman organized a platoon of volunteers to cross the bridge in the face of fierce machine gun fire. One charge shook the bridge but failed to bring it down and, in the chaos that followed, Timmerman led the platoon across the span, followed by a detail of engineers. While Timmerman's platoon fought the Germans on the hill across the river, engineers cut the wires to TNT charges fastened to bridge supports. Bradley rushed the First Army across the bridge, and during the next several days the battle for the Western Front centered on Remagen.

Hitler sent in the *Luftwaffe*, his new German jets, artillery, and even fired a few V-2s from launchers in Holland in an effort to bring down the bridge and isolate the U.S. First Army. On March 11, the Corps of Engineers finished building a 969-foot heavy pontoon bridge across the river, and when the Ludendorff Bridge finally fell into the Rhine on March 17, it no longer made a difference.

With Allied forces across the Rhine, German resistance began to collapse on all fronts. In Italy, the U.S. Fifth and British Eighth Armies launched their spring offensive. North of Remagen, Montgomery's troops crossed the Rhine, as did Patton's to the south. In the east, the Red Army captured Vienna and stormed across the Oder River.

In early April, politicians stepped into the contest over who would capture Berlin. Churchill wanted it to be Montgomery. Stalin wanted it to be the Red Army. Eisenhower called it madness to fling his forces across Germany in the distant hope of reaching there before the Russians. As armies closed in from east and west, Eisenhower wanted to avoid any risk of firing into the Soviets, so he agreed to halt once his Army reached the Elbe. He did not want to sacrifice the lives of another

100,000 GIs for no military gain.

On May 2, 1945, Berlin at last fell – and with it the "thousand year" Third Reich. Only then did the horrors of Hitler's atrocities manifest themselves.

Eisenhower once said, "I hate the Germans." Now he had reason to hate them more.

Unlike Eisenhower, the American soldier was too busy fighting the war too fully understand it. Sergeant Milt Lamm spoke for thousands when he wrote: "I began my combat life all by myself in a foxhole half full of water in front of a German pillbox at Lindern, Germany. For the next several days, all I did was cringe at the bottom... while the 88's pounded us. I had no idea what was going on." For not knowing "what was going on," Lamm eventually won a Silver Star and a Bronze Star. Some GIs won medals. Others just got killed.

Above: On April 29, 1945, a platoon of the 222nd Infantry Regiment operating near Dachau, Germany, round up four of the 30 SS troopers who had been engaging elements of the 42nd Division, U.S. Seventh Army.

Left: In April, 1945, troops of the U.S. Ninth Army discover a prison camp and begin the release of hundreds of Allied servicemen from Oflag 79.

Uncommon Valor

Unlike athletes who compete to win medals, American soldiers did not go to war to be decorated. Most of them went to war because they had been drafted. Young men enlisted, some out of patriotism, others to avoid being thrust into the Army. None of them really knew how he would behave under fire. There were always a few men who believed they could win the war single-handedly, but never did and never tried.

The real heroes emerged from obscurity and, after the war ended, those who survived melded back into society. Audie Murphy was the exception because he became a movie star. But Bruce Jacobs, who wrote of heroes in the Army, told of a GI who attended a party at an Army post. The soldier, a small, unobtrusive man, climbed on the shoulders of a buddy to reach a balloon suspended from the ceiling. He lost his balance and fell at the feet of a sour-faced lieutenant colonel, who snarled, "What are you trying to do? Win the Medal of Honor?"

"Oh no, sir!" replied the soldier as he brushed himself clean. "I've got that; I was just trying to snag a balloon for one of the kids."

The Medal of Honor dates back to the Civil War, being the highest decoration for valor given by the armed forces for supreme gallantry in action.During World War II, the Medal of Honor went to only

Left: U.S. decorations and campaign medals. Top, l to r, Distinguished Flying Cross; Distinguished Service Cross; Silver Star; Bronze Star, the "V" device on ribbon signifying valor. Center, Purple Heart. Second row, l to r, Air Medal; Navy and Marine Corps Medal, authorized 1942 for gallantry not involving actual conflict with an enemy; Army Medal of Honor, highest award for gallantry; Navy Cross, established 1919 and since 1942 the Navy's second highest gallantry award; Philippine Liberation Medal, awarded for action in liberation of those islands, October 17, 1944, to September 3, 1945. Bottom row, l to r, Navy Distinguished Service Medal; American Defense Service Medal; Army Distinguished Service Medal; Asiatic-Pacific Campaign Medal awarded for thirty days' active service in prescribed area or aboard certain ships between December 7, 1941, and November 8, 1945; and World War II Victory Medal.

World War II Army Medal of Honor Recipients		
Theater of War	*Recipients*	*Posthumous*
Far East	83	50
North Africa	6	4
Sicily	4	2
Italian campaign	47	22
Aerial offensive	23	15
France/Germany	131	56
Total	294	149

294 Army soldiers and airmen, half of whose families received it posthumously. Another 139 Medals of Honor were awarded, 57 to Navy personnel, 81 to Marines, and one to a serviceman in the Coast Guard.

The medals vary slightly for each service, but they each contain a five-pointed tipped star with trefoils and hang from an octagonal pad of blue, bearing thirteen white stars, that encircles the neck.

Ranking second to the Medal of Honor in the three services is the Distinguished Service Cross, established in 1918 for the Army; the Navy Cross, established in 1919 for the Navy, Marines, and Coast Guard; and the Air Force Cross, which was not established until 1960.

Next in order of merit is the Distinguished Service Medal. These awards usually went to commanders for exceptionally meritorious service to the government and were authorized in the same years as the three crosses.

The Silver Star Medal, established for the Army in 1932 and for the Navy in 1942, is the same for all services. It is awarded for conspicuous gallantry in action, and has been often used as a substitute for men recommended for but denied a higher award.

The Legion of Merit, authorized in 1942, ranks next after the Silver Star. It is the first U.S. decoration awarded to citizens of other nations, but it is also given to officers and enlisted men of the U.S. armed forces and to nationals of other countries who have distinguished themselves through exceptional meritorious conduct in the performance of an outstanding service.

The Distinguished Flying Cross (1926) is awarded to both U.S. personnel and members of the armed forces from allied countries for heroism or extraordinary achievement while participating in aerial operations.

Several medals are awarded for heroic voluntary risk of life not involving armed combat with the enemy. These include the Soldier's Medal (1926), the Navy and Marine Corps Medal (1942), the Coast Guard Medal (1951), and the Airman's Medal (1960).

Ranking next in importance are the Bronze Star Medal and Air Medal, the former for heroic or meritorious achievement in connection with military operations against an armed enemy, and the latter for meritorious service while in flight – combat or non-combat – but in operations against the enemy.

One Commendation Medal, the Purple Heart, was once a ribbon without medal

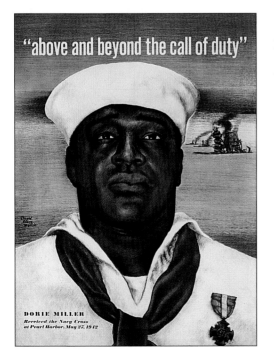

"above and beyond the call of duty"

DORIE MILLER
Received the Navy Cross at Pearl Harbor, May 27, 1942

Left: An Office of War Information recruitment poster bearing the image of Dobie Miller, who was awarded the Navy Cross at Pearl Harbor on May 27, 1942. Unfortunately, political circumstances early in the war denied blacks true recognition, and also the services of their courage and commitment in certain circumstances.

until 1932. It is awarded by the Joint Services to those wounded in combat or to the next of kin of those killed.

In all, there are about fifty different medals and decorations a soldier can earn in the service – everything from a Good Conduct Medal, Unit Citation ribbons, and campaign ribbons designating the theater in which the individual served. Small bronze stars worn on the ribbon designate the number of specific battles fought, and a silver star is the equivalent of five bronze stars. A small arrowhead was awarded to those who made amphibious or parachute landings.

During World War II there were also awards for women in the service, such as the Women's Army Corps Service Medal and a Medal of Merit for civilians and members of friendly nations who performed outstanding services.

Many career officers took extra measures to gather up medals, but the average GI drafted into the service just wanted the war to end. If he received a medal for distinguished service, at least he had something to take back to his former life.

Early in the war, "Jim Crow" segregation still flourished, confining the black soldier to mundane and often dirty tasks with the Engineer Corps. Fifty years passed before the country corrected the injustice. On January 13, 1997, seven African-American veterans received the Medal of Honor, denied them earlier only because they were black.

Yet, the second GI to receive the

Medal of Honor in World War II was what we today call a Latino minority, Sergeant Jose Calugas of the Philippines. The decoration dated from January 16, 1942, while Calugas served as a scout for the 88th Field Artillery during the Imperial Army's invasion of his country. Four days earlier the first recipient of the Medal of Honor, 2nd Lieutenant Alexander R. Nininger, Jr., fighting with the 57th Infantry on the Philippines, lost his life. He may have known Calugas. They were both with the Philippine Scouts, one the best units in the United States Army.

Twelve thousand Filipinos served in the Scouts, and most regiments, such as Nininger's 57th Infantry, were officered by Regular Army men. The Scouts had a reputation for being well-trained and combat-ready.

General MacArthur, having been recalled to active duty in the summer of 1940, commanded a district containing 11,500 miles of coastline. For every mile, MacArthur had been given one soldier to defend it. Some of those men were in the 57th Infantry commanded by Colonel George S. Clarke, a veteran of World War I.

Six weeks after Nininger reached Manila, the Imperial Navy attacked Pearl Harbor and disabled much of America's Pacific fleet. Major Royal Reynolds, commanding the 1st Battalion, made Nininger a platoon leader in Lieutenant Fred Yeager's Company A, and ordered the Scouts out to Fort McKinley. A few days later Japanese landed on the beaches and began moving inland, forming a

pincers movement to assault Manila.

To spare the city, MacArthur began evacuation, ordering the 57th to cover the withdrawal to Bataan. On New Year's Day, 1942, Nininger's regiment formed along the Abucay Line, the main line of resistance. Four days later the men went on half rations.

Company A of the 57th filed into position on the extreme right flank. They had a clear view of the field of fire and worked day and night to lay a triple row of land mines along the defensive perimeter. On the afternoon of January 9, a Scouts reconnaissance patrol spotted the Japanese moving on Bataan. After an exchange of small arms fire, they withdrew to report the enemy's approach. During the next two days, more Japanese units crossed into Bataan, taking positions off both Filipino-American flanks, and opened with artillery.

As the sun went down on January 11, hundreds of Japanese had moved into position opposite the 3rd Battalion. Then they attacked, fiercely assaulting Company I. Artillery pounded them, barbed wire entangled them, but still they advanced, using their own dead to bridge the obstructions. Company I collapsed, and the 3rd Battalion threw in Companies K and L. After they became mauled, Colonel Clarke called up the reserve.

In Lieutenant Yeager's sector, all had been quiet apart from the distant sound of firing. Nininger said that he was familiar with the terrain near Company K and could move some men into the area through an irrigation ditch. Yeager agreed to the effort and detailed a squad of ten Filipinos. Armed with an M1, hand grenades, and a pistol, Nininger led the detachment into the brush. He suspected that the ditch would take him undetected into the midst of the enemy, and it did.

To his front Nininger could hear sniper firing. A shot from his M1 sent one sharpshooter toppling to the ground. Startled, the Japanese began looking for the source of the shot. The action intensified. Nininger kept his squad controlled, and they fired only when they spotted a target. Twice he led his patrol into the midst of the enemy, smoking out snipers and shooting them down. When Major Reynolds learned that Nininger had taken a squad behind enemy lines, he ordered him out of the area. Nininger sent a message back to base refusing the order. Wounded, he would fight on. Out of M1

Below: At Pearl Harbor in May, 1945, the crew of the submarine U.S.S. *Batfish* (left) receive combat awards after completing an important and successful war patrol.

Right: On January 12, 1942, 2nd Lt. Alexander R. Nininger, Jr. of the 57th Infantry, Philippine Scouts, lost his life in hand-to-hand combat during the Japanese invasion of Bataan, earning the first Medal of Honor awarded in World War II.

Right Center: 1st Lieutenant Willibaud C. Bianchi, 45th Infantry P.S., received the Medal of Honor on February 3, 1942, after he voluntarily joined another unit attacking Japanese machine gun nests and personally silenced one with grenades. Wounded three times, he climbed on top of an American tank and continued to fire the AA gun against the enemy.

ammunition, he told his men to hold their position. Then, with a pistol in one hand and a hand grenade in the other, he attacked the Japanese still holding a salient.

With Nininger raising hell in the enemy's rear, Company K rallied and moved forward. One GI peering ahead shouted, "There he is!" Wounded three times and giddy from loss of blood, Nininger staggered after the enemy. Three Japanese suddenly emerged from the brush. With bayonets leveled, they charged him from behind. Nininger whirled and emptied the pistol into the Japanese officer and two men. They fell to the ground, and he fell beside them.

On January 12, 1942, on the blood-stained cogon grass of Bataan, Nininger died. As one historian said, his "mortal years had been pitifully few; but he had earned the special immortality that is reserved for the gallant Americans who have, over the years, given their lives so that their nation might endure."

During the battle for the Philippines in 1942, four men won the Medal of Honor – Sergeant Jose Calugas, 1st Lieutenant Willibauld C. Bianchi, General Douglas MacArthur, and 2nd Lieutenant Nininger.

Not all Americans were soldiers. Some preferred the Navy, and some of the seamen were not sailors at all but pilots. Lieutenant (j.g.) Edward H. O'Hare, an Annapolis graduate from St. Louis was one of them.

Late in the afternoon of February 19, 1942, two waves of nine Mitsubishi twin-

engined bombers attacked the carrier *Lexington*. After repulsing the first wave, all but two of the American fighters – those of O'Hare and his wingman – were back on the carrier refueling when the second wave struck. Back in the air, O'Hare spotted the bombers at 12,000 feet, but he noticed that his wingman's guns had jammed. Though alone and without support, he attacked all nine Mitsubishis, passing down the left side of the formation, banking up the right side, and repeating the maneuver five times, knocking down four of the bombers. When five of them reached the release point over the carrier, O'Hare flew through his own anti-aircraft fire to shoot down another bomber and damage a sixth. In awarding the first Medal of Honor to go to a Navy man, President Roosevelt referred to Lieutenant O'Hare's feat as the "most daring single action in the history of combat aviation."

Right: Marine Lt. Col. Harold W. Bauer (Coronado, California) of the Marine Fighting Squadron 212 was posthumously awarded the Medal of Honor for his extraordinary heroism in aerial combat in the Solomons.

Advanced three grades to lieutenant commander, O'Hare continued his daredevil flying, but on November 27, 1943, America lost one of its heroes in a fight off the Gilbert Islands. Japanese planes swarmed in force to attack American carriers off Makin Island. O'Hare took to the skies and engaged in one of the most furious dogfights of the war. He flew his plane into the middle of the fight, piercing the skies with a hail of tracer bullets. Enemy planes, engines spewing flame and smoke, careened with a scream and plunged into the ocean. Suddenly, O'Hare's plane banked and disappeared. Another Navy pilot watched as it dropped into the water. O'Hare's wingman searched in vain to find it. Rear Admiral Arthur W. Radford recommended that O'Hare receive a second Medal of Honor for saving the carriers. The name O'Hare is still familiar to anyone taking a commercial flight into Chicago's busiest airport.

By the summer of 1942, Japan's command of the Pacific ran from the Alaskan Aleutians in the north to New Guinea and the Solomon Islands off northern Australia. In square miles, the Japanese controlled more of the globe than any nation in the history of the world, but most of it was water. The end of Tojo's Imperial expansion began on August 7, 1942, when U.S. Marines landed on Guadacanal. They swept inland, captured the new airfield built by the Japanese, and renamed it Henderson Field. Then the fight really began.

On the afternoon of October 22, airplanes spotted a large force of Japanese moving eastward along the road to Henderson Field. General Vandergrift rushed two battalions of the 7th Marines to protect the vulnerable western flank.

Author Saul Brown described the actions of seven heroes who fought in the Pacific; twenty-four-year-old Platoon Sergeant Mitchell Paige of H Company, 2nd Battalion, 7th Marines, caught his attention. On October 26, 1942, Paige took his platoon to an outpost about four miles west of Henderson Field. There he set up How Company's 30-man machine gun platoon on a knoll between George and Fox Companies. He soon found himself engaged in a fierce fight for control of the position.

Paige had enlisted in the Corps the day he turned eighteen, and he did so intending to become a career Marine. He took a fancy to machine guns, and from a former company commander he learned how to modify the bolt and springs of a .30-caliber water-cooled machine gun so it could fire up to 1,300 rounds a minute. All the guns of the platoon had been altered in this manner, and when Paige placed his unit on the knoll, the men set their pieces in shallow foxholes.

Shortly after midnight on October 27, the enemy began infiltrating Paige's perimeter. He could hear soft voices speaking in Japanese just under the knoll and woke the platoon. Thirty grenades rolled down the ledge and exploded in the midst of a Japanese reconnaissance patrol. At daylight Major Odell Conoley, the battalion executive officer, stomped over to the platoon to investigate the disturbance. Paige showed him seventeen

Left: Lieutenant (j.g.) Edward H. "Butch" O'Hare, whose gallantry above and beyond the call of duty earned him the first Medal of Honor to go to a Navy man for his action in the air above his carrier, *Lexington*, on February 19, 1942. He was killed in action off the Gilbert Islands in November, 1943, and was recommended for a second Medal of Honor.

Below: For voluntary exploits above and beyond the call of duty against enemy positions during the invasion of Salerno, Italy, T/Sgt. Charles E. Kelly received the Medal of Honor.

Above: In July, 1944, PFC Galen C. Kittleson earned the Silver Star for retrieving a mortally wounded comrade while under fire during a Ranger operation on Noemfoor Island in the Philippines.

bodies. Conoley nodded approval and said, "Sergeant, you had better get your men some more grenades."

Headquarters now expected an attack, but nobody would have guessed that Lieutenant General Masao Maruyama intended to throw 16,000 men into the assault, least of all Sergeant Paige. The men of his platoon were in top physical and mental condition. For two years they had trained together and looked upon themselves as the best machine-gunners in the Corps. At dark, Paige ordered the men to keep a hundred percent watch, adding, "Don't fire until you actually see something."

During the day he had inspected his field of fire and corrected the defects. The ridge where he had placed the machine guns sloped down into a draw covered over with grass six feet tall. Shallow gullies on both flanks were filled with foliage, giving the enemy good cover. Because his guns were perched on a knoll

Right: Platoon Sergeant Mitchell Paige (seen here as promoted to 1st Lieutenant) received the Medal of Honor for almost single-handedly repulsing attacks by enemy forces at Henedrson Field, Guadalcanal, in 1942.

fifty to seventy feet above the draw, he could not lay down a grazing fire. A small number of supporting riflemen had been detailed to support his flanks, but if Fox Company needed assistance, the riflemen lay in the line of fire. Paige did not like the arrangement but, as darkness approached, he had little time to improve it.

At 2:00 a.m. he could hear muffled sounds from the jungle across the draw – the clanking of equipment, and now and then an order in Japanese. Paige crawled down the line, whispering to the men to get their grenades ready and warning them not to fire until he gave the order. He came back to the gun on his left, where Corporal Raymond Gaston reported rustling in the bushes directly in his front. Paige pulled the pin on a grenade and heard the others do the same. He spotted a dark form creeping out of the foliage toward Gaston's position and hurled the grenade. When it exploded at the feet of the infiltrator, heavy fire erupted on Gaston's flank.

Grenades rained down upon the Japanese as they spilled into the gully. American machine gun fire spat tracer bullets that swept through ranks of the enemy as they stumbled into the draw. From somewhere in the rear, Captain Louis Ditta's 60mm mortars opened, arcing shells into the expanding maelstrom. The Japanese came on, screaming "*banzai*" as they charged. In darkness they groped up the knoll, singly and in small groups, only to be cut to pieces by grenades or riddled by enfilading fire from Paige's 30mm machine guns. Several Japanese reached the number two gun and killed the crew. Spreading out, they concentrated their fire on number one gun, quickly overrunning its three-man crew.

Paige found himself in a tight situation. He turned gun number three on seventy-five Japanese spilling up the slope on the left flank and ripped the column apart. The attack suddenly ebbed, the enemy falling back to regroup.

During the interregnum, Paige prepared for the next assault but suddenly found his platoon beset by snipers who had crawled up trees and were firing at flashes from the machine guns. A third of his platoon had been killed or wounded.

Two of the guns had been damaged, another jammed, and as Paige worked frantically to remove a ruptured cartridge from the jammed gun, an enemy bullet swiped across the back of his hand and started blood flowing.

As Paige made the rounds to check on the supply of ammunition, the second wave of Japanese hit Fox Company. The enemy swept over the Marines, capturing three .30-caliber light machine guns. At 5:00 a.m. they knocked Fox Company off the spur of the ridge and threatened to overrun Paige's left flank.

Running through a hail of bullets, Paige reached the forward gun. Every man on the platoon's left flank had been cut down. He fed a belt into the weapon and fired short bursts into a column of advancing Japanese until the barrel began to steam. When the overheated piece stopped firing, he withdrew through a stream of enemy fire to the next gun. Sliding into a shallow foxhole, he swung the weapon around and dropped a dozen of the enemy in their tracks. When the gun gave out, he went to the next.

At every emplacement, he found only dead bodies. His platoon was gone, and those not killed had been removed by Navy corpsmen. Japanese soldiers were all around him, having taken possession of the knoll, but they all seemed to be in a daze. Paige bumped through them, reached the next gun, and soon had it blazing in the direction of the enemy. When he reached the end of his own line, he came in contact with two Marines

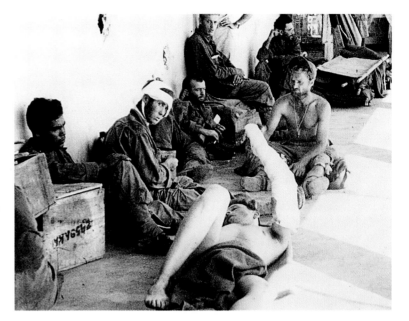

from How Company and said, "I need a gun." He grabbed a light machine gun, borrowed a few riflemen from George Company, and formed a skirmish line on the left flank. He knew that when daylight came the Japanese would see the ground they had gained, and send a third wave to overrun George Company. He ordered the Marines to fix bayonets and led them back into the fight.

Paige spotted a large group of Japanese advancing on Major Conoley's command post and opened with the machine gun, spraying 250 rounds into the enemy. Two more machine guns came up, and as another wave of Japanese showed themselves above the knoll, Paige's skirmishers knocked the enemy to pieces and sent them reeling down the hill. A few Japanese hunkered down and began crabbing their way toward one of the platoon's unmanned guns. Paige ran for it, drawing fire from snipers and a single machine gun firing near the lip of the spur. He dove into the foxhole, only to find the piece empty. He grabbed a partially loaded belt, shoved it into the breech, and got the gun working. He cleared his front of the enemy, but in doing so drew the fire from every gun that could be brought to bear on his position.

Running low on ammunition, he began to despair when three men from his platoon, whom he thought were dead, dashed across the field of fire in the early light of morning with fresh belts. All three were hit by sniper fire as they

Above: Newly liberated from Cabanatuan by Rangers on January 31, 1945, American POWs await transfer from an emergency hospital to a base facility. They were rescued by members of the 6th Ranger Battalion and their Alamo Scouts – an intelligence gathering organization of volunteers, wrapped in secrecy and set up in November, 1943, by Lt. Gen. Walter Kreuger after Gen. MacArthur forbade OSS operations within the Southwest Pacific Area.

Left: Advancing under sniper fire through a stand of tall grass, riflemen of the 6th Ranger Battalion hurry toward the Japanese prison camp at Cabanatuan on Luzon in the Philippines.

Right: First Lieutenant William D. Hawkins (El Paso, Texas) of the 2nd Marine Division, earned the Medal of Honor posthumously for repeated acts of heroism at Tarawa by individually wiping out numerous pillboxes to secure the beachhead.

Right Center: PFC Douglas T. Jacobson (Port Washington, New York) of the 4th Marine Division, earned the Medal of Honor for destroying 16 enemy positions and killing some 75 Japanese in a furious one-man assault at Iwo Jima.

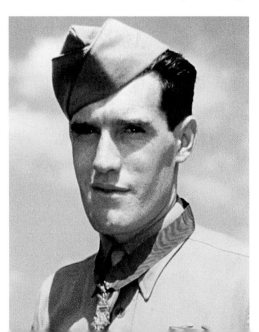

Right: PFC William J. Johnston (Colchester, Conn.), a machine gunner with the 45th Division, won the Medal of Honor for distinguished service against enemy fortified positions at Anzio, Italy.

toppled into the foxhole. A moment later twenty-four Marines came up from the command post and, with Paige, drove the enemy off the knoll and back into the jungle.

At 5:30 a.m., having about thirty riflemen from George Company nearby, Paige turned to them and said, "I'm going after those Japs and I want you to be right behind me." He slung two full belts of ammo around his shoulders, unclamped the red-hot machine gun, and started down the slope. He opened on a number of Japanese still clinging to the knoll, shot down a field grade officer, and with the men behind him screaming like Indians, swept across the draw and into the jungle. They found nothing left to shoot at. It was, said Paige later, "A strange sort of quietness." For several minutes everyone stood and listened, but the fight was over.

For his stand at the ridge a few miles west of Henderson Field, Sergeant Paige received the Medal of Honor, the second to be awarded a Marine. Almost single-handedly he had closed a crucial gap and prevented the enemy from rolling up the defensive flank of the 3rd Battalion, 7th Marines. Paige received a commission in the field and ended his career as a colonel in the Marine Corps. He never forgot the men of his platoon.

Every theater of engagement had its heroes, and the ground fighting in Italy ranked among the fiercest of the war. Forty-seven infantrymen earned the Medal of Honor, among them a mild-mannered, wavy-haired fellow who would have looked more in place at an ice cream social than on a battlefield –Charles E. Kelly. His unit, Company L, 143rd Infantry, 36th (Texas) Infantry Division, reached Oran, Algeria, in May 1943 and after three months of being schooled on amphibious tactics, headed for the west coast of Italy. Major General Mark W. Clark, commanding the U.S. Fifth Army, planned to put two corps on the beaches, one at Salerno and the other at Paestum. Kelly's 3rd Battalion, commanded by Lt. Col. Joseph F. Barnett, Jr., was to advance across the beachhead and form with the division along a rail line east of Paestum.

German mortars pounded the landing craft and pulverized the beaches. Kelly landed and raced inland. When he stopped to catch his breath, he found he had taken a wrong turn. When a machine gun opened on him, he jumped into a ditch and found himself among soldiers from a different regiment. He then doubled back to the beach, got his bearings, and in the morning found his company assembled at the base of a hill.

Colonel William H. Martin, the regimental commander, issued marching orders. The 2nd and 3rd Battalions would lead the assault. In Company L, Kelly would take the point. As the battalion approached Altavilla, machine gun and mortar fire drove Company L into a ravine. Finding his company in a tight spot, Captain Marion P. Bowden was considering his options when Kelly asked permission to look around. Bowden consented.

With four volunteers, Kelly crabbed his way forward until coming in sight of what appeared to be a mound of sandbags. One of the men lobbed a rifle grenade at the position. When it exploded, the machine gun gave a few short bursts, then fell silent again. Kelly adjusted the tripod of his BAR and opened fire. Seconds later a flurry of 80mm mortar shells drove him and his volunteers back to the draw.

Kelly reported his observations to Bowden, who sent him back up the draw, this time with 1st Lieutenant John C. Morrisey, who carried a light machine gun, and two volunteers. As the four men worked through the draw, they spotted about seventy Germans forming to attack Company L. But Kelly first wanted to knock out the machine gun. He had the range of it, pulled off ten rounds, and killed its three-man crew. The unexpected firing alerted the German combat patrol, and Kelly's BAR became the focus of their attention.

Kelly saw them coming. He whipped

Left: First Lieutenant Carlton R. Rouh (Lindenwold, N. J.) of the 1st Marine Division received the Medal of Honor for falling on a Japanese grenade on Peleliu to protect two other Marines from injury and possible death.

around and emptied his magazine on the advancing patrol. Morrisey's machine gun jammed, and Kelly had to hurry to reload. He thrust a new magazine into the BAR, pulled the trigger, and stopped the attack in its tracks. In a state of panic, the Germans withdrew in a hurry, leaving behind forty dead or wounded. But for Kelly, this was only the beginning.

Sent back with a hundred men to a temporary command post in Altavilla for ammunition, Kelly found himself in a large three-story building, built like a fortress, that formerly housed the mayor. While he was there, the Germans launched a sudden counterattack, and the house soon became the only ground in Altavilla still held by the regiment. From nearby homes, the Germans used automatic weapons to keep a steady fire pouring through the mayor's shattered windows.

Most of the GIs at the command post were at work barricading the doors. Others hung around the windows, firing back, but many of them were getting hit. Kelly bounded up the stairs to the second floor, set up his BAR, and shot the Germans trying to place a machine gun on the hill behind the house. Finding no more activity in the rear, he roved from window to window, firing into German positions no one else could hit. A GI with a light machine gun followed Kelly from one window to the next, firing intermittently to keep the Germans occupied whenever Kelly stopped to

Left: Capt. Kenneth A. Walsh (Washington, D.C.), of the Marine Fighting Squadron 124, earned the Medal of Honor for extraordinary heroism as a Marine fighter pilot during the battle for the Solomon Islands.

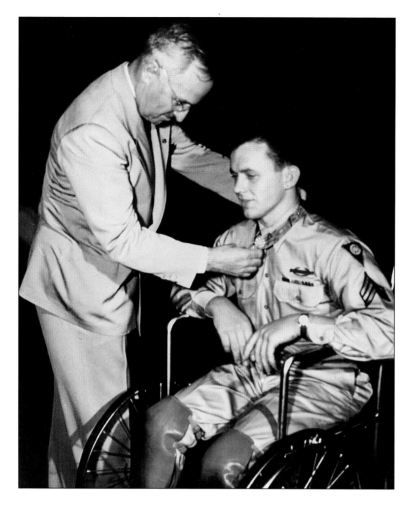

Above: Sgt. Ralph G. Keppel (Willey, Iowa) of the 329 Infantry Regiment, 83rd (Ohio) Division, is presented the Medal of Honor by President Harry S. Truman for gallantry near the village of Birgel, Germany, on December 14, 1944.

reload the BAR. A flurry of enemy bullets cut the soldier down, and he fell at Kelly's feet.

After Kelly's BAR jammed, he tossed it away and picked up another. Snapping a magazine into the slot, he went back to a window and cut down a group of Germans forming behind a building. Having disposed of them, he reloaded, went to another window, and emptied the magazine into a squad of Germans who were firing into a lower window. The red-hot barrel of the BAR turned purple and warped. Kelly discarded it and picked up a tommy gun, using it to keep the enemy at bay until nightfall.

At dawn Kelly climbed to the third floor and located a bazooka and six shells. Though not familiar with the weapon, he took it down to the second floor and fired a round into a building filled with Germans. Satisfied he could manage the weapon, he loaded it with the remaining shells and fired them into nearby homes occupied by the enemy. Finding an incendiary shell among the ammunition, he set a nearby building on fire and picked off the Germans as they fled.

Having depleted the bazooka ammo, Kelly fished through the pile of ordnance until he came across a box of 60mm mortar shells. He knew nothing about the shells, but he had watched the firing of mortars in training and knew that the shells had a safety pin that controlled the propelling charge and a cap that set off the explosion when the shell hit the ground. He pulled the safety pin, certain that nothing would happen until he pulled the second pin, but the pin stuck. He tapped the shell on a ledge, and out came the pin. He now believed he held a live shell, something he could use as a big hand grenade, but only if it landed nose first. He spotted a number of Germans creeping down a ravine and, rearing back, he held the shell like a football and hurled it out of the window. It soared through the air, plummeted into the ditch, and exploded. When the smoke and dust cleared, those who had joined him at the window observed a pile of German bodies crumpled in the ravine.

Every time a German detail came within range of Kelly's throwing arm, it was hit with a mortar shell. And when he ran out of mortars, he found a 37mm anti-tank gun, carried it into the courtyard, and fired it into the advancing enemy until an officer ordered him back inside. By nightfall, he had burned up another BAR and now had but one still useable.

When the ranking officer organized the American survivors into groups of six for the purpose of escape, Kelly remained behind with several marksmen to cover the withdrawal. When the last of the men took to the woods, Kelly could not locate his unit. Two days later he and his men turned up at Company L, by which time their commander had given them up for dead.

For services rendered on September 13, 1943, Corporal Charles E. Kelly received the Medal of Honor. Like so many veterans who returned to civilian life after the war, his neighbors in Louisville, Kentucky, found it hard to believe that such a pleasant, easy-going family man could be the famous "Commando" Kelly.

On June 6, 1944 (D-Day), Allied forces under the command of General Dwight D. Eisenhower landed on the

beaches of Normandy. During the battle through France, sixty-one soldiers earned the Medal of Honor, among them Audie Murphy, whose war began in November, 1942, when the 3rd Infantry Division went ashore in North Africa. Over the next thirty months the 3rd fought in Tunisia, Sicily, central Italy, Anzio, and France. It became among the five hardest hit U.S. divisions, with a turnover of personnel of 201.6 percent. By the end of January, 1945, one company had only two men left from the 235 who had come ashore at Casablanca. One of them was Murphy, who had risen from private to 2nd lieutenant while accumulating twenty-four decorations, including the Medal of Honor.

Many of the men who earned medals never lived to get them. At Betio in the Tarawa atoll, First Lieutenant William D. Hawkins, commanding his regiment's 2nd Scout-Sniper Platoon, landed on the island ahead of the first wave of Marines. His mission was to take out enemy machine gun emplacements on a sea wall located between two landing beaches. Using a flame thrower and grenades, he and his men cleared the pier and charged inland, attacking pillboxes and fortified positions throughout the day and into the night.

In the morning, the regimental commander gave him another difficult assignment – to knock out a group of machine guns enfilading a battalion of Marines from pillboxes. While his men laid down a covering fire, Hawkins ran from one pillbox to another rolling grenades through the firing slits. Mortar shrapnel bit into his body but he kept on going, shoving a corpsman away and saying, "I came here to kill Japs, not to be evacuated." A short time later, an explosive shell fired from a machine gun hit him in the shoulder and bled him out. Hawkins died quickly, and the Medal of Honor went to his parents.

Twenty-seven men who fought on Iwo Jima received the Medal of Honor. Private First Class Douglas T. Jacobson was one of them. After six days of relentless battle, he decided to end the fight single-handedly after sniper fire killed his buddy. With uncontrollable fury, Jacobson picked up his sidekick's bazooka, jumped up, ran toward a 20mm gun position, and blew it up. Still madder than hell, he shot a rocket into a pillbox and, running down the line, shot another one in a blockhouse. After killing seventy-five Japanese, he sat down to catch his breath, asking himself, "What the hell got into me?"

Ernie Pyle spoke for every veteran when he said, "I believe that I have a new patience with humanity that I've never had before.... I don't see how any survivor of the war can ever be cruel to anything, ever again."

Such were the lives of fighting men – common men, kind and wholesome men – who carried a spark deep inside called uncommon valor.

Left: Pfc Luther Skaggs, Jr. (Henderson, Kentucky), of 3rd Marine Division, received the Medal of Honor for gallantry at Guam. He fought on for eight hours after his leg was shattered. The award was presented on June 15, 1945.

Below: Major (subsequently Lt. Col.) John L. Smith (Lexington, Oklahoma) of Marine Fighting Squadron 223) was awarded the Medal of Honor on February 24, 1943, for outstanding heroism as commanding officer of his squadron in the Solomons Islands area, where he accounted for sixteen enemy warplanes downed.

AWAY FROM THE FRONT

On April 17, 1941, seven months before Pearl Harbor, concerned individuals in Washington established the United Services Organization – the USO – to provide recreational activities for the young men called into the service. Six major national organizations became partners in the enterprise, the YMCA and YWCA, the Salvation Army, the National Travelers Aid Association, and two public service organizations from the Catholic and Jewish faiths. Though the USO's activities were placed under the general direction of the Army and the Navy, the founding delegates agreed to finance the organization through voluntary contributions. In exchange, the government agreed to make available three hundred buildings across the country. The founders could not possibly have envisioned the financial demands of the future. Nor could the creation of the USO have come at a more propitious time. Millions of men and 200,000 women were about to join or be called into the service.

The concept of the USO took wings twelve days after its inception when Billy Rose, one of the greatest names in show business, began presenting shows for draftees assigned to military bases around the country. When the summer of 1941 came to an end, USO camp show attendances had numbered more than three million. By the time the war ended in August, 1945, attendances by servicemen and women, at home and overseas, had reached 161,000,000, and performances 293,738.

After the war started and men went abroad, the USO took their shows to the battlefield. Soldiers, sailors, and Marines did not need to leave their stations to see Bob Hope, Danny Kaye, Mickey Rooney, Jane Froman, Marlene Dietrich, Glenn Miller, and hundreds of other movie stars and entertainers, because the USO put the

Below: 10,000 GIs watch the Copacabana All Girl Review as they sing on the stage of the Glenn Miller Theater near Marseilles late in the war in Europe. Groups such as this traveled all over the theaters of war.

Below Right: In October, 1945, Danny Kaye entertains 4,000 men of the 5th Marine Division's occupation troops at Sasabo, Japan. The words chalked on the base of the stage read, "Officers keep out! Enlisted Men's country."

shows on the decks of aircraft carriers and took them right into bases and airfields in Great Britain, Morocco, Hawaii, Australia, Guadacanal and New Guinea. Wherever Bing Crosby went, he brought a "White Christmas." Duke Ellington traveled on the "A-Train," Glenn Miller came on the "Pennsylvania 65000," while the Andrews Sisters came in "Apple Blossom Time" with "One Meat Ball" and the "Boogie Woogie Bugle Boy." Marlene Dietrich formed her own troupe and took it everywhere, including Greenland, where no service-man in his right mind would apply for a three-day pass to visit the island's igloos. Singers like Jane Froman, Jo Stafford, and the Andrews Sisters put on five shows a day, seven days a week and did it fifty weeks of the year.

The first USO shows abroad went to London during the summer of 1943, taking Kay Francis, Martha Raye, Mitzi Mayfair, and Carole Landis. From there they went to North Africa and Italy. When Jo Bernier and her girls were not in Alaska, they were in Europe, right behind the front lines, living in tents and tapping their way into the hearts of men until their

feet hurt. Some of the girls went with soldiers onto the battlefield. One even fired a mortar at the enemy. When the war in Europe ended, Jo Bernier was still there and in the thick of the victory celebration.

Not all servicemen spent their R&R time at USO shows. The typical GI in Great Britain spent his off-duty hours in the town pub, an important part of every

Above: On April 13, 1945, in Kist, Germany, PFC Mickey Rooney imitates some Hollywood actors for an audience of infantrymen from the 44th Division. Rooney is part of a three-man team making a jeep tour to entertain the troops.

Left: Sultry Marlene Dietrich risked more than any other American performer when she came to Europe to entertain the troops. Being a natural-born German, she might have found herself in a bundle of trouble if captured by the SS.

Above: Frances Langford, flanked by Vera Vague, Bob Hope, Jerry Colonna, Tony Romano, and Wendell Niles, sings to wounded veterans at the Naval Hospital at Coco Solo, Canal Zone.

replied, "You're sore because you're underpaid, under-sexed and under Eisenhower."

Because of the great shortage of labor in Britain, girls were imported from all over the country to work the farms. They were called the "land army girls," and if GIs needed a little recreation, they would make their way to one of the hostels where the lasses billeted. The dances started early, were closely supervised, and ended early, because for six days a week the girls worked the fields from sunrise to late afternoon. If couples danced too closely, a buxom matron would run her hand between the dancers and growl, "Break!" But if a guy and a girl wanted to get together, they would usually find someway to do it.

Even the land army girls could not keep pace with the influx of American soldiers. By January, 1944, one million GIs were in Britain – twelve American divisions living in English cantonments. Great Britain reached the brink of its second wartime crisis – not enough women to entertain the invasion from the other side of the pond.

Somewhere between the fifteenth and twentieth mission, operational fatigue began to incapacitate a bomber crew. When an airman's eyes glazed over like he had lost his purpose in life, he became what flyers called "flak-happy" and suffered what doctors called severe emotional strain. For "flak-happy"

community and usually, from opening to closing, the center of local activity. The locals flocked to get their pint of bitter, light ale, or "arf an' arf." As one GI observed, "In such an atmosphere of timelessness, it was no wonder that... young American servicemen stood out like a sore thumb because he was always a busy and energetic person, prying in behind those solid English doors and, as a rule, being very well treated. It wasn't until a year or so later that the British began to resent the American invasion... and whispers began that we were 'overpaid, over-sexed, overbearing, and over here.'" To such allegations, some GIs

Right: On June 17, 1942, a group of African-American GIs relax at a pub near Hemel Hempstead, England, and chat with the landlord and a local "bobby" after a training march.

victims, the Air Force created for airmen the so-called "flak shack," which was not a shack at all but a lovely country estate where fliers received rest, fine food, casual exercise, sociable company, and a taste of the good life. Those who took leave and escaped the "flak-shack" went to London or sought out-of-the-way drinking establishments frequented by young women looking for a good time. Some men just hung around the base, enjoying USO shows and the girls trucked in by bus from nearby towns.

Airman Page never went farther than Norwich, a short bicycle ride from the air base, in the east of England. He met a girl at the Sampson and Hercules dance hall whose father maintained aircraft engines at the air base. She worked as a telephone operator and had two brothers serving on destroyers in the Royal Navy. She pleased Page so much that he never became "flak-happy." Instead, he got permission from the commanding officer and married the girl. Page was not unique. There were thousands of Americans just like him.

After the invasion of Normandy, every infantry battalion of the 29th Army Division received a few days' rest near a small village close to the battlefield. The village, however, was off-limits, and a cordon of grim-faced MPs with white belts, gloves, leggings, helmet liners, and arm bands patrolled the area to keep the soldiers out. To minimize the off-duty

Above: At the Dove Inn at Burton Bradstock, Dorset, England, GIs get tipsy with the locals at a pub well stocked with ale and "arf and arf."

soldier's temptation to "go on the prowl," temporary camps established on abandoned farms provided entertainment. Century-old barns and stables became the soldiers' movie theater. Film reels broke, projector bulbs failed, but for the most part every GI enjoyed the brief respite from the battlefield. One member of the Red Cross watched a Spencer Tracy movie with an outfit from the 175th Infantry, writing later, "I thoroughly enjoyed a picture while sitting for an hour and a half on a bale of horse manure." Under the circumstances, she probably had a choice seat.

When the USO went to Naples, Broadway star Ella Logan went with it. The show took place so close to the front that the sounds of artillery could be heard

Left: An American airman pays for seats at a London cinema for him and his glamorous English date, under the gaze of Errol Flynn. He and his buddies sought many forms of escape from the war for a few hours. While the reasonably well-off GIs may have pleased their socially deprived girlfriends, some British menfolk resented the "overpaid, over-sexed, and over here" U.S. servicemen.

Above: GIs at the Rainbow Corner Red Cross Club in Paris celebrate after buying the special edition of the *Paris Post*, which carried the long-awaited headline "Japs Quit."

in the distance. During one evening performance she packed the boys into a local theater, gave them a marvelous show, and closed by saying that she had wanted to bring them the "spirit of their mothers, sweethearts, or wives."

Out of the darkness came a tall, blond soldier covered with mud. He still carried his rifle and helmet, and his eyes reflected all the strain of battle. A hush fell over the audience as he walked to the stage and then up the stairs to where Ella stood. He gently took the mike from her hand, muttering that he would like to say something. With a slightly unsteady voice, he looked her straight in the eyes and said, "I've got to contradict you, Miss Logan. You don't look like anyone's sweetheart. You don't look like anyone's wife. And God knows, you don't look like anyone's mother." When he lifted her chin, she saw tears in his eyes. He leaned over and kissed her on the forehead, and

said softly, "You look like an angel." Spellbound, the theater lay hushed as the soldier clambered down the stairs, stole down aisle, and disappeared into the night.

On January 16, 1945, James C. Fry took took 350th Infantry Regiment of the 88th "Blue Devil" Division into Montecatini, Italy, for a wintry week of R&R. For most, it was the first shower and change of clothes the boys had enjoyed for weeks. But what soldiers seldom witness on the front lines is what lies behind them – half-starved families having neither food nor money.

A few flurries fell that day outside the mess hall, and standing at the end of the line were dozens of hungry waifs waiting for scraps to take home to their families. Fry observed a small blonde girl about eight years old standing in front of the group and clutching a small pail. She patiently watched as the soldiers piled high their mess kits. Fry studied her for a few moments and began to feel a sudden clutching in his throat. He walked into the mess, picked up a large piece of bread, smothered it with butter and jam, and walked it back to the girl with the pail. He stood for a moment waiting for her to eat it, but she gave the tasty morsel a woeful stare and dropped it into the bucket. Fry then realized that the girl had instructions from her parents to not eat anything, but to bring home whatever food she could grub. He continued to watch her, and noticed how men as they finished their meal would pass by and scrape their scraps into her bucket, dumping

Right: On September 24, 1942, Marines on Guadacanal go to the posted "Latest News." One GI points to the location of Japan on the map, while the chap on the right seems more interested in the baseball scores.

Left: Ted C. Needham has acquired quite a collection of Japanese souvenirs at Saipan. With a captured enemy machine gun in one hand and a Japanese pastel parasol in the other, the rugged Coast Guard defender probably has plans to ship the kimono draped around his shoulders and the other loot home to his girlfriend.

everything on top of the buttered and jammed bread. "She was barefooted," Fry observed, "and snow was beginning to fall. Occasionally she would lift a foot and rub it against her leg." When her pail was full, she scampered away. He then realized that the men in the regiment always took a little more than they could eat to feed the children.

Ernie Pyle noticed that wherever Americans went in this new bewildering and foreign world, they always befriended war's ragged and crestfallen children, giving them candy bars, chewing gum, and sometimes a handful of rations in exchange for a grateful smile. But wherever else the soldier went, he manifested a strong craving for drink and feminine companionship, sometimes in off-limits establishments. The easiest way for a soldier to lose his hard-earned stripes was to be caught drunk and disorderly in an unauthorized area by the Military Police and put on report. The loss of pay always hurt more than the loss of stripes, and most of the men obeyed the rules.

In the Pacific, downtown Honolulu presented an interesting spectacle on weekends when hundreds of servicemen

Below: Americans practise amphibious operations after debarking from an LCI at Nelson's Bay, New South Wales, Australia. After a hot day of training, they'll have a short pass to visit a nearby town, competing with tough Australians for the gals.

Right: Crew members from the U.S.S. *Altamama* relax with a bottle of beer and a cigarette on a beach at the fleet recreation park at Espiritu Santo in the New Hebrides.

congregated on the street outside the city's Recreation Center and waited for the girls to come and the dancing to start. The town merchants knew where to put their businesses. May Cohn sold uniforms on the corner. Between her store and the Recreation Center was Playland, which offered attractions not found next door. On the other side of the Center was Ray Kahne's Jewelry Mart, where servicemen had the choice of buying a bauble for an alluring hula girl or a gift for the loved one left behind. MPs and SPs (Shore Patrol), aware that most of the men wore few if any stripes on their sleeves, kept a close watch on the area as girls began to make their nightly debut. Unlike in Great Britain, few relationships ended in marriage.

On Christmas Day, 1941, the light cruiser *Marblehead* stopped at Surabaja in the Dutch colony of Java. A group of enlisted men went ashore and soon got mixed up with a fortune teller. All the sailors were impressed by the wisdom of the soothsayer except Shipfitter Bernard J. Wardzinski, who refused to go near the man. Wardzinski said he already knew his fortune, and when pressed by his friends to reveal it, he answered, "I'm going to die...soon [and] I don't need this guy to rub it in." Having heard Wardzinski's remark, the seer assured the others that, "Soon all of you will be in a great battle, in which many will be killed." After living through a severe bombing, Wardzinski died from poisonous gas in a flooded compartment. Others died, too, but at the time nobody admitted to taking the fortune teller seriously. One sailor recalled, however, that "it sure scared the hell out of some of us."

Right: The late and beloved Ernie Pyle, the Scripps-Howard columnist who followed the war from Europe to Okinawa, shares a cigarette with men from the 1st Marine Division a few days before he was killed by Japanese machine gun fire.

Machinist's Mate Dale Johnson loved his wife very much and thought she would be pleased with a few gifts from the Dutch Indies. He shopped about and spent a bundle of money on exotically painted curios. When he got back to the ship he noticed small stickers pasted to the back of each item. Inked in tiny blue letters were the words "Made in U.S.A."

During the early months of the war, Darwin, Australia, became one of the Allies' staging areas in the South Pacific. Most sailors had never been there before, and when *Marblehead* received orders for Darwin, the crew rejoiced at the opportunity to get ashore for some badly needed feminine attention. What they found was a "bleak, barren town about three blocks long and two blocks wide." It reminded them of an old western frontier town, except that the buildings were made of corrugated iron. Owners had boarded up all the windows to keep drunks from throwing beer bottles through the panes. The rainy season had just begun, and the town's streets ran like a sea of red mud. Captain A. G. Robinson turned to his executive officer and said, "Look at this God-forsaken place. It hasn't one redeeming feature."

But, for the enlisted man, every shore leave had at least one redeeming characteristic. They trundled into Darwin's dinky restaurants, drank large quantities of beer, ordered a big steak for the main course, and then ordered another for dessert. Three of the sailors from the engine room got into a fight with each other and ended up in the ship's sick bay. Assistant Medical Officer T. C. Ryan expressed his disapprobation by withholding anesthetics when he sewed up their scalps. By the time the stitches were in, the men were sharing Lucky Strikes again.

Darwin became a base for the Army and the Navy, and the headquarters for the Air Forces in the Far East. Marines used it as a staging area for the invasion of the Solomons. Not until the Japanese pulled out of Guadalcanal did Marines on the island get a leave and, more often than not, it was a sick leave with a trip back to Darwin. "We were [physically] beat," Warner Pyle recalled. "That constant strain of combat, the lousy diet and, above

all, the goddamn malaria had turned us into scarecrows. We were a mess."

Some malarial recovery cases went to Melbourne, where the typical male native on the street was either less than eighteen or more than fifty – the other Aussies being with the ANZACS, fighting on both fronts. A Marine on Guadacanal did not collect his pay until leaving the island, and now he had a bundle of cash to blow. "You got PFCs taking a suite at the Hotel Australia," one Marine recalled. "A girl wants to go to dinner – okay, honey, where to? These guys are taking the dolls to the best places in town. You never saw a Marine without a beauty on his arm, maybe two."

While 1st Division Marines enjoyed the companionship of the Melbourne girls, thousands of ANZACs came home. "Hell," said a Marine, "they'd been away fighting the Germans for two or three years. What do they find – these bloody Yanks with their women. What a battle! They had those big boots and we had our

Above: On February 12, 1944, an Army Pictorial Service Photographer caught this picture of a "Duck" set fire by German shells at Nettuno, Italy.

Below: A group of African-American GIs serving with an Engineer Battalion show their Technical Sergeant the latest news – "Victory in Europe."

Above: On May 8, 1945, members of the Medium Automobile Maintenance Ordnance Company, Third Army, at Dorfen, Germany, break out the beer to celebrate a victory toast to V-E Day.

sorts of bad things to follow. When they came on board, Lieutenant John P. Bracken, junior officer of the deck, asked the meaning of their tardiness. The soberest of the group replied, "We got drunk, sir." Bracken looked the boys over. They were dirty, tired, and weaving about on their feet. "This has been a lousy Christmas," said Bracken. "None of us have gotten any gifts. But I'm going to give you one. Go sleep it off with a happy heart. Nobody's name goes on report."

Many of the Marines that ended up in the Solomons received their pre-combat training at Camp McKay on North Island, New Zealand. Most of the country's young men were with the ANZACs, so the friendly New Zealanders reached out to the Marines and gave them a second home. The men obtained passes, developed strong ties with New Zealand families, and married local girls. One day the 8th Marines boarded transports to practise amphibious landings on an island in New Hebrides. Instead, they landed on Tarawa. Some of their names went to the Graves Registration Service, an organization established to keep track of those who died, even if their remains could not be found.

In places like Tarawa, Saipan, Iwo Jima, and Okinawa, nobody took time to pack the dead into coffins and send them home. After all identification had been stripped off the bodies, bulldozers dug deep trenches and buried the dead in mass graves. After the fighting stopped, a detail

belt buckles. There were fist fights all over town. Many of us thought we should have been given a combat star for the battle of Melbourne." With the girls, however, "there was plenty of hanky-panky going on," but there were also lasting relationships that led to marriage.

During one Christmas of loneliness, a group of sailors went ashore on an island in the Dutch Indies and got "thoroughly soused on Bols gin." Their passes expired at 9:30 p.m., but none of the men was in condition to heed the time. When the Shore Patrol rounded them up and hauled them back to the ship, every sailor envisioned being put on report with all

Right: Hundreds of New Yorkers gather at Times Square to celebrate V-E Day while the theater in the rear advertises the film "Maidanek," held over by popular demand to reveal to the world Nazi atrocities.

came through, planted small crosses, and looped dog tags over each cross. Sailors received a traditional burial. Regardless of rank, a seaman's grave was the sea.

On March 3, 1945, forces under MacArthur killed the last of 20,000 Japanese defending Manila and took possession of the city. Fighting continued to persist south of the city as MacArthur pressed forward to clean out pockets of resistance. Tankers could not penetrate the jungles in southeastern Luzon and spent weeks of idleness caught between the front and the base at Manila. There was not much to do, recalled Tom Howard of the 754th Tank Battalion, so, "We learned to live off the land. We fixed fish by drying, [and] we boiled... dried sugar cane... and made sugar bar candy." Others dug wild peanuts and sweet potatoes, cooking the batch into a paste, drying it, and later mixing everything together with water to make a soup. Using bows and arrows provided by Filipinos, the tankers became hunters, amusing themselves by killing wild chickens and cockatoos for meat. Fruits and berries grew all over the jungle, but some were poisonous. Filipinos taught the men to capture monkeys and use them

to test the edibility of each fruit. If monkeys rejected the treat, it would probably be poisonous. Having no enemy to kill, the tankers had found ways to kill time. They did not mind. They had been in 112 days of continuous combat without a break.

On VJ-Day, August 15, 1945, the war came to an official end, although fighting continued for many weeks on some of the isolated islands in the Pacific. Most American soldiers, sailors, and Marines finally got a rest, but they had nowhere to go to celebrate. Eventually, many of them landed in Japan as an occupation force and for the first time viewed the horrible bomb damage inflicted upon Hirohito's cities. Nothing, however, compared to the scene at Hiroshima and Nagasaki. Donald Cortright went to Hiroshima shortly after the war ended, and in a letter home, wrote, "My God, oh my God! I'll never forget that sight as long as I shall live." From the center of the city he looked about and said, "I cannot use enough superlatives to describe that awful scene to you. Around us lie about six square miles of nothingness. Just rubble... piled about two feet high."

The Red Cross established several

Above: On August 15, 1945, in Sydney, a sailor with the U.S. Navy performs an impromptu duet with an Australian digger during victory in the Pacific celebrations in the city.

hospitals outside Hiroshima where American nurses and medics worked with Japanese and American doctors to save the people suffering from radiation. Most of the civilians who survived the blast soon fell sick. On August 20, Mrs. Nakamura, who had suffered no cuts or burns, began combing her hair. Clumps fell out, so she stopped combing. Four days later she became bald. Mr. Tanomoto, who lived in the suburb of Ushida, lay shivering with fever in a bedroll on the floor of his half-wrecked home. Perfectly healthy physicians and Red Cross workers in Hiroshima and Nagasaki became ill with the same sickness. White blood counts plummeted to half normal. Then came spot hemorrhages. A doctor treating the patients confided to a Mother Superior at the Red Cross Hospital, "All these bomb people will die – you'll see. They go for a couple of weeks and then they die." Not all died. By November, 137,000 of Hiroshima's former inhabitants were building shacks outside the city that had been their home.

The Army sent Lieutenant John D. Montgomery, of Kalamazoo, to Hiroshima to form a planning commission and decide what the new city should be. With more than 92,000 people killed or missing and another 37,000 dying, the young lieutenant could find no place to start. His planning commission

stumbled about the city, every day uncovering hundreds of bodies baked in the ashes. "Hiroshima," said Montgomery, "was a graveyard. There was nothing to do but be sickened by the horror and devastation surrounding us." Montogmery laid down a few new streets, got the electrical and water systems running, and then went home, disconsolate and lightly radiated.

But earlier, in Europe, the place to be on VE-Day was on leave in Paris. Hotels were jammed with servicemen. Some of them were enjoying their first good bath in weeks when the bells started ringing, horns blew, and pandemonium erupted on the streets below. Corporal Bill Wilson from Cleveland, Ohio, jumped back into his freshly cleaned and pressed uniform, bounded down the stairway, and pressed through the doors of the old Hotel Du Paris to the street. "I hadn't gotten three steps through the door," said Wilson, "when some girl grabbed me and kissed me. Then I realized it was going on all over town. Everybody kissing everybody, so I said to myself 'what the hell' and grabbed a girl near me and gave her one helluva smacker. She kinda reeled back and said, 'I think you a bad boy,' and then she gave me another one that I don't think I'll ever forget."

Wilson had never seen so many people in one place in his life, not even on D-Day when he had come across the Channel and landed on Utah Beach. Lights in Paris came alive that had not been lit for years, bottles of wine passed through the crowd, musicians blared horns from windows and balconies. "You'd think it was New Year's Eve in Central Park," Wilson recalled, but the crowning memory occurred early in the evening.

"I went to a park where someone had turned on a fountain, and there were men and women standing under the spray and kissing, so I waded in with my freshly polished shoes and nice clean uniform and grabbed the first girl not wrapped up with some other guy. Then more girls waded in, and the pool began to fill, and before I knew it, I had to take my wallet out of my pants and shove it in my shirt because by butt was getting wet. I was trying to button my shirt when some gal grabbed me and we both took a tumble into the water. Well, we got up laughing, and the girl was so damned cute, wet hair and all, that we dragged ourselves out of the water, went into a restaurant dripping wet, and had ourselves a good, hot meal. I can't tell you what happened next, but it was a hell of a good night. If more wars ended like this, we'd be fighting all the time."

Without the correspondents who covered the war, the intimate relations between the fighting man and his new military environment might have gone untold. They provided the human side of the war. American magazines and newspapers sent seven hundred correspondents abroad to cover the camps, the foxholes, the fighting ships, and the battlefields. They flew in bombers over Germany, went ashore with the Army at Normandy, rolled across France on tanks of the 3rd Armored Division, landed with the Marines on Iwo Jima, rode by mule across Sicily, and plodded by foot through the jungles of New Guinea and Bougainville. They wrote the story of the war through the perspective of the American soldier and kept the folks at home informed every mile along the way. Between 1942 and 1945, they sent home more than five hundred million words. Through them, every father, mother, child and sweetheart came to know men like MacArthur, Eisenhower, Halsey, Spaatz, Spruance, Nimitz, Patton, Bradley, and Vandergrift, the commanders who looked after their loved ones in the service.

The men and women who fought in the war told their own stories best through the millions of letters they sent home. Without them, the human side of the war would have been lost to posterity. The fear, pain, exhaustion, dirt, filth, stench, and bloodied fields experienced by millions of fighting men may have passed into oblivion. But what meant the most to the folks at home were the words, "We've been in a hard fight, mother, but I came out of it in good shape. I think the war is about over." The American fighting man never tried to understand tactics and strategy. He just did what he was told, and he did it well.

Left: One of the most famous pictures of the war was taken on the streets of New York when a sailor, having learned of the surrender of Japan, took hold of a nurse and gave her a kiss; the image joins with the raising of flag on Iwo Jima as one of the classic photographs of the war.

UNDERCOVER HEROES

Right: General William J. "Wild Bill" Donovan, a legendary World War I hero who had won the Medal of Honor, was a ruddy-faced Wall Street lawyer when President Roosevelt called him to Washington and urged him to organize what became the Office of Strategic Services (OSS). Here, Donovan is seen during a visit to Detachment 404, Frankfort Place and Kandy in July 1945.

U nlike Great Britain, the United States had much to learn about the spy business. In 1940, at Churchill's request, President Roosevelt sent an old friend, William J. "Wild Bill" Donovan, to meet with British intelligence. Though Donovan's credentials as a prominent attorney may not have qualified him as the best choice for the job, he was a highly decorated officer from World War I, having received the Medal of Honor, the Distinguished Service Cross, the Distinguished Service Medal, and the Purple Heart with two oak-leaf clusters. More importantly, Donovan was a person whom Roosevelt trusted.

At the time, the United States had no director of intelligence and no concept of what was required to develop a central agency. Each of the armed services operated its own intelligence branch, as did some departments of the government, but no vehicle existed for unifying and distributing collected intelligence. After Donovan brought back glowing reports of the British system, Roosevelt felt he needed to craft a centralized intelligence unit.

In July, 1941, Roosevelt named Donovan as Coordinator of Information (COI), a department which soon outgrew itself the moment America entered World War II. On June 13, 1942, the COI's propaganda activities were transferred to the Office of War Information. Donovan

stayed on to head the Office of Strategic Services (OSS), which was put where it belonged, under the Joint Chiefs of Staff. When peace came in 1945, the OSS had 30,000 persons operating in a multiplicity of top secret roles throughout the world.

Donovan organized the OSS into four branches of intelligence, the largest being Research and Analysis (R&A), which digested intelligence and reported it objectively. The other branches did everything else. They ran spies, engaged in sabotage, supported resistance groups in occupied countries, conducted raids of their own, and planted false information. They were supported in this work by highly skilled technicians, men like the fictional "M" in James Bond movies. They provided agents with miniature cameras, custom-made radios, special weapons, and a variety of unique gadgets designed to meet the requirements of the mission. Although the OSS operated in all theaters

Below: An OSS technical officer examines some of the many weapons developed and used by the outfit, including the silenced M3 smg, silenced .22-cal pistol, Liberator pistols, clam mines, spring cosh, detonator delay devices, and small objects such as time pencils and incendiary devices that could be carried in operatives' pockets.

of war, it was most effective in North Africa and Europe.

General Eisenhower had not quite decided what to think of Donovan's OSS until he arrived in Great Britain for his first chat with Winston Churchill. While dining at Chequers, Churchill's country home, the prime minister gradually introduced Ike to the wizard world – the silent, unseen, and most intense battle between Great Britain and Germany to uncover each other's secrets. Already, Britain's Special Operations Executive (SOE), a branch of the secret service, had underground operatives working in Poland, France, and Norway, agents in Germany, and saboteurs infiltrating Holland and Belgium. Many of them were highly trained, multi-lingual civilian agents and amateur adventurers, not military personnel.

Then came Ultra. Churchill called it the most valuable secret of the war. Before he said more, he made Eisenhower promise to never go into a war zone or fly over one. Churchill exposed no one to Ultra without demanding the same promise because the Germans had methods for prying information out of captured prisoners.

The Germans believed they had developed an impenetrable and unbreakable encoding machine, one they called Enigma. It consisted of two machines similar to

electric typewriters but connected together through three rotating drums. An operator could type a clear message, set the drums to scramble it, and transmit it in code. To unscramble the message, the receiver used the same Enigma settings and produced a clear typewritten page. The Germans believed that if the enemy captured an Enigma machine, the message could never be unscrambled without knowing the exact settings, which approached being infinite in number.

Listening to the dummy message was simple; it was sent by radio in plain German with the secret message coded and embedded. German confidence emanated from Enigma's ability to produce several million different cipher alphabets by merely changing the keying. The British broke the system using two Enigma machines stolen by Polish intelligence agents in 1939, and the Germans did not know it. All of this work was accomplished through the use of spies, double-agents, traitors, and Britain's own technical experts. At Bletchley Park in England, scientists then built what was thought to be the first computer, which allowed operators to break into the key and read most German messages, though days were sometime lost deciphering. Espionage, however, worked both ways, and the Germans were also breaking the British codes.

Churchill said he used Ultra discriminately, since he did not want the Germans to suspect that their code had been broken. Yet, when enemy

Above: Weapons such as these were supplied and used by the OSS and Britain's SOE for emergencies and silent killing. On the left is the Liberator, a .45-cal single-shot smoothbore designed for partisans. It is shown with packing case, simple visual instructions, and wooden ejector rod. Top right is the Welrod 9mm single-shot silenced pistol, accurate at 15-30 yards. Below it is the High Standard Model H-D .22-cal semi-automatic pistol. Bottom is the High Standard Model B .22-cal semi-auto pistol.

Left: Comdr. George L. "Gravey" Graveson, CV(S),USNR, OSS Communications branch, worked behind the scenes, as did most OSS officers, coordinating covert operations in France that led to the liberation of Paris.

Above: The OSS recruited Sicilian-Americans, taught them covert warfare, made them into paratroopers, and on July 11, 1943, began dropping them into the Sicilian countryside at night.

Above Right: "Lucky" Luciano never became a war hero, but he used his connections from his jail cell to help the OSS recruit men from "Murder, Inc." to serve as operatives working behind the lines in Italy.

Right: At left background in picture is Lieutenant Ray Kellogg, USNR, OSS officer in charge of a fast patrol boat operating in North African waters from 1944.

paratroopers dropped secretly into Crete, the British, though militarily weak in the area, inflicted casualties severe enough to make a less arrogant enemy suspicious that their code had been violated.

During the Battle of the Atlantic, Ultra led planes and destroyers to German submarine "wolf packs." When preparing for D-Day, Ultra gave Eisenhower pinpoint information of the size and deployment of German troops. And, in August, 1944, Ultra warned the Allies of the time and location of the German counterattack, enabling American forces to stop the assault in its tracks. Ultra became probably the best kept secret of the war. Not until 1974 did any but the highest ranking officers in the services know of its existence, and when its secrets were revealed hundreds of exasperated World War II historians had to go back and rewrite their books.

Eisenhower quickly realized that the Allies had a tool of immense value, so he put it to work with Donovan's OSS to set the stage for Operation Torch, the invasion of North Africa. Attacking North Africa became a difficult choice for Roosevelt. Polls showed that the American public considered Japan their number one enemy – only 34 percent nominated the Germans. Invasion became doubly difficult because the American landing sites at Algeria, Oran, Casablanca, and Safi were

controlled by the Vichy French.

Donovan had sent Marine Col. William A. Eddy to Tangiers in September, 1941, and already had American Consul Robert Murphy and other operatives there to pave the way for Torch. Eddy's OSS organization in Oran and Algeria, however, failed to disrupt Vichy control, and when the Americans landed on the wrong beach they found themselves fighting the French before they could fight the Germans. In the meantime, the French allowed Germans to come into Tunis and no French officer in Algiers would issue orders to resist.

The early shortcomings of the OSS in North Africa had nothing to do with Ultra and everything to do with their own bumbling among Frenchmen with different political ambitions. Neither Eddy nor his OSS partner, Murphy, could bring three Frenchmen competing for individual power together. Eisenhower resolved the issue more by force of arms than by negotiation, and the final outcome pushed the OSS farther up the learning curve.

When planning the invasion of Sicily, the OSS recruited the Mafia through "Lucky" Luciano, who was in prison in New York for crimes that included racketing in prostitution. If Luciano would use his connections to get the Mafia in Sicily to cooperate with the OSS, the Office of Naval Intelligence promised to petition the governor for executive clemency. Luciano agreed. The conspiracy worked marvelously because there were millions of Americans of Italian descent who could speak the language fluently.

Donovan searched for an ideal volunteer for the mission and found Max Corvo, an army private of Sicilian descent. Corvo added 12 more Sicilian-Americans and two lawyers to his team to recruit spies and act as organizers in Sicily. The OSS officer who trained Corvo's team recalled that some of the men came from Murder, Inc., and Philadelphia's "Purple Gang."

Above: The OSS worked closely with indigenous resistance forces. Here, an OSS officer gives Free French Navy seamen instructions in the use of 75mm anti-aircraft artillery.

They all shared one characteristic. They were "tough little boys from New York and Chicago, with a few live hoods mixed in." They all seemed anxious "to get over to the old country and start throwing knives." When Corvo's group infiltrated Sicily, they did not find many local volunteers willing "to take a shot at their relatives." The scheme put a few operatives into Italy, where the OSS began engaging in covert activities, to which, since he had no knowledge of them, Eisenhower could hardly have given his approval.

After American forces landed in Italy, the OSS transferred most of their operations from Algiers to Caserta. Here they set up some of the first paramilitary teams, bringing in enormous quantities of arms, supplies, and equipment and distributing them to resistance groups in the Balkans and western Europe. This opened clandestine communications channels and paved the way for the overall acceptance of Donovan's activities in Europe.

Few people understood how Donovan's organization operated in the field. Edward Hymoff, a demolition expert, remembered working with the OSS in Italy and having "no immediate superior." He had been sent there to collect, coordinate, and supervise the shipment of supplies to OSS units in

Left: Casualty rates among OSS agents remained low, but five members of a Sussex team were caught, interrogated, and summarily executed by the Germans. Six others escaped.

Right: The French resistance was active in the days prior to D-Day. American Pvt. Winifred D. Enson (right), of Company B, 509th Parachute Infantry Battalion, thanks Marc Rainaut (left) for saving his life.

Yugoslavia. No questions would be asked unless the "equipment or weapons or demolitions didn't arrive on time to be sent off to destinations behind enemy lines. And," Hymoff recalled, "I was just a lowly Private First Class, about the last person who would carry any clout in an organization chock full of stripes and brass like OSS. Which was one of the things I liked about OSS. It was so un-military."

In 1943 the OSS began to train their operatives in much the same manner as did Britain's SOE, whose veterans had become experts at infiltration. The SOE worked hand-in-hand with resistance movements on the European continent and supplied them with arms, money, communications equipment, and on occasion, air support.

Donovan had his own ideas of what he expected of an operative. He preferred men who had been with airborne units because they had already accepted "hazardous duty behind enemy lines" and were physically fit. He liked bright young men, usually junior or non-commissioned officers who had experience of leading men and could speak at least one foreign language. He also liked lawyers, because they had been trained in guile and could convincingly talk themselves out of difficult situations. He ran candidates through a battery of interviews, tests, and psychological examinations before thrusting them into training for guerrilla warfare.

Right: At Milton Hall, England, Jeds go through intensive training with the British SOE. Here two Jeds scale a brick wall, using a rope fastened to a three-prong hook.

Some of the training areas had been established right under the noses of the public. The Congressional Golf Course in Washington served as a night-stalking area with sentry posts, railroad trestles, power transformers, and other appurtenances resembling those a guerrilla team would target when behind the lines. GIs surviving the course without being cut from the roster went on to a former boys' camp (now Camp David) in western Maryland for more training, this time in self-defense and weaponry from an officer of the SOE. His philosophy was simple: "A well-trained man had nothing to fear from close combat. Rather, if this man was properly armed, all nearby adversaries had everything to fear." For an operative to reach this level of competence he had to become so proficient with a variety of foreign weapons that he could use any one of them instinctively and hit a target without aiming at it.

Vernon A. Walters, who later rose to the grade of lieutenant general, got his early training at Camp Ritchie. He remembered being in class all day and spending every night working on map problems while "wandering around the Maryland countryside." Farmers in the area had given the Army permission to cross through their property, but, said Walters, "Not many of them expected us to move across their land in the middle of the night wearing German uniforms and helmets. More than once we were chased by angry farmers who thought that paratroopers had landed."

For American OSS agents, training continued in the Scottish Highlands where brisk winds swept off the Hebrides Sea and encrusted the heights with ice. SOE teams whipped operatives into shape by taking them on twenty-mile hikes across windswept moors, lugging a shoulder weapon, ammunition, and a loaded rucksack. One American trainee remembered wading through a half-frozen bog surrounded by ridges when mortar shells began falling too close for comfort. After a shell landed exactly where he had been lying, "I was on my feet and running low toward the ridge line, my heart thudding in my ears like a jackhammer." Running beside him was a cross-country star at West Point, probably the fastest runner in the group. "But," said the fleet-footed soldier, "he sure as hell couldn't catch me that morning."

After three more months of training, the operatives were broken into teams of three for infiltration into France. Each team consisted of a British or American officer, a French counterpart, and an enlisted radio operator. The team would parachute into a specific sector of France to organize, equip, train, and lead a French Maquis resistance group. The objective was to arm tens of thousands of resistance

volunteers to support the Allied invasion of France during the spring and summer of 1944. The mission carried the codename Jedburgh, and the individual units were called Jedburgh or Jed-teams. Once dropped behind enemy lines, each team would train a resistance group but keep it undercover until Eisenhower sprung the invasion. Then, while Allied forces attacked the Germans along the front, the Maquis, led by Jed-teams, would harass the enemy from the rear and disrupt their supply lines.

The SOE had been long at work behind enemy lines, but not on so grand a scale. They depended upon the classical wartime use of spies and saboteurs, but rendered it far more effective by employing aircraft and submarines to deliver the operatives. Both sides produced audacious special agents, trained in silent killing and equipped with gold coins, counterfeit notes, booby-trap devices, portable communications systems, and light weapons. Each tried to break into the other's systems, leading to a growth in the number of double-agents. Code messages directed to guerrilla organizations and sabotage groups were mixed with skillfully camouflaged propaganda broadcasts that seemed to originate inside German-occupied territory. The Germans were experts, but the British and Americans were better. One OSS agent planted a microphone in the *Luftwaffe's* Paris headquarters.

Yugoslavia, Greece, Albania, Italy, and most of France gradually filled up with Jed-teams of Englishmen and Americans who fought beside local partisans and transmitted detailed information on enemy dispositions, resulting in air strikes and

Left: Part of the Jed obstacle course includes a tower of connecting bars which agents in training must scale and descend in a specified amount of time.

Below: An important phase of Jed training included demolition of bridges and railroads behind enemy lines. At Milton Hall, England, new Jed members learn the tricks of the trade from experts.

Above: The OSS sent their operatives to the far reaches of the war. Here in Ceylon, OSS personnel take time out for a picture with the camp pin-ups.

Below: The valuable undercover and guerrilla training work carried out by the OSS teams in the Pacific area was recognized by British Admiral Lord Louis Mountbatten, Allied Supreme Commander in South East Asia, shown here visiting Detachment 404, Kandy.

Clifford Cole's B-17 lost two engines to flak before reaching the target. He dropped out of formation and turned back for England. The crippled aircraft attracted a swarm of German fighters, which the gun crews fought off until they ran out of ammunition. At 22,000 feet, with the left wing on fire and the volatile oxygen tank ruptured, the crew jumped. Cole lost consciousness when he began the descent but woke up just in time to see his B-17 explode in mid-air. When he landed on the ground he strained his back, but he managed to crawl into a pile of brush where he hid until dark. Then, using his button compass, he began a painful trek west, hiding and sleeping in hedgerows during the day. On the fourth day he fell into the hands of a friendly Belgian boy who turned him over to resistance volunteers specially trained to rescue downed pilots.

Cole endured quite an experience reaching safety. He hid in tunnels, caves, and attics. Dressed in country clothes and wearing wooden shoes provided by the Belgians, he traveled by bicycle and then by train to Brussels. There he stayed at a home adjacent to German military headquarters, which was cleaned daily by his hostess. The man of the house worked for the Brussels telephone company and spent his time "repairing the lines" so he could listen in on headquarters' conversations and relay intelligence to the OSS or SOE at Bletchley Park.

Belgian resistance verified Cole's American identity and issued him forged identification papers, a passport, a photograph, and a new set of civilian clothing. An undercover nurse in a white uniform took Cole to the train station and guided him into Paris, along with four other downed airmen. He stayed briefly at an apartment with a man who worked at a local plant that supplied trucks to the Germans. "He told me," said Cole, "that he and his fellow workers were sabotaging as many of the trucks as possible by filing deep scratches in the cylinders, pouring sugar in the gas tanks, and many other ingenious tricks."

The following evening another operative came and conducted Cole to a bus containing, among others, the same airmen he had seen on the train. After passing many

commando incursions. But there were differences in political strategies. The OSS believed that when working with resistance units, all political animosities should be suspended to fight a common enemy. Official British policy sided with a country's monarchy and supported those resistance groups who were royalists at heart. Because communist activity existed everywhere in Europe, the problem of local politics caused no end of trouble for the OSS.

The OSS, working with the SOE, planted agents in every country in Europe, and their activities encompassed more than local resistance and sabotage operations. During the 95th Bomb Group's August 12, 1943, raid on Bonn, Captain

checkpoints, the bus stopped at a farmhouse at the foothills of the Pyrenees Mountains. Even though he still had a tender back, Cole scaled the snow-covered range and spent the night in a winery outside the Spanish town of San Sebastian and the next day in a nearby barn. That night a car from the British embassy gathered up the men, took them into Madrid, gave them fresh clothes, and transported them to Gibraltar. A major came up from Cole's unit in Great Britain and ushered him back to England. There he learned that his entire crew had been taken prisoner, the exception being the tail gunner, who had gone down with the plane.

The OSS and SOE had established elaborate channels for getting downed flyers out of harm's way. Like Cole, hundreds of men were saved by well-organized resistance movements which were trained, armed, equipped, and provided with funds through the OSS and the SOE.

There were also double-agents in the field, as Leroy Lawson, a navigator with the 335th Squadron, soon discovered. After ditching his plane over Holland, the Dutch resistance found him and sent him to a house in Brussels. Everything went well until Lawson reached Paris, where a guide met him at the train station and ushered him into a room at a hotel three blocks away. "Wait here," said the guide, "I'll be back in a few minutes." Moments later the door burst opened. Three men brandishing Lugers snapped him up and said, "For you the war is over." The Gestapo threw Lawson in jail with two sergeants, both of whom grumbled that they had gotten to Paris through that same house in Brussels. After intensive questioning, mixed with threats of being shot as spies, the Germans sent Lawson and the other men to a prisoner of war camp, where they all remained for nineteen months.

Soon after Patton's Third Army captured Palermo, the OSS sent a team under Lieutenant John Shaheen, USNR, on a PT boat with a letter from the government "to a certain Rear Admiral (Massimo Girosi) in the Italian Navy." The letter offered favorable inducements to the admiral in exchange for surrendering the Italian fleet. Shaheen's mission was to land, deliver the letter through an agent,

and if possible bring someone from the admiral's staff back to parley. Lieutenant (jg.) Richard H. O'Brien took Shaheen's team up to the Gulf of Gaetei and on August 12, 1943, put them ashore north of Naples. The OSS agent disappeared into the woods but never returned to the boats waiting at the rendezvous. After a few weeks passed, confirmation came that the letter had been delivered, and soon afterwards, the Italian Navy surrendered.

The OSS recruited Turhan Celik, a sophomore at Robert College in Istanbul, to get chummy with a beautiful young lady who claimed to be married to a Canadian. His assignment, to find out whether she planned to leave the country. Celik could speak many languages fluently, including Italian, which had a special significance to the OSS because the lady was a German spy. Using the name Ted Andrews, he made love to her and won her confidence. As the affair progressed, she asked if he could help her obtain a passport to Canada. Celik passed the request to the OSS; it was

Above: OSS Maj. Peter J. Ortiz (third from right), a veteran of the French Foreign Legion and the U.S. Marine Corps, addresses a group of Maquis in Occupied France.

Below: In preparation for a drop into Occupied France, a Jedburgh team huddles for last minute radio instructions before departing on their mission.

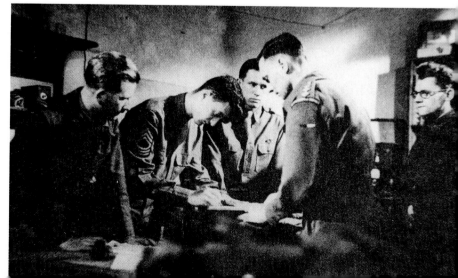

Above: At Area T, Harrington Airdrome, England, a Jed-team converges by the low-flying B-24 that will drop them behind enemy lines in Occupied France.

were problems. More than 5,000 resistance fighters followed Charles De Gaulle, calling themselves the *Forces Françaises de l'Interieur* (FFI). Another group, calling themselves the *Communist Franc Tireurs* et Partisans (FTP), had almost as many men under arms. Though the FTP usually cooperated with the Jed-teams, they resisted close alliances with the Gaullists. After D-Day, the OSS needed to bring the two resistance groups together for unified operations against the Germans and sent Jed-teams into occupied France to do it. One of these three-man teams was commanded by Lieutenant John K. Singlaub, who had been trained on the Congressional Golf Course in Washington, D.C., and in the Highlands of Scotland for exactly this type of mission.

On Friday, August 11, 1944, a British Stirling bomber flew over the Massif Central section of France and dropped Singlaub, French Lieutenant Jacques Le Bel de Penguilly, Technical Sergeant Tony Denneau, the radio operator, and cargo pods filled with weapons and ammunition into a field not far from the Corrèze River. With Singlaub's Jed-team came a ten-man reconnaissance detail of French Special Air Service (SAS) troops.

Before the air drop, the mission had been spelled out in detail. In the Corrèze section of Massif Central the Germans had several thousand veteran troops, supported by armor and artillery, posted in four heavily fortified garrisons along Highway 89. The Jed-team's objective was to close the road to the Germans and keep them off

exactly what they wanted, and they provided the documents. Celik later discovered how he had been used. The mysterious Austrian-Turkish beauty was actually a German spy responsible for the deaths of several American airmen shot down in Austria. She could not be touched in neutral Turkey, but the OSS had her arrested in Damascus, and the Syrians executed her. Not all operations had a pleasant ending.

By D-Day, Jed-teams formed by the OSS and the SOE had helped organize and equip eighty Maquis companies – 8,000 resistance fighters – in France, but there

Right: The OSS recruited men of foreign extraction because of their language skills. Here a former tsarist officer, multi-linguist Serge Obolensky (left), chats with fellow operatives before flying to Sardinia.

Left: OSS and SOE personnel, and agents trained by them, were frequently para-dropped behind enemy lines, or flown in at night by short take-off and landing light aircraft, such as these Stinson L-5s operating in Burma in May 1945.

General Patton's flank. To do this, Maquis units were to be trained in sabotage methods, ambush techniques, and in the use of weapons dropped in cargo pods. The team's other role was to lead the Maquis units in raids upon the Germans and keep the resistance supplied with ammunition by coordinating future weapons drops with London.

Men who operated behind enemy lines needed a facile mind, fluency in a foreign language, an ability to take command of any situation, and enough bluff to save their skins when confronted with adverse conditions. To eliminate the German threat along Highway 89, Singlaub knew that he needed to bring the Gaullists together with the communists in order to coordinate raids on the outposts. If the enemy could be driven out of any of their four strongholds and forced to take to the road, the others would follow. Ambushes could be set up along the highway and the enemy withdrawal blocked and bloodied.

The Germans held an almost impregnable position in the town of Egletons, between Brive-la-Gaillarde and Ussel. Marquis units had set up roadblocks around the town in an uneasy alliance with communist counterparts. The team faced a difficult situation. It needed to keep the

concentration of both factions on the enemy and not on each other. During the day-long attack on August 15, the Germans could not be driven from their fortress, and enemy Heinkels and Fw 190s flew in with sticks of heavy bombs, making life uncomfortable for the Frenchmen. Sergeant Denneau radioed the RAF for support. A time was set for bombing the enemy out of their works, but nothing happened.

While the Jed-team waited with the Maquis for the RAF, General Alexander Patch put the U.S. Seventh Army ashore on the French Riviera and began his push north. That same day, Maquis at Ussel broke through the German defenses and captured the entire garrison. A day later, the larger enemy garrisons at Brive and Tulle agreed to surrender, but only to an American officer. Singlaub was the only American officer in the Corrèze district and made the short trip south in a "shaky little Renault." After signing the surrender agreement, the Maquis led the enemy off to improvised POW camps in the hills. But not all the Germans had surrendered. Two thousand infantrymen had broken away and were on the road with 150 trucks and two armored cars mounting automatic weapons.

The only way to stampede a moving column was to ambush it at different points along the road, and for such an operation the Jed-team needed help from the communists. Singlaub pulled the units back from Egletons, split them into ambush teams, and placed them at hand-picked sites near the road. The German column took heavy losses as it moved to Egletons, where it picked up the garrison and continued its withdrawal. The Jed-team established more ambushes to greet the enemy column as it rumbled north. During two weeks involving daily skirmishes with the enemy, the Jeds worked with the French resistance, and cleared the Germans out of the Corrèze area. Then, knowing that the German First Army, still garrisoned in southwest France, would eventually be forced to withdraw, they trained the Maquis in the use of 2,000 captured German weapons to meet the next enemy withdrawal.

Jed-teams operated in unorthodox ways. In Czechoslovakia, during the

Right: On May 6, 1945, PFC Edeleanu chalks news on the bulletin board outside the Intelligence tent at Kyaukpyu Camp a day before operatives from Detachment 101, Ramree Island, Burma, depart by convoy for Rangoon.

summer of 1944, a British team working with the resistance had collected a number of downed airmen, hid them in a hotel in Banska Bystrica in Slovakia, and called for the OSS to get them out of the country. During a bombing raid headed for central Europe, three B-17s slipped out of formation and dropped into an abandoned airfield near Tri Duby. As six OSS agents lowered themselves through the forward hatch, the ragged airmen waiting for rescue stopped short, one of them staring at the leader's uniform and saying, "What the hell's the Navy doing here?" But then Sp(X)2/c Charles Heller, the radio operator, made his appearance dressed in Army fatigues, a green Navy jacket, and a white sailor's cap. Before anyone else could ask, "What the hell unit is this," the OSS loaded sixty airmen on the planes and sent them back to Brindisi. The Jed-team, with Sgt. Joseph Horvath as interpreter, remained in Slovakia to train the resistance.

Before the war ended, the OSS group in Slovakia grew to twenty men, mostly specially trained soldiers. They repatriated another twenty-six men, and ended the war captured by the Germans. Fifteen of the OSS operatives, including a war correspondent and his photographer, were tortured and executed by the Gestapo. Three GIs survived and two barely escaped during one of the enemy's most intensive anti-guerrilla campaigns.

Toward the end of 1944, the OSS planted more Jed-teams trained for combat missions behind enemy lines. Like the French Maquis, the units were composed of internationally integrated

groups formed into platoons of thirty to forty men, led by an officer, and often containing a sprinkling of British commandos or American Rangers. About 1,500 men, experts in sabotage and organizing resistance fighters, infiltrated enemy territory. General Donovan vicariously envied these men. He knew what they did and at times spoke a little too openly about their exploits. William E. Colby, Director of the CIA from 1973 to 1976, served as a Jed officer and in March, 1945, led a thirty-man combat team of Norwegian-Americans on a mission into Norway. During World War II, spying and infiltration became both an art and a science.

The OSS did not get established in China until April 15, 1943, when Donovan negotiated an agreement with General Tai Li, Chungking's national intelligence and police director. Jed-teams were slow in coming. Bases needed to be established, and Chinese nationals trained. Jed-leaders organized their teams based upon the requirements of the mission. Problems in China mirrored the problems of bringing the French together in North Africa. Chinese communist forces fought the Japanese and the Chinese nationalists. In Vietnam, Ho Chi

Below: Accompanied by Brig. Gen. Lucian K. Truscott, Jr., William Darby (pointing) inspects U.S. Rangers training in Scotland. Truscott was the U.S. Army advisor and attached staff chief of combined operations. Darby organized the Rangers.

Minh worked with the OSS, but only because it served his political purpose.

Captain Singlaub eventually found himself in Kunming, China, to command a Jed-team for a very special mission. With ten men he parachuted onto Hainan Island to rescue from a Japanese prison camp hundreds of starving Australian and Dutch prisoners of war. The Japanese officer in charge did not know the war had ended, so Singlaub had to bluff his way into the compound by using authority he did not have, that of a commissioned major. The ruse worked, and a few days later Japanese guards conveyed their former prisoners to rescue vessels waiting at the island port of Sanya.

OSS operatives performed a multitude of covert duties, acting as intermediaries between the enemy and the Allies. They hastened the collapse of the Italian front through a fascinating secret negotiation. After late summer, 1944, the Nazis had made various efforts to sound out their different enemies on a possible separate peace. Himmler, perhaps hoping to save his own skin, sent S.S. General Karl Wolff to northern Italy to try and cut a deal with Italian partisans working with the OSS. When this failed, Himmler's principal Italian representative, Colonel Friedrich Dollmann, together with Wolff's adjutant, contacted an American OSS agent in the Swiss border city of Lugano. Wolff himself was smuggled into Switzerland where, on March 8, he was received in Zurich by Allen Dulles, head of OSS operations in Europe. On March 19, still in Switzerland, Wolff met two Allied generals wearing mufti, one of whom, Lyman Lemnitzer, was to become the U. S. Joint Chiefs of Staff and after that NATO commander. By the end of April, terms of capitulation had been agreed, and on May 2 they were finally implemented.

By war's end, the men and women of the OSS represented the intelligentsia of World War II. They were among the brightest and best trained American soldiers, sailors, and Marines in the service. They came from all walks of life, and each of them was chosen because of special analytical, technical, or combat talents. Not much is known about most of them, except what people have read in the cloak and dagger works of fiction that

came after the war, or the James Bond movies watched by millions time and again. What can be said of the combat Jed-teams is that no work of fiction can accurately describe what some of those volunteers endured. Those who died executing their missions too often passed into the vacuum called "missing in action."

In the end, General Donovan, though always controversial, did a creditable job organizing and staffing the OSS. To Donovan's credit, the OSS survived to become the Central Intelligence Agency. The CIA is no longer a department filled with GIs, but during World War II an American soldier created the service and other American soldiers made it work.

Above: Somewhere in England, a squad of U.S. Rangers train with tommy-guns as they prepare for their mission. All the Rangers are enlisted men except for Lt. Eugene Dance, third from right.

Below: Taking a break from their secret communications work are OSS operatives at Commo Camp "Y", Ceylon, July 24, 1945. They and their comrades were frequently in danger and, while little was known about them then, or publicized since, their efforts were invaluable to the Allies' war effort in the Pacific and Far East theaters.

COUNTING THE COST

Right: Coast Guardsmen know that "you have to go out, but you don't have to come back." The statement comes home to a young man killed at his battle station in combat during the Coast Guard's role in Europe's liberation.

Below: A lone bugler blows taps at the conclusion of Memorial Day observances for thousands of American servicemen buried at Margraten Cemetery in the Netherlands.

No war is ever fought without a "Butcher's Bill," and no conflict ever produced more casualties than World War II. After 1941 no American put on a serviceman's uniform without contemplating the prospect of being killed or wounded. Youngsters having that innate exuberance to believe that harm only ever comes to others experienced a rude awakening when they filled out the standard ten-thousand-dollar life insurance policies and named their mothers as beneficiaries.

As their training progressed, servicemen began reading battle reports in the newspapers about hundreds of thousands of Chinese killed by Tojo's Imperial Japanese Army. China's military casualties eventually topped 3,211,000, of which nearly half were killed, but the toll on civilians was enormous, estimates placing the dead at more than 35 million.

After 1941, the press shied away from publicizing battle losses so as not to upset recruiting, but the perceptive inductee soon came to understand that, if sent into battle, he could return home in a wheelchair or perhaps not at all.

Soldiers landing on foreign soil often admitted having premonitions of death. Others voiced confidence that they would never be harmed. James Jones, who survived to write the autobiographical novel *The Thin Red Line* believed that a soldier must go into battle with the expectation of being killed. "Only then can he function under fire," said Jones. "He knows and accepts beforehand that he is dead, although he may still be walking around for a while." Those who fought beside Jones understood his philosophy, but few of them agreed with it.

Nobody wanted to be killed, and nobody wanted to be wounded, but every battle became an affair for the oddsmakers. GIs lurking around headquarters of the VI Army Corps overheard a senior officer predict casualties of 30 percent when Allied forces stormed the beaches at Anzio. Word traveled fast, and some 30,000 men of the VI Army Corps quickly calculated that at least 9,000 of them would be either killed or wounded.

For the average infantryman, war continued to be a new experience, but he already understood the concept of casualties. One in ten would die. The others would go on with life, some without an arm, a leg, or an eye. By the time the VI Corps broke out of its beachhead and linked up with the Fifth Army, Allied forces tallied 7,000 dead and another 36,000 wounded. So much for the oddsmakers.

Battles like the four-month stalemate at Anzio did not make for heartening letters home. GIs ducked the issue of regimental losses, writing loved ones that they had been in combat and survived without a scratch. Those who had received a belly-full of shrapnel put the best face on their condition by promising a rapid recovery and a trip home.

Medics who circulated through the battlefield collecting casualties often found a letter clutched in the hand of a dead soldier – his last message home, one that never got into the mails. One

medic found a GI braced against a rock near Salerno. The soldier's entrails spilled through a slit in his stomach. He could not speak, but he reached his bloody hand into his breast pocket for a letter written during the night, held it to his heart, and died.

Every branch of the service had its casualties, but none more so than the infantryman at the front. It took a year after the war ended to sort things out. Of ten million men serving in the Army Ground Forces between 1941 and 1945, battle casualties fleshed out at 949,000 with 175,000 killed in action. Thus the chance of being hit was one in ten, and of being killed, not much less than one in fifty. The odds dramatically changed for the soldier in a combat unit, the infantry suffering 264 casualties per 1,000 men per year and the armored units 228. Field medics, combat engineers, and tank destroyer groups sustained similar casualty rates. A few stories circulated about medics being unwilling to expose themselves during a fire fight, but those instances were rare. There are more stories to be told of medics tending to the wounded while wounded themselves, and on many occasions dying from their unattended wounds in order to save others.

Casualties, however, were not evenly spread throughout an infantry division.

Above: On July 17, 1944, French civilians at Carentan, France, erected this silent tribute to an American who fell in the crusade to liberate their country.

Right: Wounded by shrapnel on August 9, 1943, in Sicily, PFC Roy Humphrey receives a pint of blood plasma from medic PFC Harvey White, who is intently watched by grimacing bare-footed civilians

Below: In an underground bombproof surgery behind the front lines on Bougainville, an American Army doctor operates on a soldier wounded by a Japanese sniper.

Nor were they evenly spread throughout the war. The heaviest toll fell upon rifle companies, where combat losses could equal or exceed the number of men originally assigned to it. The most intense ground fighting took place in Europe between June, 1944 (D-Day), and June, 1945. During the first six months of that period, 12,000 to 18,000 GIs were killed each month and another 40,000 to 60,000 received wounds. Few riflemen escaped unharmed.

Conversely, most other soldiers saw little or no combat because they played supporting roles to the men who actually did the fighting. The reason for so large a number of support troops involved logistics. Because all supplies emanated from the United States, they had to be transported and distributed to bases in North Africa, Europe, Australia, China, and the islands of the South Pacific.

In June 1941 the U.S. Army Air Corps became the U.S. Army Air Forces (USAAF), and throughout World War II it remained attached to the U.S. Army. General Henry "Hap" Arnold built the Air Force from 20,000 men in 1939 to a multi-faceted command composed of 1,900,000 men and women and 422,000 civilians, including female ferry pilots known as WASPS. Unlike other branches of the service, the number of U.S.A.A.F. personnel wounded was relatively small, but 40,000 airmen were killed, mostly in combat, and another 35,000 lost their lives in training or on non-combat missions. Strategic bombing, compared with the cost of ground warfare, was to have saved lives, but it fell short of its objective. With so great a majority of men and women in the U.S.A.A.F. serving as

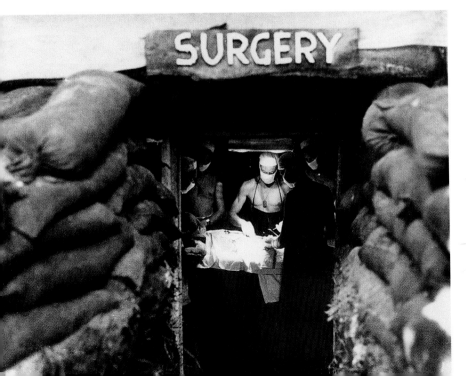

SURGERY

Left: On August 9, 1944, this group of nurses arrive at a field hospital in France after performing nearly three years of service in England and Egypt.

ground personnel, the death ratio of those who flew was the highest in the war.

In 1944, German flak destroyed 3,500 bombers and their fighters destroyed 2,900 more. For all the years of combat in Europe, the Air Force lost 10,000 bombers of all types and another 8,000 were damaged beyond repair. Some of the bombers carried a crew of ten. The Army Air Force as a whole suffered more than 120,000 battle casualties.

The men of the Marine Corps sustained the heaviest percentage of casualties in all branches of the services. In 1933 the Marine Corps numbered 20,000 men. At the peak of operations in the South Pacific, it counted 500,000 men, including 10,000 pilots. Though the majority of Marines performed non-combat roles, 92,000 men – nearly 20 percent of the Corps – ended the war as casualties, and 24,500 of them died. Nearly all the losses in the Marine Corps occurred among its six infantry divisions.

Organized along the lines of an Army combat division, a Marine division consisted of three regiments. These grew into Regimental Combat Teams (RCTs) – overstrength regiments containing about 7,500 officers and men, many of whom performed support occupations requiring minimal risk. These became the regiments formed into battalions that attacked the Japanese-held islands in the South Pacific.

On Peleliu, the 1st Marine RCT suffered 1,749 casualties; on Iwo Jima the 26th RCT reported 2,675 casualties; and on Okinawa the 29th RCT sustained 2,821 casualties. During the height of operations in the Pacific, it was unusual for a Marine rifleman to go through a single combat without a scratch. Unless

Below: Some men never get over losing a buddy. This Coast Guardsman stands in silent reverence beside the grave of a comrade killed in the Pacific.

Right: In the mud and snow of December, 1944, German POWs are put to work digging graves for members of the 101st Airborne who were killed defending Bastogne during the Battle of the Bulge.

the wound was serious, the typical Marine applied first aid to himself and never reported it.

In 1975 the Army Medical Department looked at three categories of treatment for the years 1942 to 1945 – wounded in action, non-battle injury, and disease. When the fighting in North Africa and the South Pacific began piling into the statistics, wounded in action rates climbed steadily, occasionally spiking as high as 100 per thousand during periods of heavy fighting. In 1944, one hundred thousand infantrymen fell during the months of June, July, and August, mainly because beachhead operations were the costliest of all.

GIs engaged in amphibious assaults were most often struck in the upper body. Tank crews suffered burns. Despite wearing the M1 helmet, infantrymen in the field were often shot in the head while crouching or lying prone. Non-battle injuries and disease remained almost flat throughout the war, but the numbers approached the same ranges as wounded in action, varying between fifty and one hundred cases each month of the war.

Friendly fire, parsed into the word "amicicide," also took its toll. Such casualties resulted mostly from artillery shells landing short of their objective. Through miscommunication or a sudden advance of infantry, American bombing raids also took their toll. Because of a persistent pattern of mistakes made by the Air Force, soldiers in Europe called it "the American *Luftwaffe*." In July, 1944, one massive strike against German positions made by the Eighth Air Force during Operation Cobra (the breakout from the Normandy beachhead) wounded 700 GIs, killed 131, and took the life of Lieutenant General Lesley J. McNair, Chief of Army Ground Forces.

Jungle warfare in the South Pacific introduced a new dimension to friendly fire. Because infantry used a perimeter defense against Japanese infiltration, a nervous soldier, especially during the night, might fire at anything that made a noise, and if he lost his sense of direction, he could pump a few rounds into his own perimeter, sending bullets whizzing through the platoon and into support groups in the rear. One young Marine guarding a perimeter for the first time "heard a strange noise, fired at it, and then called out, 'Who went there?'"

Below: American losses at Saipan were horrendous. During dedication ceremonies at the 4th Marine Division cemetery on the island, an honor guard fires a volley in salute to those comrades lost in battle.

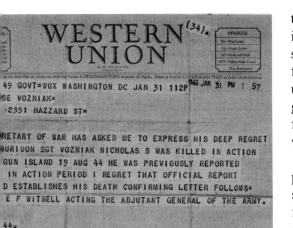

Days of endless fighting wore quickly on the nerves of the infantryman. One soldier squatting in a foxhole on Guadacanal turned to his buddy and said, "I can't see that damned sniper, but I wish he'd put a bullet in my ass so I can get the hell out of here." In France, a corporal chatted with a friend who had been wounded in the shoulder, and as an ambulance hove in sight, he lit a cigarette for his buddy and said, "Congratulations, you lucky dog. If I survive this bloody war, I'll see you stateside. If not, I'll see you in hell." Words such as those gave great encouragement to the wounded, but doctors disappointed three out of four by returning them to the battlefield.

GIs called tickets home a "million-dollar wound," and as the war dragged on the number of self-inflicted injuries began to climb. They were usually caused by a bullet in the foot or the lower leg, easily detected by powder burns, and not the type of wound received in battle. The cases were few and prosecutions even fewer. If a doctor suspected the wound to be self-inflicted, he would patch-up the suspect and send him back to his unit, offering words of encouragement, such as, "Now you can get back to your regiment and show them the stuff you're really made of."

Only a small number of wounded died, mainly because infantrymen had been trained to administer their own first aid, carried dressings as part of their battle kit, and knew how to apply tourniquets. If a GI was hurt badly, a buddy attended to the wound until a medic arrived. Stomach wounds ranked among the most serious. The jungles, where heat and humidity were high and

the disease rate enormous, made the islands a much less healthy place to survive an injury than did Europe. But fighting in the South Pacific had an upside. Japanese artillery, mortars, and grenades were so inferior that shell fragments sometimes causes nothing worse than bruises.

Every soldier carried a sulfanilamide packet. It contained twelve tablets for swallowing, and a small sack in powder form for sprinkling on a wound. Using it as instructed saved hundreds of soldiers wounded on the battlefield. "There was one sidelight on it," said one GI. "Some of the wounded soldiers didn't have any sulfanilamide left, because they had used it all to cure venereal disease. They said a venereal case could be knocked out in four or five days with it, and thus a man did not have to report in sick."

Jungle diseases afflicted healthy men, but never so seriously as wounded men. Malaria prevailed throughout the region, as did dengue fever, scrub typhus, diarrhea, parasites, swimmers' itch, tree sap dermatitis, and every other skin ailment known to man, including a peculiar disorder called "blue nail" which resisted all forms of treatment. Twenty years after the war ended, men back in

WAR DEPARTMENT
THE ADJUTANT GENERAL'S OFFICE
WASHINGTON 25, D. C.

IN REPLY REFER TO:
AG 201 Vozniak, Nicholas S.
PC-O 030027

blc/bj

1 February 1946

Mrs. Rose Vozniak
2351 Hazzard Street
Philadelphia, Pennsylvania

Dear Mrs. Vozniak:

It is with regret that I am writing to confirm the recent telegram informing you of the death of your son, Sergeant Nicholas S. Vozniak, 13,052,332, Air Corps.

Your son was reported missing in action 19 August 1944 on Pegun Island, Mapia Islands Group. It has now been officially established from reports received in the War Department that your son was killed in action 19 August 1944 when the scouting party of which he was a member was ambushed by the Japanese.

One of the party managed to crawl back to the beach to warn a second group of men and was again shot. Information obtained when the island was occupied was that all of the men in the scouting party had been killed by the Japanese but that the body of one of them had been washed away. The remaining bodies were found but identification could not be established.

I know the sorrow this message has brought you and it is my hope that in time the knowledge of his heroic sacrifice in the service of his country may be of sustaining comfort to you.

I extend to you my deepest sympathy.

Sincerely yours,

Edward Witsell
EDWARD F. WITSELL
Major General
Acting The Adjutant General of the Army

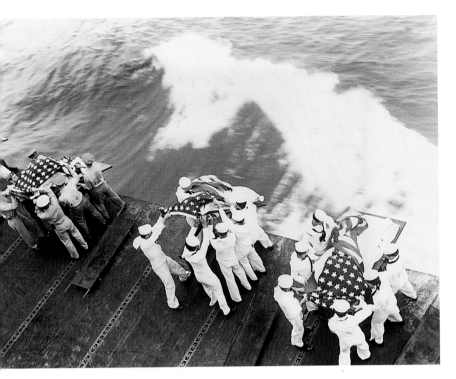

Above: On April 9, 1945, Japanese planes bombed and strafed the carrier U.S.S. *Hancock,* killing twenty-eight sailors. Three of the men killed are covered with the American flag before sliding into the depths, as viewed from the carrier's deck edge elevator.

Below: In May, 1942, with their hands tied behind their backs, Samuel Stenzler, Frank Spear, and James M. Gallagher (l to r), survivors of the Bataan Death March, wait exhausted along the road to the Cabanatuan prison camp.

Pacific, the wounded were often transferred to an island beachhead hospital with minimal capabilities, and while waiting for evacuation they sometimes suffered a second wound from enemy aircraft.

In Tunisia, Bill Mauldin struck up a friendship with an Army nurse, Mary Ann Sullivan, who worked with doctors on a mobile surgical truck, one that would rush into the "thick of things, and operate on wounded men" while snipers' bullets whizzed and ricocheted around them. Mauldin became so impressed with Sullivan and her unit that he "arranged officially with General Headquarters to be wounded in Mary Ann's vicinity."

Company commanders dreaded the chore of writing letters to families of men lost in combat. After a while the letters became more matter-of-fact and less deeply personal. War had its way of wearing off the tender edges of sympathy. In Orval Faubus's letter to the widow of a sergeant, he wrote, "He was leading his squad in the attack on the morning of our first assault on enemy lines. He was struck by small arms fire and killed. There was no suffering. His body was recovered and is now buried in an American cemetery on the northern coast of Normandy." The letter conveyed an aspect of heroism and sacrifice, but not much sympathy.

When a family recovered from the shock of losing a loved one, they would paste a gold star in the window – a symbol shared by an increasing number of neighbors. Later a parcel would arrive with the soldier's personal effects, and the misery would begin all over again. If the family wished, the Graves Registration Service would disinter the body if they could find and identify it, and ship it stateside. Over time, 280,000 bodies – battle and non-battle deaths – crossed the oceans for reburial in the family plot.

The number of unknown soldiers began to mount, especially in the Far East. When Germans collected American dead, they used a GI's dog tags to identify the corpse and buried it as they did their own, using an identification disc, half of which went into the grave with the body. For the Japanese, the preferred method for disposing of dead Yankees was to

civilian jobs still suffered periodic bouts of malaria, mainly in the form of chronic chills and fever.

Getting a wounded soldier in the jungle to a battalion aid station became a perplexing problem if a litter was required. Unlike in Europe, there were few roads and not much transportation nearby, and many infantrymen bled to death from internal injuries while waiting for transportation. The patient had the best chance of recovering from invasive surgery if the fragments could be removed within six hours after penetration. In Europe, medical care facilities kept much better pace with the Army and surgical centers were set up not far from the main battlefield. In the South

throw them on a fire. GIs reciprocated, using bulldozers to bury masses of the enemy. Most soldiers missing in action in the South Pacific were never found, the exception being those repatriated from prisoner camps.

More than 120,000 army personnel became prisoners of war (POWs), and all but 25,000 of them were captured in Europe. Oddly enough, GIs in a combat zone never contemplated capture in the same way they envisaged death or dismemberment. Seldom did they get any warning when it happened, the exception being places like Bataan and Corregidor in the Philippines where senior officers surrendered the entire force. Otherwise, a soldier had little opportunity to prepare for his capture.

In the South Pacific a soldier attempting to surrender stood an equal chance of being shot by his captors, and many soldiers chose to die in battle rather than play the odds. The Japanese were especially ruthless. If they found Japanese coins in a POW's pockets, they shot the soldier on the pretext that he had killed one of their number to get them. Those who survived the Bataan Death March admitted after being released that, had they known how they would be treated, they would have taken

refuge in the jungle and fought beside Filipino guerrillas. After 1942, most of the Americans captured by the Japanese were airmen. Prisoners captured by the Japanese suffered under the worst conditions for more than three years, and thirty-five percent of them died in prison camps.

Few GIs fell into German hands until 1944 and 1945. POWs taken by the Germans fared much better, their captivity lasting less than a year and their death rate about equal to one percent.

Germany ratified the 1929 Geneva Convention covering prisoners of war, but not Japan. During the war, Germany applied the provisions to prisoners of the western Allies, but more than half of the Russians taken by the *Wehrmacht* mysteriously disappeared. Japan advised the Swiss Government that they would adhere to the Convention's regulations to the extent that they conformed with their own rules of conduct.

Both Germany and Japan violated provisions of the Convention. Hitler issued orders that all prisoners taken during commando raids be shot on the spot, and during the Nuremberg trials Field Marshall's Wilhelm Keitel's involvement in carrying out the order led to his execution for war crimes. Japan's army regulations stipulated that POWs were to be treated with "a spirit of good will and... never be subjected to cruelties or humiliation." The regulations made good reading but were never

Above: American POWs celebrate 4th of July in the Japanese prison camp at Casisange in Malaybalay, on Mindanao, Philippines. It took courage to arrange a celebration so contrary to Japanese regulations, and ingenuity to assemble a "feast" and take a photograph such as this.

Left: A lanky GI, hands clasped behind his head, follows a long line of American soldiers surprised and captured by the Germans during the Battle of the Bulge.

Above: A young German soldier, armed with only a Luger, leads a column of American prisoners through the Ardennes. Neither Germany nor Japan adhered strictly to the Geneva Convention concerning captured enemy.

administered with any consistency.

Some Japanese soldiers schooled in the philosophy of fighting to the death believed that enemy servicemen who surrendered were weak and dishonorable and therefore deserved to die. Those American servicemen lucky enough to reach a POW camp received wretched treatment. As one prisoner recalled, "All our guards are misfits – deformed, alcoholic [and] insane. Depravities of all types stood guard around us, hating us and hating the world because of themselves."

Because Japan needed fighting men in the South Pacific, they used captured Koreans and other indentured Orientals to guard the camps. POW camp commanders mistreated the guards, so the guards mistreated the prisoners. Barely a day passed without some number of prisoners being pummeled with a rifle butt or knocked senseless for failing to respond to orders spoken in a foreign tongue they did not understand. An officer who had fought in Europe before going to the South Pacific declared, "I didn't always have that feeling in Europe about some poor German family man but I felt with a Jap it was like killing a rattlesnake." The sentiment was even shared by generals, one saying, "In the last war, I looked at dead Germans and I thought about their wives and children. [With] these [Japanese] bastards, that doesn't even occur."

Justification for such strong feelings was formed when a postwar survey of POWs released from Japanese camps showed that more than 90 percent of the prisoners had been beaten. The survey also showed that the average POW lost sixty-one pounds in a Japanese camp compared with thirty-eight pounds in a German camp. In Japanese camps, no facilities were provided for health care, and if a POW required surgery, a sharpened spoon handle in the hands of a willing inmate served as a scalpel.

Death from disease and malnutrition among prisoners could have been

Right: Being captured was never a pleasant experience. Here a group of grim-faced American POWs arrive at Stalag Luft 111, a special holding pen for fliers.

avoided had the Japanese permitted the Red Cross to bring in medicine and food packages from home. Boxes from home that made it to the camp were often stolen by the guards. Half of the POWs surviving Japanese prisoner camps returned to civilian life with permanent disabilities and qualified for Veterans Administration benefits.

After *kamikaze* attacks began in the South Pacific, a conference among high-level American Naval officers concluded in their minutes that: "All agree the only way to beat the Japs is to kill them all. They will not surrender and our troops are taking no chances and killing them anyway." Despite such bellicose outbursts, soldiers fighting on the ground were much less vindictive than the officers in the war room, mainly because killing had never been among their former professions.

According to the provisions of the Geneva Convention, prisoners could not be forced into labor that provided a military benefit for the captors. While the Germans ignored the rule to a lesser degree – such as forcing prisoners to clear away rubble caused by bombing raids – the Japanese set prisoners to work building military infrastructure, such as airfields in the Philippines and railroads into Burma, the latter involving the film-famous "Bridge on the River Kwai."

For American labor, the Japanese paid ten cents an hour. Instead of money, the

GI received mostly chits showing that his earnings had been invested in Japan's postal savings. Most prisoners ignored the scam. Working outside the camp gave them an opportunity to escape, but few tried. If a prisoner succeeded, Japanese camp commanders had the habit of rounding up all the escaper's buddies and standing them before a firing squad.

By early 1945, POWs began to witness signs of impending liberation. Some had squirreled away small radios and caught snippets of war news. Hope revived, and as each day passed it grew stronger. In Germany, Allied aircraft became more prevalent, camps were vacated, and prisoners marched to new compounds located deeper inside Germany. In the South Pacific prisoners suddenly found themselves herded onto freighters and carried off to Japan. Some never reached the island, falling victim to attack by American aircraft or submarines. Rescued by a seaplane, one prisoner referred to his brush with death on a burning Japanese freighter as "being as close to hell as a man could get."

A few years after the war, a group of veterans from the South Pacific went to work at a manufacturing facility in Muncy, Pennsylvania. Still enraged over Japan's sneak attack on Pearl Harbor and

Above: Unlike the emaciated forms liberated from Japanese prisons on the Philippines, POWs in German camps fared better, as did the three rescued GIs chatting with the MP on the left.

Left: When Rangers rescued 511 Leathernecks and civilians from the Cabanatuan prison camp on Luzon, some of the men had lost a hundred pounds. Though they relished a change into fresh clothes, hardly anything could be found that would fit.

Above: For the first time in forty-two months, American POWs liberated from the Japanese prison camp on Formosa enjoyed a hearty meal. Most of the men, such as Jimmie R. Murphy (left) and Wilbur F. Hansen were suffering from malnutrition.

Below: On June 20, 1945, the great day for many came when the *Queen Mary* arrived at New York with thousands of troops from Europe. For them, the fighting had ended, though the war in the Pacific continued for another two months.

the war that followed, they became annoyed when learning that the owner of the company had invited a number of Japanese to tour the factory. The old soldiers united in a pact to drive away the visitors. There were no riots or group demonstrations, but as Tojo's survivors strolled with their cameras from one work station to another, they were met by a new form of sneak attack. Hurled from undetected locations – some suspected the overhead bridge crane – exploding M1 firecrackers fell at the visitors' feet, causing them to hop through the guided tour and retreat to the safety of the board room for an apology.

The American soldier paid dearly for the war, but so did the world. More people were killed or maimed in World War II than in any war before or since. Up to 60 million people died, and most of them were civilians. Those who died can never be counted to the last man, woman, and child. The United States reported 405,000 killed, the United Kingdom 330,000 (including civilians), Australia 23,000, and Canada 42,000. Before 1940 and after November, 1942, the French Army lost 200,000 dead, while another 400,000 civilians lost their lives in air raids or concentration camps.

Actual Soviet losses were never counted, but in 1990 the government announced that 8,668,000 military personnel had been killed in what Stalin had called the Great Patriotic War. A better estimate might be 10 million with another 18 million wounded. At least 7 million Soviet civilians lost their lives because of the war. They were mostly Ukrainians and White Russians who died as a result of deprivation, reprisal, and forced labor.

German military losses approached 4 million and civilian losses from bombed cities 750,000. Japan lost 2 million soldiers, sailors, and airmen killed, and a million civilians. How many people died in German and Soviet camps will never be known, but the number probably exceeded 12 million persons, half of them Jewish.

The countries caught in the middle of the war suffered equally, if not worse. Poland lost 6 million – 20 percent of her prewar population – and more than half were of Jewish descent. Yugoslavia lost 1 million, the Dutch and the Greeks, more than 200,000 each. The number of casualties from the invaded countries of the Far East will never be known.

It was during America's Civil War that Major General William Tecumseh Sherman coined the phrase, "War is hell," but never could he have envisioned the slaughter of civilians during World War II. The hammermill of death ground up its victims and passed on, leaving only scars on the topography and sadness in the hearts of men. As a whole, America's soldiers and civilians got off easy.

Millions more people were crippled physically, millions of others permanently damaged mentally – some on the front lines, some in concentration camps,

and some in bombed cities. The mushroom clouds over Hiroshima and Nagasaki confirm the lesson that man's inhumanity to man knows no limit and that science will provide mankind with the means of destroying himself. Never in the long history of the world had there been a Butcher's Bill so immense.

The average serviceman never understood – after all the killing and spilling of blood – how the faulty political settlements in Asia and Europe at the end of the war created problems that could lead to World War III. He was not at Yalta with Roosevelt, Churchill, and Stalin, or at the last wartime summit meeting with Harry Truman at Potsdam in July, 1945. From those meetings he could not predict his future, for he trusted the leaders of the world to make a permanent peace. He did not know that Churchill wanted to preserve the British Empire while Roosevelt wanted to end European colonialism, nor that while both men agreed that the nations of Europe should be free and self-governing democracies, Stalin wanted just the opposite – to impose his personal communistic dictatorship on the countries of eastern, central, and southern Europe.

The GI went home happy to be among the living, proud of his service, yet saddened by the loss of those who had become his buddies. If he served as a rifleman on the front lines, he counted himself among the lucky. He came home

with silver stars, bronze stars, purple hearts, oak leaf clusters, campaign ribbons, a good conduct medal (even if he had been bad), an honorable discharge, or – for those who survived after serving above and beyond the call of duty – the Medal of Honor. He could not predict the Korean War, the Cold War, or the Vietnam War. To him, wars were over, or so he thought.

Alvin Bridges had joined the Army in February, 1942, "to get something to eat." The Army made him an MP and sent him to France. After the war he returned home and eventually became the police chief for Bay City, Michigan. Twenty years later, after watching politicians manipulate world affairs in their quest for power, he looked back on World War II and lamented, "It was a useless war, as every war is."

Alvin Bridges was not a politician. He was only a GI – an American soldier. He did not create wars – he just fought them.

Left: On May 25, 1945, American troops head for Le Havre, France–the first to be sent home and discharged under the Army's point system.

Below: On September 2, 1945, as the battleship U.S.S. *Missouri* ties to the pier in Tokyo Bay for the surrender ceremony, sailors, spectators, and photographers scramble to grab points of vantage to capture the scene.

BIBLIOGRAPHY

Ambrose, Stephen E. *American Heritage New History of World War II*. New York: Penguin Putnam, 1997.
Band of Brothers: E Company, 506th Regiment, 101st Airborne, From Normandy to Hitler's Eagle Nest. New York: Simon & Schuster, 1992.
Citizen Soldiers: The U.S. Army From the Normandy Beaches to the Bulge to the Surrender of Germany. New York: Simon & Schuster, 1997.
Ike's Spies: Eisenhower and the Espionage Establishment. Garden City: Doubleday & Company, 1981.

Astor, Gerald. *A Blood-Dimmed Tide: The Battle of the Bulge by the Men Who Fought It*. New York: Donald I. Fine, 1992.
Crisis in the Pacific: The Battles for the Philippine Islands by the Men Who Fought Them. New York: Donald I. Fine, 1996.

Bailey, Ronald H., et al. *The Air War in Europe*. Alexandria, Va.: Time-Life Books, 1979.

Balkoski, Joseph. *Beyond the Beachhead: The 29th Infantry Division in Normandy*. Harrisburg, Pa.: Stackpole Books, 1989.

Berry, Henry. *Sempre Fi, Mac: Living Memories of the U.S. Marines in World War II*. New York: Arbor House, 1982.

Bergerud, Eric. *Touched with Fire: The Land War in the South Pacific*. New York: Viking, 1996.

Boswell, Rolfe. *Medals for Marines*. New York: Thomas Y. Crowell Co., 1945.

Braun, Saul. *Seven Heroes: Medal of Honor Stories of the War in the South Pacific*. New York: G. P. Putnam's Sons, 1965.

Brown, Anthony Cave. *Bodyguard of Lies*. New York: Harper & Row, 1975.
The Secret War Report of the OSS. New York: Berkeley Publishing, 1976.

Davidson, Edward, and Manning, Dale. *Chronology of World War II*. London: Cassell & Company, 1997.

Dunnigan, James E. and Nofi, Albert A. *Dirty Little Secrets of World War II*. New York: William Morrow and Company, 1994.

Eisenhower, John. *The Bitter Woods: The Battle of the Bulge*. New York: G. P. Putnam's, 1969.

Ellis, John. *On the Front Lines: The Experience of War Through the Eyes of the Allied Soldiers in World War II*. New York: John Wiley & Sons, 1980.

Faubus, Orval. *In This Faraway Land*. Conway, Ark.: Privately printed, 1971.

Frank, Richard B. *Guadacanal*. New York: Random House, 1990.

Freeman, Roger A. *The Fight for the Skies: Allied Fighter Action in Europe and North Africa, 1939-1945*. London: Arms and Armour Press, 1988.

Fry, James C. *Combat Soldier*. Washington, D.C.: The National Press, 1968.

Giles, Janice Holt, ed. *The G.I. Journal of Sergeant Giles*. Boston: Houghton, Mifflin Company, 1965.

Goodson, James A. *Tumult in the Clouds: A Story of the Eagle Squadron*. New York: St. Martin's Press, 1983.

Hastings, Max. *Overlord: D-Day and the Battle for Normandy*. New York: Simon & Schuster, 1984.

Hawkins, Ian L., ed. *COURAGE*HONOR*VICTORY*. Winston-Salem, N.C.: Hunter Publishing Company, 1990.

Hoyt, Edwin P. *Now Hear This: The Story of American Sailors in World War II*. New York: Paragon House, 1993.
The GI's War: The Story of American Soldiers in Europe in World War II. New York: McGraw-Hill, 1988.

Hymoff, Edward. *The OSS in World War II*. New York: Richardson and Steirman, 1986.

Hynes, Samuel. *Flights of Passage: Reflections of a World War II Aviator*. Annapolis: Naval Institute Press, 1988.

Jablonski, Edward. *Air War: Terror from the Skies-Tragic Victories*. Garden City: Doubleday & Company, 1971.

Jacobs, Bruce. *Heroes of the Army: The Medal of Honor and Its Winners*. New York: W. W. Norton & Company, 1956.

Kennett, Lee, *G.I.-The American Soldier in World War II*. New York: Charles Scribner's Sons, 1987.

Lewin, Ronald. *Ultra Goes to War*. London: Hutchinson, 1978.

MacDonald, Charles B. *A Time for Trumpets: The Untold Story of the Battle of the Bulge*. New York: William Morrow & Company, Inc., 1985.

Marshall, George O., Jr. *My World War II: The Home Letters of George O. Marshall, Jr., U.S. Army, 1943-45*. Athens, Geo.: University of Georgia Press, 1983.

Mauldin, Bill. *Up Front*. New York: W. W. Norton & Company, 1968.

May, Elaine Tyler. *Pushing the Limits: American Women, 1940-1961*. New York: Oxford University Press, 1994.

Miller, Arthur. *Situation Normal....* New York: 1944.

Miller, Francis, et al. *The Complete History of World War II*. Chicago: Progress Research Corp., 1948.

Miller, John. *U.S. Army in World War II: The Reduction of Rabaul*. Washington, D.C.: Office of the Chief of Military History, 1959.

Murphy, Edward F. *Heroes of World War II*. New York: Ballantine, 1991.

O'Neill, William L. *World War II, A Student Companion*. New York: Oxford University Press, 1999.
A Democracy at War: America's Fight at Home and Abroad in World War II. New York: Free Press, 1993.

Peckham, Howard H., and Snyder, Shirley A., eds. *Letters from Fighting Hoosiers*. Bloomington, Ind: University of Indiana Press, 1948.

Perry, George Sessions and Leighton, Isabel. *Where Away: A Modern Odyssey*. New York: Whittlesey House, 1944.

Phillips, James H., and Bovee, Donald E., comp. *The Medal of Honor of the United States Army*. Washington, D.C.: Government Printing Office, 1948.

Pogue, Forrest C. *The Supreme Command (From the United States Army in World War II)*. Washington, D.C.: Office of the Chief of Military History, 1954.

Pyle, Ernie. *Brave Men*. New York: Holt, Rinehart and Winston, Inc., 1944.
Ernie's War: The Best of Ernie Pyle's World War II Dispatches. New York: Simon & Schuster, 1986.
Here Is Your War. New York: Henry Holt and Company, 1943.

Schaffer, Ronald. *Wings of Judgment: American Bombing in World War II*. New York: Oxford University Press, 1985.

Smith, Richard Harris. *OSS: The Secret History of America's First Central Intelligence Agency*. Berkeley: University of California Press, 1972.

Smith, S.E. *The United States Navy in World War II*. New York: William Morrow & Company, 1966.

Spector, Ronald H. *Eagle Against the Sun: The American War with Japan*. New York: The Free Press, 1985.

Stouffer, Samuel, et al. *The American Soldier*. 2 vols. Princeton: Princeton University Press, 1949.

Sulzberger, C. L. *The American Heritage Picture History of World War II*. New York: Simon & Schuster, 1966.

Terkel, Studs. *"The Good War": An Oral History of World War II*. New York: Pantheon Books, 1984.

Tobin, James. *Ernie's Pyle's War: America's Eyewitness to World War II*. New York: The Free Press, 1997.

Walters, Vernon A. *Silent Missions*. Garden City: Doubleday and Company, 1978.

Weiss, Robert. *Enemy North, South, East, West*. Portland, Ore.: Strawberry Hill Press, 1998.

Welker, Robert H. *A Different Drummer: The Odyssey of a Home-Grown Rebel*. Boston: 1958.

Wilson, George. *If You Survive*. New York: Ballantine, 1987.

Index